Yale Studies in
Hermeneutics

Yale Studies in Hermeneutics

JOEL WEINSHEIMER, EDITOR

Introduction to Philosophical Hermeneutics

JEAN GRONDIN

FOREWORD BY HANS-GEORG GADAMER
TRANSLATED BY JOEL WEINSHEIMER

Yale
University
Press
New
Haven and
London

Originally published as Jean Grondin,
*Einführung in die philosophische
Hermeneutik.* Copyright © 1991 by
Wissenschaftliche Buchgesellschaft,
Darmstadt, Germany.

Printed in the United States of America.

Library of Congress Cataloging-in-
Publication Data

Grondin, Jean.
[Einführung in die philosophische
Hermeneutik. English]
Introduction to philosophical hermeneutics /
Jean Grondin ; foreword by Hans-Georg
Gadamer ; translated by Joel Weinsheimer.
    p.   cm.—(Yale studies in hermeneutics)
Translation of: Einführung in die philoso-
phische Hermeneutik.
Includes bibliographical references and
index.
ISBN 978-0-300-05969-4 (cloth: alk. paper)
        978-0-300-07089-7 (pbk.: alk. paper)
1. Hermeneutics—History.   I. Title.
II. Series.
BD241.G69512   1994
121'.68—dc20   94-12360
                                                    CIP

A catalogue record for this book is available from the British Library.

The paper in this book meets the guide-
lines for permanence and durability of the
Committee on Production Guidelines for
Book Longevity of the Council on Library
Resources.

10   9   8

For
Paul-Matthieu and Emmanuel

Contents

Foreword

The "universality of hermeneutics" is less the name of a certain position than a demand for a certain kind of distinction. The term *hermeneutics* goes far back and traverses a long history from which there is still much to learn today. However, the term *universality* presents a challenge, as it were—one that indicates not so much a philosophical position as a philosophical task. Thus I am very happy to be able to introduce Jean Grondin's book, already known to me in German, to the English reader. At the outset of the long history of the concept of hermeneutics stands Aristotle's work of that title, which basically treats of propositional logic. Even this narrower way of posing the question, which implies the bracketing out of nonpropositional forms of speech, views itself as being bound up with all the claims for universality that have always been acknowledged as belonging to the universality of logic, the logos, and language. From the beginning, then, it was understood that language usage, which has assumed such prominence in modern hermeneutics, pertains in principle to all the special interpretive disciplines. This is the case in juridical as well as in theological hermeneutics, and ultimately the ancient word *hermeneutics* connotes "translation" in the broadest sense.

When the age of metaphysics came to a close, and the modern sciences' claims to possess a monopoly on knowledge were consequently reduced, the attempt to develop a genuine universality could look to this ancient conception for a starting point. There were, however, deeper-lying reasons when, beginning in the Romantic age, hermeneutics expanded to the point that it comprehended the theory of the human sciences as a whole. Thus it came to include not only jurisprudence and theology but also philology and all its related disciplines.

It was above all Wilhelm Dilthey's descriptive psychology that marked an important step in this direction. But it was only when Dilthey and his school gained influence on the phenomenological movement, polemically with Husserl, but productively with the young Heidegger, that understanding was no longer merely juxtaposed with conceptualization and explanation, and that it was not limited to its use in the sciences. Quite the contrary, understanding came to be seen as constituting the fundamental structure of human Dasein, and thus it moved into the very center of philosophy.

Thereby subjectivity and self-consciousness—which, for Husserl, expressed themselves in the transcendental ego—lost their primacy. Now, instead, there is an Other, who is not an object for the subject but someone to whom we are bound in the reciprocations of language and life. So, too, understanding is no method but rather a form of community among those who understand each other. Thus a dimension is opened up that is not just one among other fields of inquiry but rather constitutes the praxis of life itself. This certainly does not exclude the possibility that the sciences go their own way and have their own method, which consists in objectifying the objects of their research. However, there is a danger here of limiting ourselves to a theory of science which, in the name of methodological rigor, robs us of certain experiences of other people, other expressions, other texts and their claim to validity.

One need only think of the great effort that structuralist poetics has put into shedding some light on myth—and yet without even coming close to realizing the aim of letting myth speak more clearly than before. The same could be said for the semantics that objectified the world of signs and the textuality that has made possible new and interesting steps toward scientific knowledge. By contrast to these, hermeneutics encourages not objectification but listening to one another — for example, the listening to and belonging with (Zuhören) someone who knows how to tell a story. Here we begin to glimpse the je ne sais quoi that we mean when we refer to people's understanding one another. It is Grondin's special merit to have worked out this "inner" conversation as the real foundation of hermeneutics, which (as I indicated in *Truth and Method*) plays an important role in Augustine and in other contexts such as process theology.

Hans-Georg Gadamer

Preface

In a preface, an author is permitted to say something about himself and his relation to what he has written. Alongside the text proper, the purely accidental impulse that motivated it can emerge more clearly.

As I worked on this book in the late fall of 1988, I found myself having difficulty conceptualizing the universal claim of hermeneutics. That phrase seems to mean so much, and to draw so much criticism, that I couldn't see my way through it. Wittgenstein remarks, "A philosophical problem has the form: I can't find my way around," and so at first I comforted myself in the knowledge that there might be something philosophical about my situation. Somewhat later I met with Hans-Georg Gadamer in a Heidelberg pub to discuss this and other matters with him. In a formulaic and unsophisticated way, I asked him to explain more exactly what the universal aspect of hermeneutics consisted in. After everything that I had read, I was prepared for a long and rather vague answer. He thought the matter over and answered, concisely and conclusively, thus: "In the verbum interius."

I was astonished. This is nowhere emphasized in *Truth and Method*, let alone in the secondary literature. The universal claim of hermeneutics is to be found in the "inner word," which Augustine discussed and to which Gadamer had devoted a little-noticed chapter of his magnum opus? Somewhat nonplussed, I asked him to elaborate on what he meant. "This universality," he continued, "consists in inner speech, in that one cannot say everything. One cannot express everything that one has in mind, the logos endiathetos. That is something I learned from Augustine's *De trinitate*. This experience is universal: the actus signatus is never completely covered by the actus exercitus."

I was confused at first, because this seemed to run contrary to the basic tendency of Gadamer's philosophy, since he takes it as an absolute principle that hermeneutic universality consists in the fact that everything can be expressed in real language. Language can overcome all objections to its universality, because such objections themselves must be capable of being formulated linguistically. For Gadamer everything is supposed to be language: "Being that can be understood is language," as his most often cited maxim puts it in expressing this universality.

What did his gesture toward the verbum interius have to do with these matters? Does it represent a late self-interpretation, a self-correction, or only a passing thought to be ascribed no fundamental significance? For some months I remained without a clue in this respect, until I was reading through *Truth and Method*, along with the original version preserved in the University of Heidelberg library. There it occurred to me that the universal claim of hermeneutics could indeed be derived only from the doctrine of the verbum interius — that is, from the insight (stemming from Augustine read through Heidegger) that spoken discourse always lags behind what one wants or has to say, the inner word, and that one can understand what is said only when one derives it from the inner speech lurking behind it. That sounds outmoded and very metaphysical: alongside language there is also the world of the verbum interius behind or within it. As we will see, however, this insight alone is capable of undermining the metaphysical and logical priority assigned to propositions. According to the classical logic that nurtures the metaphysics of substance, everything is fully expressed in the proposition. What is expressed propositionally is self-sufficient and is to be judged on the basis of its own evidence.

For hermeneutics, by contrast, the proposition is something secondary and derivative, to put it in the hyperbolic language of *Being and Time*. Clinging to propositions in their disposability conceals the struggle with language comprising the verbum interius, the hermeneutic word. By the inner word, however—and this should be made emphatically clear—is meant no private or psychological inner world existing prior to its verbal expression. Rather, it is that which strives to be externalized in spoken language. Externalized language is the site of a struggle which must be heard as such. There is no "preverbal" world, only world oriented to language, the world which is always to be put in words, though never entirely successfully. This is the uniquely hermeneutic dimension of language.

The present introduction is an attempt to depict philosophical hermeneutics from this point of view. My reference to the conversation with Gadamer is not meant to imply any presumptuous claim that my interpretation is "authentically" Gadamerian. Such references are highly problematical, and so I hesitated for a long while before mentioning it in this connection. Finally, however, I was encouraged to do so by the example of Walter Schultz, who referred to his own talks with Heidegger, since they had contributed substantially to the formulation of his interpretation of Heidegger.[1] The same may have occurred in my discussions with Gadamer. Yet an interpretive orientation occasioned in this manner can succeed only at a certain cost and risk. Specifically, my concern—independent of Gadamer, on my own responsibility, and in the context of the present state of philosophical conversation—is to introduce readers to the philosophical dimension of hermeneutics. (Hence I shall disregard the particularities of individual hermeneutic disciplines such as philology, theology, history, and the social sciences.) Within the context of the verbum interius, I shall attempt to reconstruct the historical problematics of philosophical hermeneutics as faithfully as possible and so will be referring to authors seldom read today. Of course, this makes it necessary to show that the perspective of the verbum interius is in fact central.

I am deeply indebted to the Alexander von Humboldt Foundation and the Canadian Council for Research in the Humanities for making this work possible. Meetings with colleagues have given decisive impetus to the present investigations. I am grateful to Ernst Behler, Otto Friedrich Bollnow, Luc Brisson, Rüdiger Bubner, Hans-Georg Gadamer (who permitted me to refer to our conversation), Hans-Ulrich Lessing, Manfred Riedel, Frithjof Rodi, Josef Simon, Alberto Viciano, and Joel Weinsheimer. Let me end these acknowledgments by expressing the admiration in which I have long held their work. However philosophy tries to purify itself critically and argumentatively, without *thaumazein* before what it brings to thought, it would never even begin.

Introduction to Philosophical Hermeneutics

Introduction

Since its emergence in the seventeenth century, the word *hermeneutics* has referred to the science or art of interpretation. Until the end of the nineteenth century, it usually took the form of a theory that promised to lay out the rules governing the discipline of interpretation. Its purpose was predominantly normative, even technical. Hermeneutics limited itself to giving methodological directions to the specifically interpretive sciences, with the end of avoiding arbitrariness in interpretation as far as possible. Virtually unknown to outsiders, it long maintained the status of an "auxiliary discipline" within the established disciplines that concerned themselves with interpreting texts or signs. Thus the Renaissance formulated a theological hermeneutics (hermeneutica sacra) and a philosophical hermeneutics (hermeneutica profana), as well as a juridical hermeneutics (hermeneutica juris). The idea of an art of interpretation can, of course, be traced much farther back, at least to the patristic period, if not the Stoic philosophy (which developed an allegorical interpretation of myth), or even to the tradition of the Greek rhapsodes.

Philosophical hermeneutics, by comparison, is of very recent date. In the ordinary, narrow sense, this term refers to the philosophical position of Hans-Georg Gadamer, and sometimes that of Paul Ricoeur. Significant forms of hermeneutics undoubtedly existed before then, but they hardly presented themselves as fully developed philosophical conceptions. Even if Schleiermacher, Droysen, and Dilthey—the fathers of contemporary hermeneutics—did make decisive contributions to the growing awareness of hermeneutic problems, they did not pursue the work they initiated primarily under the rubric of hermeneutics. Even though Gadamer's philosophical endeavors would have been impossible without Heidegger, Heidegger nevertheless could not help stating: "'Hermeneutic philosophy'—that's Gadamer's business."[1] No really ground-breaking innovations in hermeneutics have appeared since Gadamer's, though his philosophy has stimulated numerous debates, especially with ideology critique and Derridean deconstruction.[2]

Although Gadamer's hermeneutics defined the field, for the purpose of introducing philosophical hermeneutics, it is advisable to take a somewhat broader view of the matter. Gadamer's expressly Heideggerian origins indicate that Heidegger's thought belongs within the parameters of a philosophically motivated hermeneutics. The entire career of Heidegger's thought— his late philosophy after the "turn," as well as the early lectures published only recently—had a path-breaking influence on Gadamer. In his highly significant essay "The Universality of the Hermeneneutic Problem," which initiated the debate with Habermas, Gadamer mentioned that he called his perspective "hermeneutic" in "connection with a manner of speaking that Heidegger had developed early on"[3]—that is, earlier even than *Being and Time*. Heidegger's "hermeneutics" cannot be understood by reference to *Being and Time* alone. It would not be substantially incorrect to infer that Gadamer's hermeneutics was much more deeply influenced by the early lectures than by *Being and Time*, even if Gadamer had not admitted that he viewed Heidegger's work of 1927 as a "hurry-up job done for extraneous reasons," if not "a let-down."[4] Without falling into the exaggerations implicit in a degrading classification of Heidegger's main philosophical work, Gadamer's admission might well imply that only now is it possible to undertake an appropriate evaluation of Heidegger's philosophical hermeneutics as developed in his earlier lectures and elaborated by Gadamer.

In order to contextualize this new hermeneutics, we will need to return to the older—as it were, pre-philosophical—tradition of hermeneutics to which

Gadamer continually refers and from which he distinguishes himself. Rich in tradition and receptive to it, hermeneutics must itself be deduced from its own origins. We need to trace the connection not only to its classic beginnings in Schleiermacher, Droysen, and Dilthey but also to the often underestimated hermeneutics of the Enlightenment, the initial theories of interpretation originating in early Protestant theology, and the pioneering work of the patristic period.

In doing so, we need to avoid presenting the history of hermeneutics as a teleological process, which, starting in antiquity and proceeding through the Reformation and Romanticism, was brought to consummation in philosophical hermeneutics. This is the way hermeneutic history has in fact often been presented, beginning with Dilthey's path-breaking essay "The Rise of Hermeneutics" and then radicalized by Gadamer and the overviews influenced by him. It always follows something like this pattern: During antiquity and the patristic period, there were at first fragmentary hermeneutic rules. Then Luther and Reformation theologians fashioned a systematic hermeneutics, which first became a universal theory of understanding in Schleiermacher. Dilthey broadened this hermeneutics into a universal methodology of the human sciences, and Heidegger located hermeneutic inquiry on the still more fundamental ground of human facticity. Gadamer ultimately reformulated universal hermeneutics as a theory of the ineluctable historicity and linguisticality of our experience. Universal hermeneutics, finally, was extended into such fields as critique of ideology, theology, literary theory, theory of science, and practical philosophy.

This universal history of hermeneutics, conceived quasi-teleologically, however, has aroused considerable skepticism, especially among philologists and literary critics.[5] Objections arose to the unitary conception of hermeneutic history initiated by Dilthey and Gadamer and then repeated in compendiums and overviews, a history supposedly coming to fruition "in a sequence of teleologically related steps or phases."[6] What is correct in the classical representation of hermeneutic history, however, is the idea that early hermeneutics resembled a technical theory, and as a rule such theory was of much less universal application than present-day philosophical hermeneutics. Yet the skeptics about traditional hermeneutic history are right to suggest that the two projects, theoretical and philosophical, have little to do with each other and that hermeneutic history has unfolded in anything but a teleological manner.

Modern history of hermeneutics, like every other, is written after the fact—that is, it is a construction. For the most part, this history proceeded without taking much cognizance of itself. As late as the seventeenth century it still had no name. What was earlier called ars interpretandi was taken up and furthered by various branches of knowledge, such as criticism, exegesis, and philology. Even modern hermeneutics has not developed in a linear manner toward a philosophical telos. Luther is customarily considered responsible for discovering or revitalizing hermeneutics. This is the view taken by the Protestant Dilthey (which Gadamer considers compelling), as well as by the Luther scholar, Gerhard Ebeling.[7] The principle of sola scriptura does indeed suggest the existence of a fully worked-out hermeneutics, but Luther did not himself develop such a program. Rather, he wrote exegeses and delivered lectures without specifying any hermeneutical *theory*. It was rather his collaborator, Flacius Illyricus, who conceptualized this specifically modern principle of scriptural interpretation, a theory that remained the fundamental basis of exegesis until the late eighteenth century.

During the seventeenth century, in the meantime, an embryonic universal hermeneutics was developed along rationalist lines by such authors as J. Dannhauer, G. F. Meier, and J. M. Chladenius.[8] These general theories of interpretation broke through the limits of the regional hermeneutics—that is, the manuals—that were specifically designed to help in elucidating Scripture or classical authors. Consequently, the development of the first supraregional art of interpretation cannot be justly ascribed to Schleiermacher. The place of Schleiermacher's hermeneutic theory is anything but patent. This is due first of all to the fact that Schleiermacher, who thought of himself primarily as a theologian, never published his hermeneutics himself. The single piece of hermeneutic work that he saw through the press, the lectures "On the Concept of Hermeneutics" (1829), offers a discussion of Wolf and Ast's contributions rather than a comprehensive conception of hermeneutics. He treated his hermeneutics, which was to be articulated within the horizon of dialectics, in lectures that F. Lücke first published in 1838 under the title *Hermeneutik und Kritik*. Beyond the confines of theological hermeneutics, Schleiermacher's fragmentary sketches enjoyed little attention.[9]

August Böckh, who attended these lectures, was strongly influenced by them. Böckh based his *Enzyklopädie und Methodenlehre der philologischen Wissenschaften* on the lectures he gave after 1816 (that is, before they were published by Lücke). Following his mentor's example, Böckh did not himself publish the encyclopedia; that was left to his student Bratuschek, who brought it out in 1877.[10] Böckh wanted to present a methodology of the philological sciences based on Schleiermacher's hermeneutics of understanding. By so doing he tied hermeneutics to the methodological demands of the inexact sciences—a connection which, though foreign to Schleiermacher's intentions, was furthered by Droysen and Dilthey. Droysen likewise endeavored to formulate a methodology for historiography, and he, too, presented it in lectures never published in their entirety. In 1868, however, he printed his compact *Grundriß der Historik,* which was widely influential. In 1937, Rudolf Hübner published Droysen's lectures on history. Incidentally, in neither the *Grundriß* nor the published lectures is the name of Schleiermacher or the word hermeneutics once mentioned.

Schleiermacher's significance for hermeneutics and its "history," only now becoming manifest, was displayed above all by Wilhelm Dilthey. As a student of Böckh's, Dilthey became acquainted with Schleiermacher's work at an early age. In 1860, at twenty-seven, he received the Schleiermacher Foundation prize for his essay titled "The Hermeneutic System of Schleiermacher in Comparison with Earlier Protestant Hermeneutics," an essay that probably represents the first and most important history of hermeneutics, though he never published it. Dilthey's preoccupation with Schleiermacher later intensified: in 1864 he wrote a Latin dissertation under Trendelenburg on Schleiermacher's ethics, and he followed this in 1867 with the first volume of his Schleiermacher biography. He never published the second volume, which was to have presented a systematic view of Schleiermacher's philosophy and theology, including his hermeneutics, probably by appropriating materials from his prize essay of 1860. (Work pertinent to that project was gathered from the posthumous remains and published in 1966 by M. Redeker.) In the decades that followed, Dilthey devoted himself to his lifelong project: a methodology of the human sciences that was to bear the ambitious title "A Critique of Historical Reason." Of this project, only the first, predominantly historical part appeared in 1883 with the title *Einleitung in die Geisteswissenschaften.* In this work, remarkably, Schleiermacher and hermeneutics are absent. Whether they were to receive treatment in the second volume, as girders in the "foundation" of the human sciences, remains open to speculation. Apparently Dilthey envisioned the foundation of the sciences of man as belonging to descriptive psychology, not hermeneutics. Throughout his whole life (though this is a matter of debate in Dilthey scholarship), he seems to have maintained the foundational status of psychology. To be sure, we can trace important insights that can be called "hermeneutical" everywhere in Dilthey's work—for instance in the treatise of 1895, "Über erklärende und beschreibende Psychologie"; but hermeneutics, specifically so called, reappears in the foreground only in the brief study of its rise dating from 1900.

This piece marked the rise of the history of hermeneutics as well. To chart the rise of hermeneutics Dilthey reached back, almost literally, to his longer article of 1860, as if nothing had happened in the intervening forty years. There, for the first time, occurs the idea that hermeneutics should disclose all the general rules of interpretation that underlie the human sciences, for all of these sciences depend on interpretive knowledge. So conceived, hermeneutics—as universal guarantor of validity—could serve something like the function of grounding the interpretive sciences (Dilthey doesn't spell out the details). It is important to mention, however, that this intuition occurs primarily in the handwritten additions to the 1900 essay, and these remained unpublished until the fifth volume of the collected works appeared in 1924. The view, now become standard, that Dilthey's hermeneutics was to offer a methodological basis for the human sciences is, as we will see, less Diltheyan than is often thought, and so is in need of revision.

Hermeneutics was laden with heavy philosophical importance primarily by Dilthey's student and stepson, Georg Misch. In the preface to the fifth volume of his edition of Dilthey's works, Misch portrayed the path of Dilthey's thought as a logical series of steps, beginning from the early projection of a positivistic and psychological grounding of the human sciences up to the complete development of a universal philosophy of historical life, in which hermeneutics was to play a decisive role, and which was even to be called hermeneutics. Thereby Misch was of great help in clarifying conceptually where the late Dilthey was headed. Suddenly, hermeneutics became the catchword of a philosophical generation that began to deviate from the straight and narrow confines of the dominant neo-Kantianism and that gladly took Dilthey as the prophet of a nonpositivistic philosophy open to the historical facticity of life. What all this enthusiasm concealed, however, was Dilthey's own positivistic starting point and the de facto secondariness of hermeneutics in his texts. Under the influence of Misch's life philosophy, the systematic and theoretical starting point to which Dilthey gave his full attention retreated behind the hermeneutic motif, and this finally tended to conceal his methodological ambitions.[11] A useful monograph by O. F. Bollnow (1936) fixed the image of a coherent path of Diltheyan thought that departed from an epistemologically laden psychology and ultimately opened up the possibility of grounding the human sciences hermeneutically.[12]

In the course of their own emancipation from neo-Kantianism, the early Heidegger and young Gadamer found in Dilthey a precursor in their search for an existential or hermeneutic reconceptualization of philosophy. Heidegger revealed his revolutionary intentions under the rubric of a hermeneutics of facticity. For some reason, however, Heidegger declined to publish the germinal hermeneutic ideas that so fascinated audiences of that time.[13] Nevertheless, in *Being and Time* his conception arrived at its first published expression and caused vast reverberations. His insights into the ontological circularity and fore-structure of understanding marked a new beginning for hermeneutics. Yet, because *Being and Time* offered only meager remarks on this theme, it remained difficult to understand what Heidegger meant, exactly, by hermeneutics. Indeed, in *Being and Time,* a mere half-page at the end of Heidegger's otherwise elaborate Section 7 on phenomenology is devoted to situating and systematically defining hermeneutics as a philosophical program.[14] There we learn only that the word *hermeneutics* derives from *hermeneuein* and that Heidegger's usage corresponds to "the primordial signification of this word, where it designates the business of interpreting." After further explaining the secondary significations of the word, Heidegger adds that hermeneutics in the *primary* sense will mean an "analytic of the existentiality of existence," though he offers no more detailed clarification of the relation between hermeneutics and analytic(s). In the years that followed, the analytic of existence, hermeneutics of facticity, and ontology of Dasein all came to function as vague synonyms for what *Being and Time* was doing. Whether Heidegger intended the word *hermeneutics* to designate some specific meaning—and therefore to situate it in a tradition relatively unknown outside theology and the school of Dilthey—could not be immediately ascertained.

At first, the purely "hermeneutic" character of Heidegger's thought remained overshadowed by his other concerns. It seemed, at least in comparison, as if his hermeneutic preoccupations had given way to the ontological and related transcendental claims of the whole. This is what Gadamer may well have been feeling when, as mentioned above, he described *Being and Time* as a "publication very quickly thrown together," one in which "Heidegger, contrary to his deepest intentions, once again assimilated himself to the transcendental self-conception of Husserl."[15] In spite of the respect for Heidegger's philosophical accomplishments of 1927 that Gadamer expresses elsewhere, these words evidence a certain disappointment, as if Heidegger had betrayed his more genuine and fundamental insights. Other members of

Heidegger's audience, we know, thought so, too—for instance, O. Becker, K. Löwith, and later O. Pöggeler.[16] Yet whether Heidegger really concealed his earlier hermeneutics of facticity in *Being and Time* or just moved beyond it, we will not finally be able to determine until the early lectures and manuscripts have been published in their entirety.

At present we can be sure only that a reconstruction of Heidegger's hermeneutics has to begin with the early program of a hermeneutics of facticity, especially because Gadamer's usage of the word *hermeneutics* accords with the meaning prevailing at that time, and he has tied his own hermeneutics in *Truth and Method* far more closely to the hermeneutics of facticity than to that of *Being and Time*.[17] The retreat from a hermeneutically understood philosophy that began in *Being and Time* intensified in the late works, which virtually never refer to the concept of hermeneutics at all. Nevertheless Heidegger's late thought concerning the historicity of being swarms with hermeneutical insights—for example, the dependence of previous philosophy and history on metaphysics—though such insights are not called "hermeneutical." Nevertheless, in Heidegger's thought after the "turn," Gadamer brilliantly discerned nothing less than his teacher's return to his earlier hermeneutic ideas.[18]

In retrospect we can see that it was thanks to Gadamer that the hermeneutic insights of the turn, on which *Truth and Method* is based, were connected to the hermeneutic inquiry of the early Heidegger.[19] Thereby, as the classic formula has it, Gadamer thought with Heidegger against Heidegger—that is, against Heidegger's apparent abandonment of hermeneutic thought, but with his program for a hermeneutics of our historical facticity, now to be followed through consistently. Gadamer's achievement consists in having shown how the historicity of being pertains to understanding our historically situated consciousness and the human sciences in which that consciousness expresses itself. The present introduction proposes to survey the development of this hermeneutics as understood by Heidegger and the older tradition.

It is always difficult to orient oneself in the vast field of present-day philosophy. For just this reason we need to make the attempt again and again. More than twenty years ago K.-O. Apel began with the premise that philosophy proceeds in three primary directions: Marxism, analytic philosophy, and phenomenological-existential-hermeneutical thought.[20] Among these three "schools," philosophical Marxism has certainly suffered some loss of currency. The tradition of critical social theory deriving from Marx and Lukács hardly represents itself as Marxism anymore or, at least, not as historical Marxism. In the eighties, after Apel proposed his tripartite division, the appeal to Marx (then still a common denominator for the German and French traditions that set the tone for Continental philosophy) became suspect for historical reasons that need not concern us here. An author like Habermas, for example, who during the seventies was still engaged in the reconstruction of historical materialism, now supports his critical theory (apart from its sociological and juridical aspects) with arguments drawn from hermeneutics, analytic philosophy, and pragmatics. And K.-O. Apel too presents his normative theory as transcendental hermeneutics or transcendental pragmatics.

In fact, of Apel's three strands, only two—analytic philosophy and the phenomenological-existential-hermeneutical tradition—remain. The triple designation of the latter is meant to represent a historical development. If Continental philosophy was first described as phenomenology broadly understood (Husserl, Scheler, Lipps, Heidegger, and in substance N. Hartmann), immediately after the war it came to be designated by the term existentialism (Jaspers, Heidegger, Merleau-Ponty, Sartre), defined as the concretization of the phenomenological viewpoint. Thereafter, having acquired the reputation of being faddish, existentialism gave way to hermeneutics (Heidegger again, Gadamer, and more broadly the transcendental hermeneutics of Habermas and Apel, as well as postmodernism). The term *hermeneutics* came to comprehend things as various as Gadamerian philosophy itself, the rehabilitation of practical philosophy—often caricatured as "neo-Aristotelianism"[21]—that arose under Gadamer's influence (H. Arendt, J. Ritter, M. Jonas, M. Riedel, R. Bubner, and others),[22] the historical and relativist wing of theory of science (Kuhn, Feyerabend) and of philosophy of language (Rorty, Davidson), and also Nietzschean postmodernism and the neostructuralist avant-garde.[23] Nowadays, all of these are conceived as belonging to "hermeneutics." Here, however, we will need to define hermeneutic philosophy more strictly and circumscribe it within narrower limits.

Along with Continental hermeneutic philosophy, analytic philosophy remains dominant, especially in Anglo-Saxon countries, though it has endured fundamental changes affecting its self-understanding. Following the steps of the late Wittgenstein and under the auspices of the older pragmatic tradition (Peirce, James, Dewey), Quine, Goodman, Rorty, and Davidson have gradually detached analytic philosophy from its early program of logical critique of language. In doing so, they reoriented it toward general questions such as the possibility—given perspectivism and cultural relativity—

of binding truth, as well as of responsible behavior and knowledge, a task that had been entrusted to Continental philosophy since the advent of historicism. Today, quite unlike formerly, it seems that analytic philosophy stands for no precisely formulable program. In the very pursuit of its own tradition, analytic philosophy came to the recognition that it is faced with the same challenges as is transcendental hermeneutics on the Continent. Both are impelled toward a pragmatic philosophy of finitude that must take its chances and weigh its risks. That is one way of describing the dissolution of philosophical analysis, or at least its convergence with hermeneutic philosophy.[24]

Such a convergence, of course, does not lend itself to being easily identified with any particular philosophical problematic. For that very reason, our task here must be to work out a special form of hermeneutic philosophy, one that can legitimate philosophy's classical claim to universality under today's conditions—that is, under the banner of historical consciousness. Only thus can we speak of a hermeneutic contribution to present-day philosophy.

Yet what is meant by universality? Although the word is in constant use, it cannot be said that the concept of a "universal claim" (either of hermeneutics or of philosophy) is very clear. Neither the Gadamerian claim to universality—which seems to pertain to language, historicity, and his own philosophy as well—nor its denial by Habermas and Derrida has achieved any final clarity. One might well suppose that "universality" refers to the universal validity of some proposition. If so, it would be easy to show that hermeneutics is stuck in a logical or pragmatic contradiction. Some have tried to construe the universal claim of hermeneutics as climaxing in the thesis that everything is historically conditioned, a thesis supposed to be universally valid. If this thesis is meant to apply universally, then it must apply to its own claim, which must itself be historically limited and therefore not universal. The universal claim of hermeneutics is thus considered self-contradictory.

This argumentative strategy creates the impression that historical consciousness could be somehow eluded by showing that its universalization involves an untenable aporia. Thus the supposedly saving world of logic is reinstated: not everything is historical because universal historicism is self-contradictory. As Heidegger remarked early on, however, these formalist arguments that try to outsmart genuine historicity with the help of logic have something of an "attempt to bowl one over."[25] Elaborating Heidegger's thought, Gadamer discerns in such arguments a "formalist illusion" that misses the truth of the matter: "That the thesis of skepticism or relativism refutes itself to the extent that it claims to be true is an irrefutable argument.

But what does it achieve? The reflective argument that proves successful here rebounds against the arguer, for it renders the truth value of reflection suspect. It is not the reality of skepticism or of truth-dissolving relativism but the truth claim of all formal argument that is affected."[26]

As philosophical hermeneutics can show, to appeal to the logical contradictoriness of universal historicity is to remain in the rut of historicism. Historicism, one could affirm with good reason, is the central and most crippling problem facing philosophy since Hegel, namely, the question concerning the possibility of binding truth and thus conclusive philosophy within the horizon of historical knowledge. Are all truths and rules of conduct dependent on their historical context? If so, the specter of relativism and nihilism lurks nearby. The fundamental question must undoubtedly be taken seriously. If the cultural horizon is the final determinant of acceptability, then how can a perverse way of life (and for German philosophy after the war, the extreme example of National Socialism became paradigmatic) be defined or criticized by comparison to what is only another lifestyle? Metaphysical inquiry into historicism tried to solve this problem by claiming to transcend historicity. This it did by way of an appeal to a supratemporal authority, either secular or sacred, intended to guarantee the validity of allegedly unhistorical norms, or by recourse to the ultimacy of logic, or sometimes by certifying its own foundational status. What all these attempted solutions share with historicism is their common metaphysical cornerstone, namely, the idea that in the absence of absolute truth everything is irredeemably relative. Ultimately, however, these solutions were themselves overtaken by historicism: they, too, showed themselves to be historically conditioned, since they were continually being outmoded and the particularities of their perspectives superseded.

The philosophical achievement of hermeneutics lies perhaps less in having solved the problem of historicism than in its departure from it. Heidegger and Gadamer folded historicism back upon itself, so to speak, and thereby they manifested its own historicity—that is, its secret dependence on metaphysics: the dogmatic thesis of historicism that everything is relative can be made meaningful only against the horizon of a nonrelative, absolute, supratemporal, metaphysical truth. Only by supposing absolute truth possible and using it as a criterion could an opinion be judged merely relative. What does this absolute truth look like, however? There can never be an answer that all will acknowledge and accept. Philosophical hermeneutics suggests that historicism's pretension to supratemporal truth derives precisely from the denial of its own historicity. Significantly, the truth considered to be absolute has only a negative definition: the nonfinite, the nontemporal, and so forth. What expresses itself in these terms is the self-negation of human temporality. The search for absolute norms, measures, and criteria testifies to the metaphysical origins of historicism, its subservience to the logic of thought that represses time.

Repudiating the metaphysical obsession with the supratemporal, whose covert historicity we have shown, philosophical hermeneutics situates the paradigmatically fundamental problem of temporality within the framework of a hermeneutics of facticity. How this regression articulates itself philosophically we will see in the pages that follow. Here we can already see, however, that such thought about finitude is anything but uncritical. It would be presumptuous to suppose that a temporal being has no means of critique at its disposal. The fallacy lies, rather, in thinking, along metaphysical and historicist lines, that credible criticism can derive only from supratemporal authorities or norms. The fact is just the opposite. Human begins are fundamentally critical *because* they are temporal, and they oppose evil by appeal to their own interests and aspirations, which can only be understood temporally. We need no supratemporal laws in order to denounce Hitler's dictatorship or other lesser evils. Such madness is criticized primarily in the name of the pain and suffering it causes. This critique can dispense with the support of nontemporal principles. Suffering, whether felt or anticipated, whether of a greater or lesser degree, always makes the best critical argument; and hermeneutics can increase sensitivity to it. One might object that evil cannot always be prevented in this way. True enough, but if principles could be found that would prevent injustice, no discussion of the means and ends of social justice would ever be necessary.[27] The call for vigilance and critical thinking, coupled with a warning against metaphysical utopias, is not the least significant contribution hermeneutics has made to this important discussion.

The universal claim of hermeneutics has still not been clarified, however. What is the point of trying to erect such a claim? In what follows we shall consider this question at length. The history of hermeneutics is disjointed in just this respect, for the universal claim has manifested itself in various forms. Thus it would be worthwhile to inquire into hermeneutic history by investigating the universal claims that constitute it. Such will be the guiding thread of the present introduction: What kinds of universality are claimed by the various forms that hermeneutics has taken in the past, and what kind can be claimed by that of today? This question will need to be directed to the whole corpus that has been constituted over time by hermeneutical self-reflection.

The claim to universality must de facto have already been immense for such modes of inquiry as those practiced by the early Middle Ages, when all knowledge derived from the interpretation of a single (holy) book; and the same must be true of the Enlightenment, as exemplified in the universalist hermeneutics of Chladenius and Meier, which in the spirit of Leibniz portrayed all knowledge as the explication of signs. In all probability, such claims prepared the way for modern forms of hermeneutics—for example, the semiotic.

By way of beginning, it seems advisable to view the universality of hermeneutics as a universal *problem*. What has raised hermeneutics in our time to the status of prima philosophia is probably the omnipresence of interpretive phenomena. Beginning at least with Nietzsche's insight into universal perspectivism ("there are no facts, only interpretations"), addressing the problem posed by this omnipresence has been the order of the day for philosophy. Nietzsche is probably the first modern author to have made us conscious of the fundamentally interpretive character of our experience of the world. Hardly limited to such purely interpretive sciences as scriptural exegesis, classical philology, and law, the horizon of interpretation comprehends all the sciences and modes of orienting one's life. The interpretive tendency was furthered by a revaluation of empiricism and inductivism within theory of science, a revaluation that found consequences of hermeneutic significance in Kant's distinction between phenomena and things in themselves: knowledge is not a reflection of things as they are, independent of us; it is a schematized and interested construction of phenomena. For Kant this fact presented no danger to objectivity, since all humankind is equipped with fundamentally the same categories of understanding. It became a philosophical as well as universal problem, however, when with Nietzsche people discovered that these categories—that is, reason and its verbal embodiments—could be subject to historical, cultural, and even individual perspectivism. This perspectivism is no ultimate for Nietzsche, however; it has its foundation in the will to power. Every perspective stands under suspicion of being not an adaptation to the world's own order but an attempt to control it in the sense of a will to power. Nietzsche's panhermeneuticism feeds into a certain pragmatism that looks forward to the renewal of pragmatic thought in analytic philosophy as well as Continental hermeneutics. What legitimates any given perspective is the value it has for life, its contribution to stimulating or stabilizing a given form of the will to power. This doesn't necessarily lead to defeatism, nihilism, or disorientation, however. The perspectives are not all of equal value, since some prove to be more fruitful than others. The mistake, in Nietzsche's view, lies rather in equating what is merely a fruitful perspective with the thing itself.[28]

In its universality such perspectivism may appear extreme. Nonetheless, Nietzsche has thereby indicated an essential characteristic of our modern world-picture. What distinguishes the modern understanding of the world, as Habermas has most recently pointed out,[29] is its "reflexivity"—that is, it reflexively recognizes itself to be an interpretation. Our knowledge knows about itself as knowledge and interpretation of the world as well. It does not identify itself with the world itself or its mere reflection. The mythic interpretation of the world, by contrast, is not aware of itself *as* interpretation. It equates itself, so to speak, with the world in itself. Habermas catches myth's reflective deficiency in the happy phrase: "the reification of the world-picture."[30] It is in the modern, demythologized world-picture that our interpretations of reality have first emerged *as* interpretations, exposing themselves as such for discussion and critique. Habermas and Nietzsche are at one concerning the fundamentally hermeneutical—that is, interpretive and ultimately pragmatic—horizon of our world-picture. Both bear witness to the universality of the hermeneutic problem, though, to be sure, without taking it to its ultimate conclusion. In the face of this thoroughgoing perspectivism, Habermas considers it appropriate to discuss our worldviews, although or even because they are known to be perspectives, and to hold those viewpoints to be (pragmatically) legitimate that have proved themselves capable of consensus. The fact that a given consensus can be artificially produced— for example, by force—makes Habermas hesitate to identify any actual consensus with the true one. He must resign himself to the idea that truth is tied to the contrafactual anticipation of an *ideal* consensus. At best this contrafactual idealization functions as a goad spurring us on to further critique,[31] and so it finally remains problematical what, if anything, can be deemed true or legitimate.

Nietzsche refuses to use such metaphysical idealization to escape the agonistic conflict of fundamentally heterogeneous, power-based perspectives. But how can we be sure that everything is perspectival? Isn't perspectivism itself only one perspective among others? We can answer first that the *suspicion* of perspectivity is certainly universalizable. That a given view of the world is merely a perspective conditioned by interests serving the will to power is a suspicion that can be used to criticize any conception.[32] The position under suspicion has the burden of proving, if it can, that it is *not* a one-sided perspective. The perspective of perspectivism, then, does not necessarily lead to resignation and the belief that "anything goes." It is a critical and hermeneutical perspective espoused by a philosophy whose job is to protect us from knowledge claims that cannot be proven.[33]

Within the spectrum of present-day hermeneutics, Nietzsche can be considered a representative of the "hermeneutics of suspicion." This is a phrase coined by Paul Ricoeur to characterize the interpretive strategy that distrusts immediate meaning, tracing it back to an unconscious will to power.[34] Along with Nietzsche as representatives of the hermeneutics of suspicion, Ricoeur names Freud, who reduces meaning to unconscious drives, and Marx, who links it to class interests. On the other side, and exhausting the spectrum, he places the hermeneutics of faith, confidence, or attestation which takes meaning phenomenologically, as it is given. Whereas the hermeneutics of suspicion looks backward, thereby reducing claims to meaning to the economy or energies that function behind them (impulses, class interests, will to power), the hermeneutics of confidence is oriented in a forward direction, toward the world that presents us with meaning to be interpreted. Such faith does not surrender to the lure of immediate meaning, however. Rather, it learns from the hermeneutics of suspicion and cooperates in destroying the illusions of false consciousness, insofar as they can be demonstrated. This destruction leaves the question of meaning completely open. The consciousness that has been freed of its illusions strives to orient itself just as it always has. That is, critically informed faith concerns itself with truth claims that disclose the possibility of meaning—and thus with the verbum interius behind every explicit meaning. This faith in meaning, without which language would remain empty of significance, can lay claim to universality. The hermeneutics of suspicion must be subordinate to that universality insofar as suspicious hermeneutics performs its destructions by appeal to a "true" consciousness, even if this truth functions only as a regulative idea.

Thus it is that the problem of universality manifests itself within the horizon of hermeneutic thought. Reflection on interpretation has allowed present-day philosophy to renew its concern with the universal. By thematizing the fundamentally hermeneutic character of our relation to the world, hermeneutics by no means relinquishes philosophical universalism. It realizes it.

I
On the
Prehistory of
Hermeneutics

1. Linguistic Delimitations

The development of explicit hermeneutical reflection bears the signature of modernity. As shown above with reference to Nietzsche and Habermas, what distinguishes the modern world-picture is its consciousness of being perspectival. As soon as it becomes evident that worldviews do not merely duplicate reality as it is in itself, but are instead pragmatic interpretations embraced by our language-world, then hermeneutics comes into its own. Only with the advent of modernity has this occurred. For this reason, it is hardly accidental that the Latin word *hermeneutica* first emerges in the seventeenth century. Yet modern insights can be traced back to antiquity, where the cosmos was much less univocal than the common platitudes would have it. Along with the rationalist Eleatics and Platonists there was also a host of relativistic Sophists who were thoroughly familiar with the conditioned and perspectival nature of human standards. So it remains a question how far back the history of hermeneutics reaches. The answer, of course, depends on how one defines hermeneutics. Thus to delimit our topic we need some linguistic signposts.

In present-day usage, the word *hermeneutic* is afflicted by a vast amorphousness which, as in the case of most other philosophemes, may well explain why it has prospered. Such concepts as hermeneutics, interpretation, explication, exegesis are often used synonymously. An interpretation of Hegel, for example, can describe itself, without qualification, as being a hermeneutics of Hegel.[1] In the business of interpretation today, "hermeneutic preconsiderations" means the same thing as preliminary explanations. For the sake of defining our terms, then, it seems advisable to narrow the concept of hermeneutics somewhat, first of all confining its meaning to *theory* of interpretation. We can leave the term theory undefined, because various hermeneutics have various conceptions of what theory means. On one hand, it is a *Kunstlehre* (Schleiermacher)—that is, a methodical exposition of rules governing the interpretation of texts—and its purpose is primarily normative and technical. Such a theory is intended to show how interpretation should be conducted so as to exclude arbitrariness from the universe of interpretation. On the other hand, others encourage hermeneutics to renounce this technical task in order to assume the more comprehensive form of a philosophy or phenomenology, with the task of analyzing the originary phenomenon of interpretation or understanding. In its phenomenological guise hermeneutics apparently no longer teaches anyone how to interpret but instead shows how interpretation is de facto practiced. Fundamentally, theory means either a normative and methodological hermeneutics or a phenomenological hermeneutics.

The concept of interpretation varies in inclusiveness as well. If one maintains, for example, that language is always already interpretation, then theory of interpretation becomes general theory of language or knowledge. Yet though language is inalienably tied to interpretation, a historical introduction to hermeneutics such as this cannot hope to offer a general theory of language (though we will be able to treat hermeneutics' contribution to language theory). Here, too, it seems necessary for heuristic purposes to employ a narrower concept of interpretation. Accordingly, we will take interpretation as referring to what occurs when a really or apparently unfamiliar meaning is made intelligible (not necessarily made credible, because incredibilities can be understood). Hermeneutic theory concerns itself with just this process of interpretation. This seems unimportant enough if interpretation were taken to be merely a tiny fraction of human experience. It assumes universal relevance, however, as soon as we become aware that all human behavior is based on making sense of things, even if only unconsciously; and ultimately this is the best evidence for the universal claim of hermeneutics. Beginning in the twentieth century this universality penetrated philosophical consciousness, whereas earlier, apart from a few exceptions, the process of interpretation was treated as a special and local problem, governed by auxiliary normative disciplines within the individual interpretive sciences.

A thoroughgoing history of hermeneutics cannot afford to forget these "provincial" origins. Especially fruitful for opening up a hermeneutic archaeology is the fact that at certain pivotal periods—times at which hermeneutics went into high gear, so to speak—the problem of interpretation became particularly pressing. Even if constructed retrospectively—that is, even if they derive from the expectations of present-day historiography—experiences of rupture in tradition infused the problem of interpretation and hermeneutic theory with renewed explosiveness. Thus, in post-Aristotelian philosophy, for example, a theory of allegorical interpretation was developed for revaluing the rationalizing myths that had become incredible and offensive. Using this theory, allegorical interpreters gave new currency to what had been merely alien meaning. To be sure, interpretive violence is often the price to be paid for papering over breaks in tradition. For this reason, the advent of Christ, which appeared to interrupt Jewish tradition, called special attention to the principles of interpretation. In the early Middle Ages as well, interpretation necessarily assumed a prominent place, since all knowledge depended on interpreting Scripture and the works of the Fathers. When medieval hermeneutics was transformed during the Reformation by the introduction of the rule of *sola scriptura,* hermeneutic reflection acquired renewed energy. Thus the Reformation is often celebrated, by Dilthey, for example, as the beginning of hermeneutics. It must be admitted, however, that the treatises produced by Reformation theologians in their dispute with Catholic orthodoxy swarmed with rules drawn from the Church Fathers, so that this pivotal period is much less revolutionary than the classic history of hermeneutics, itself indebted to Protestant theology, would suggest.

In the seventeenth century, beginning with J. C. Dannhauer, quite a number of now almost forgotten general theories of interpretation sprang up. In the spirit of rationalism, their avowed purpose was to offer rules and methods for discerning the true sense of a text. Stimulated by Kant's Copernican revolution, which assigned subjectivity a new, constitutive role in cognitive processes, romantic hermeneutics broke with rationalism. At first, romanticism limited itself to offering subjectively tinged canons of interpretation—here, too, by means of a thoroughgoing transformation of older materials. In the later nineteenth century the subjectivizing tendencies of Kantian critique sparked the emergence of historicism, which confronted hermeneutics with the radical problem of theorizing the objectivity of the human sciences in such a way as to match the standards of the natural sciences. Authors such as Böckh, Dilthey, and Droysen found themselves faced with the Kantian task of formulating a critique of historical reason. The foreseeable future of hermeneutics then seemed to be comprehended in the task of methodologizing the human sciences. Later the very process of alienation caused by the obsession with methodology and epistemology led to Heidegger's universalization and radicalization of hermeneutics. "Making sense of things," the beginning and end of hermeneutic endeavor, was no longer a marginalized epiphenomenon limited to text-based disciplines; it was instead a fundamental aspect of existence for a being that understands itself in time, and whose own being is concerned with being. Now indisputably philosophical, this has remained the nature of hermeneutics up to Gadamer and Habermas.

Before then, the history of hermeneutics remained in what might be called its "prehistory." In what follows we will trace its most important stages, beginning with the etymology of the word.

2. The Semantics of *hermeneuein*

The notion that the purpose of hermeneutics is to make meaning intelligible finds its first confirmation in the etymology of the term. We have been taught by G. Ebeling to distinguish three senses of hermeneuein: expression (utterance, speaking), explication (interpretation, explanation), and translation (acting as an interpreter).[2] It is not difficult to understand why the second two senses are designated by the same verb. To translate—that is, carry-across unfamiliar sounds into familiar language—is to interpret in a certain sense. The translator's job is to explain or make sense of what a strange text is trying to say. Thus there remain only two fundamental senses of hermeneuein: expressing and interpreting. Here again the two share a common term because both of them, equally aiming at understanding, have to do with similar movements of spirit—though as J. Pépin puts it, the one is directed outward, the other inward.[3] In "expression" spirit, as it were, makes what is contained within knowable from without, whereas "interpretation" tries to penetrate an uttered expression to see the spirit contained within it. What is involved in both is making sense or communicating it. Interpretation inquires into the tacit, inner sense behind the explicit; speaking ex-presses the inner.

This explains why the Greeks think of saying as hermeneuein: "interpreting." Speaking is merely the translation of thoughts into words. Thus the title of Aristotle's logical and semantic treatise Peri hermeneias—whose subject is propositions (logos apophantikos)[4] that can be either true or false—was consistently translated in Latin as De interpretatione. The utterance (hermeneia) is always a translation of the soul's (that is, inner) thoughts into externalized language. A sentence thus mediates between the thoughts and the addressee. This Greek conception of discourse reaches its apex in the Stoic distinction between the logos prophorikos and the logos endiathetos (between uttered and inward logos). The first concerns only the expression (hermeneia), whereas the second concerns the inner, the thought (dianoia).[5] The hermeneia is simply the logos comprehended in words—its radiance ad extra. Mutatis mutandis, interpreting the spoken word involves proceeding in the opposite direction: inward, toward the logos endiathetos. In both cases, hermeneuein proves to be a process of mediating meaning that proceeds from the outside to the inside of meaning.

Usually the concept of hermeneutics is taken to be a modern phenomenon. And that is true insofar as one is thinking about the word hermeneutica, which entered common usage around 1619. That term, however, is merely the Latinized rendition of the word hermeneutike, which is first to be met with in the Platonic corpus (Politikos 260 d 11, Epinomis 975 c 6, and Definitiones 414 d 4). Hermeneutike has a sacred or religious function in the Politikos. The Epinomis associates hermeneutike with mantike, or soothsaying, since both are kinds of knowledge that do not lead to sophia because the interpreter understands only what is said as such (to legomenon), without knowing whether it is true (alethes). He comprehends a meaning, an utterance, though he cannot determine its truth—which is the first and foremost business of sophia.

Can we differentiate between mantike (soothsaying) and hermeneutike (divination, perhaps)? Neither the Epinomis nor the Politikos is very clear on this issue (because they merely list hermeneutike within a host of other sciences). What is clear, however, is the reason why mantike, at least, can lead to no kind of sophia or truth whatever: a madness (Gr. mania) dwells within it. Plato remarks in the Timaeus (71a-72b) that those in the grip of madness lack the self-possession necessary to assess the truth of their visions, even if the visions are of divine origin. The mad are so outside themselves that they cannot rationally interpret their own experience.[6] Who does possess this competence? According to the *Timaeus*, it falls to the prophet (prophetes). He alone can communicate the truth to be found in the vision of the possessed. Hermeneutike is not mentioned in this connection, and so we might ask whether its activity belongs to the mania that energizes mantike or to the prophet. In Plato's texts the answer to this question is not all that clear. In other Greek texts, too, the meaning of prophetes remains rather ambiguous: sometimes it designates the one who *receives* direct inspiration by the divine and communicates it to others, sometimes the one who *explains* the words of a divinely inspired person.[7] In both cases, however, it is assigned a mediating function, and it is viewed as succeeding on either of two different levels. It has to do with the mediation between either gods and men (through the medium of the one possessed, the prophet), or between other people and the mediator himself.

The task of mediating falls to the hermeneus too. In an often quoted passage Plato refers to poets as the hermenes tôn theôn (*Ion* 435e). In this dialogue, moreover, the rhapsodes who perform the poets' works are described as interpreters of interpreters (hermeneon hermenes, *Ion* 535a). Just like the prophet, the hermeneus seems to mediate both between god and man as well as between people and the (manic) mediator. Thus the hermeneus is the mediator of something mediated, the mediator of a hermeneia—a function that can go on indefinitely, since it always leaves more to say than can be precisely captured in words.

The mediatory function of the hermeneutic led antiquity to make an etymological linkage between the semantic family of hermeneus and the mediator-god, Hermes. This connection is probably more plausible than true, and philologists today regard it with almost universal skepticism.[8] Yet a better etymology is still to be found, and none has met with consensus. So at present the etymological origins of hermeneuein must remain an open question.

So far, with respect to the semantic level of hermeneuein, we have occupied ourselves with its religious function. An alternative, secular level of meaning is to be found in the pseudo-Platonic *Definitiones* (414 d 1), where the adjective hermeneutike means "signifying something." This meaning—which is broader than the strictly religious meaning—typifies the semantics of the word hermeneia. It means not only utterance but also language generally,[9] translation, interpretation, and also style and rhetoric (elocutio).[10] The

Peri hermeneias (Latin, *De elocutione*) of Demetrius, for example, is nothing but a treatise on stylistics.[11]

Here, too, the unitary function of hermeneia is patent. It always involves reproducing something already thought in such a way as to make it intelligible, for what is "style" but an adept way to further meaning? This sense of the term dominated early Latin as well as patristic writing, since hermeneuein was translated as interpretari, and hermeneia as interpretatio, even if utterance alone was meant. Boethius (c. 475–525) defines the matter nicely: interpretatio est vox articulata per se ipsam significans.[12] Philo of Alexandria (c. 20 B.C.–A.D. 50) also understands hermeneia as the spoken logos;[13] and the Church Father, Clement of Alexandria (c. 150–215), likewise considers he tes dianoias hermeneia as the manifestation of thought in language.[14]

Most important to philosophical hermeneutics is the wide range of relations (implying no ambiguity, since it is highly consistent) that antiquity glimpses between language, reproduction or interpretation of thought, and hermeneuein. For the interpretation or translation which was then generally called hermeneia means precisely reversing the process to which the word speaking (Sprache) always refers, namely, making oneself understood. In modernity, hermeneutics has merely recuperated this ancient insight in asserting its universal claim.

3. Allegorical Interpretation of Myth

Recognizing the obvious fact that language is always interpretatio, however, marks only the beginning of interpretation theory. It does not constitute a hermeneutics in any systematic sense. Making things understood becomes an acute problem only when it no longer works. The necessity for express consideration of interpretation—of the primordial event of language as interpretatio (repetition of thought)—is owing to the experience of unintelligibility. And nothing is more human than this experience.

Such consideration first begins when understanding is put to the test by passages in religious and mythic tradition that have become objectionable. Especially during the Hellenic period, when philosophy had reached the point of identifying the divine with the rational logos, to speak (as Homer often did) of all too human goings-on, such as chicanery and jealousy, on divine Olympus, no longer seemed appropriate to godliness or rationality. Thus such passages required "allegorical" reinterpretation. The beginnings of this process are commonly traced back to Stoic philosophy, which worked out a procedure for systematic, rationalizing, and hence allegorical interpretation of myth.

More generally, insofar as allegorical *practice* serves to accommodate ancient wisdom to the Zeitgeist of later times, it certainly occurs earlier than Stoicism, as indicated by the fact that Plato and Aristotle had also offered rational interpretations of myth. Even the rhapsodes, no doubt, had to take the current taste of their audiences into account, if only by adapting their manner of presentation to them (hermeneia!). So, too, early rabbinical interpretation of Scripture avoided the literal sense on those occasions when it gave offense.[15] This practice lies at the heart of hermeneia understood as the mediation or communication of meaning. Once we appreciate the full breadth of the concept of hermeneuein, we come to see that behind what is literally said, something other, something more lies hidden; and discovering it requires all the more hermeneutic effort when the immediate sense, the literal, is unintelligible.

It was the Stoa who first systematized this practice, raising it thereby to the status of a conscious method. Yet given the fragmentariness of our information about them (not a single, complete Stoic treatise is extant), it is doubtful or, at any rate, difficult to determine whether the Stoa arrived at what could be called a genuine *theory* of allegory. Indeed, the word allegoria is not to be found among the Stoics.[16] The synonymous term hyponoia, however, was in circulation among them, and Plato and Xenophon had used it in an allegorical sense. Hyponoia is a form of indirect communication that says one thing in order to make something else understood—a process that the verb allegorein makes explicit: it signifies to mean something different (allos) than what is said (agoreuein)—even than what is "publicly said" (here agora can be heard, too). Behind the sense that is out there in the open, in the agora, there is something other, something deeper that first seems alien to the agora (the obvious interpretation).

The practice of allegoresis, that is, allegorical interpretation of myth, thus consists in discovering something more profound behind the shocking literal sense. The offensiveness or absurdity of the immediate meaning serves to indicate that an allegorical meaning is intended which the knowledgeable reader or hearer can unlock. But what constitutes this other kind of meaning? Doesn't the danger of arbitrariness begin to loom large as soon as one bids farewell to the literal? Even if this danger cannot be avoided, and even though allegoresis had for just this reason already fallen into discredit in antiquity, the allegorical interpreter will insist that the literal meaning must always be exceeded even to understand *it* aright. Etymology was one of the preferred means of doing so. The Stoics were of the opinion that the earliest ancients carried the as yet unfalsified logos within them and thus could penetrate the essence of things.[17] This capacity is especially evident in a passage from Cicero's *De natura deorum,* where a speech ascribed to the Stoic Balbus is described. Balbus is trying to prove that the Greeks had converted moral qualities and beneficent natural forces into gods. Saturn, for example, means time, since Saturn means "sated by years" (quod saturetur annis).[18] Thus etymology could give access to hidden dimensions of meaning surpassing the literal.

The expression *allegoria* actually derives from rhetoric and was formulated by a grammarian, Pseudo-Heraclitus (fl. first century A.D.), who defined allegory as a rhetorical trope whereby it was possible to say one thing and at the same time allude to something else.[19] Allegory does not first enter the scene with the self-conscious act of interpretation; it is already at home in language. It dwells, as it were, immanently within the expressive function of language: its capacity to let something else be heard in the utterance. It seems clear enough that the Stoic distinction between the logos prophorikos and logos endiathetos prepared the way for the formulation of the rhetorical concept of allegory.[20] Spoken discourse is not sufficient unto itself; it points to something else, whose sign it is. Interpretation and understanding clearly have to do with this inner logos, not with the word itself. Language invites us to recognize the literal logos within its limits and then surpass them. Before it became a technique of interpretation, then, allegory (like hyponoia) simply designated a form of speech, indeed a rhetorical form, since rhetorical acts are concerned with communicating meaning. Thus scholars began to distinguish between allegory, the original figure of speech, which aims at something beyond the literal, and allegoresis, which means the explicit interpretive act of tracing the literal back to the meaning communicated through it (that is, just the reverse of allegory).[21]

The motives of allegorical interpretation of myth—or allegoresis—are threefold.[22] The first is moral: it is intended to purify written tradition of scandalous material. According to Pseudo-Heraclitus, allegoresis functions as an antipharmakon tes asebeias: an antidote for impiety. The second, related motive is rational. The Stoa wanted to show that rational interpretation of the world was compatible with myth, since this compatibility would support their conviction that the all-encompassing logos was the same everywhere.[23] Finally there is what might be called a utilitarian motive of allegoresis. No author of that period wanted to be in a position of contradicting the authority of the ancient poets. For the Stoics it was extraordinarily important to maintain the authority of myth. Earlier, suspicion of impiety led merely to the repudiation and mythic interpretation, as is the case in Xenophanes[24] and frequently in Plato.[25] The Stoics could afford this erosion of authority no longer. They needed the support of tradition in order to maintain their closed worldview, despite their now tenuous relation to the ancient world of the Greeks. The more distant and problematic tradition becomes, the more pressing it is to preserve it by any means—including the artificial means of allegoresis.

None of these three motives is completely outmoded, even now. Today, too, allegorical interpretation is on occasion pressed into service in order to reinterpret morally objectionable passages, harmonize reason with poetry, and leave the authority of the classics unimpaired. To the extent that it derived from these motivations, the Stoic doctrine of an inner and outer logos as concretized in allegorical interpretation of myth gave substantial impetus to the development of hermeneutics.

4. Philo: The Universality of Allegory

In discussing the Stoics we have carefully avoided speaking of a hermeneutic *theory*—that is, a hermeneutics. The earliest general contours of such a theory are to be found in Philo of Alexandria (c. 20 B.C.–A.D. 50), an author of the Jewish tradition heavily influenced by the Stoics. Philo is universally considered to be the father of allegory,[26] though he nowhere spells out his allegorical method.[27] He is primarily a practitioner of allegoresis applied to the Old Testament, reflecting only seldom on the principles underlying his procedure.

Philo's allegoresis has an apologetical motive. It is employed when literal interpretation involves the danger of misunderstanding the myth. How can we tell whether a passage of the Bible is to be interpreted literally or allegorically? According to Philo, the author (that is to say, God) ensures that the text will be understood allegorically by scattering objective signs or grounds of allegory in the text.[28] The first book of Moses, for example, speaks of two trees in paradise, the trees of life and knowledge (Gen. 2:9), whose difference from ours makes a literal interpretation implausible. Thus Scripture itself contains indicators of allegory—for example, aporias, absurdities, strangeness or errors in the literal, which can only have been intentional in the author of Scripture, since divine revelation can contain no falsehoods.[29] On occasion it reveals spiritual and divine mysteries which the "carnal" sense is fundamentally unsuited to convey. In such cases, it is the content itself that necessitates taking the allegorical path.

Philo compares the relation between literal and metaphorical to that between body and soul—a metaphor whose enormous influence justifies extensive quotation from the following crucial passage:

> The interpretations of the Holy Scripture are made in accordance with the deeper meanings conveyed in allegory. For the whole of the Law seems to these people [that is, the exegetes] to resemble a living being with the literal commandments for its body, and for its soul the invisible meaning stored away in its words. It is in the latter that the rational soul begins especially to contemplate the things akin to itself and, beholding the extraordinary beauties[30] of the concepts through the polished glass of the words, unfolds and reveals the symbols, and brings the thoughts, thus bared, into the light for those who, with a slight jog to their memory, are able to view the invisible through the visible.[31]

The fact that allegoresis is intended to reach something high and invisible implies that such meaning is not immediately accessible to all readers. Only the initiated, only interpreters with the proper vocation and experience can penetrate to this higher meaning that God hides from the common reader restricted to the literal. As Philo shows, only those who have the capacity to comprehend the little hints of the invisible to be found in the visible (tois dunamenois ek mikras hupomneseos ta aphane dia tôn phanerôn theôrein) are in a position to grasp the deeper meaning of Scripture. Thus Philo often avails himself of the language of orphic mysticism to describe how the interpreter rises to the level of allegorical meaning. This level is meant not for the many (pros tous pollous) but the few (pros oligous) who concern themselves with the spirit, not the letter.[32] The key to Scripture belongs only to those within the esoteric circle who are worthy of the invisible. In fact it is apparent that religious discourse itself invites allegorical understanding if the next world is conveyed by means of a thoroughly this-worldly language. That the spoken logos, the logos prophorikos, is always the sign of another, invisible logos could only add further impetus to that notion.

Generally speaking, from the Stoic to the patristic period, there was a broad conviction that everything religious must involve something symbolic, indirect, and mysterious.[33] After all, religion is concerned with spirit—that is, with the esoteric—and allegory is what discloses spiritual or pneumatic meaning. Over time arose the sense that religion consists *entirely* of mystery, as seemed perfectly appropriate from the point of view of its subject matter (the divine) and of its human addressees (who are dependent on the body).

Even if on occasion Philo emphasizes the autonomy of the literal meaning and warns his readers against the dangers of radical allegorization, he himself does not wholly escape them. In his work are to be found passages suggesting that *everything* in Scripture consists of mystery. The first practical theory of allegory that antiquity offers, then, culminates in the intuition that allegory is universal. What appears here for the first time on theoretical terrain (it was already implicit in the semantics of hermeneia, though in a nontheoretical way) is a distant prefiguration of the universal claim of hermeneutics. It implies that everything literal (Wörtliches) must be related to something pre-verbal (Vorwörtliches) in order to be fully comprehended. Scripture does not suffice in itself;[34] it needs the light shed on it by another— a requirement that allegory strives to fulfill. Its universalization indicates why it is necessary to retrace the logos prophorikos to the spirit that animates it. For the interpreter, this goal alone is what is important.

Yet universalizing allegory, a process which cannot be resisted given that no written word suffices unto itself, can lead to abandoning the verbal logos, disregarding the expressive intent that is manifested there and only there, and this can open the door to interpretive arbitrariness. Thus Philo's mode of allegoresis had acquired a bad reputation even in antiquity. He had distanced himself too far from the primacy of the literal interpretation of law that distinguished Judaic interpreters of the Torah who were less infected than he by the orphic mysticism of Greece. It was probably for this reason that his influence on Palestinian exegesis was small, and he was silently excluded by rabbinical Judaism from its canonical tradition.[35]

5. Origen: The Universality of Typology

On early Christianity, by contrast, Philo's mode of allegoresis was far more influential. From the beginning, Christianity faced the special challenge of spreading the message of Jesus and extending its implications for Judaic law. On the basis of his teaching, the Mosaic law and especially its messianic prophecy could no longer be understood literally. Since Jesus explicitly appealed to its authority, however, Christians could not simply put the Judaic tradition behind them. Thus it seemed advisable to interpret it allegorically and to relate it exclusively to the person of Jesus. Jesus was the spirit to be gleaned from the letter of the Old Testament. Moreover, the words of Jesus himself pointed in this direction, at least according to the fourth Gospel: "Search the scriptures; [they] . . . testify of me" (John 3:39). "Had ye believed Moses, ye would have believed me: for he wrote of me" (5:46).

It was hardly evident that this was the case. Judaic messianism anticipated the coming of a powerful ruler who would restore the kingdom of the Jews to its old majesty—certainly not someone, crucified as a blasphemer, who wanted to revoke the law. The literal meaning of Scripture was unmistakable here. Thus an allegorical interpretation was needed that could unlock the Scriptures with the hermeneutic key offered by the person of Jesus. Much later, allegoresis relating the Old Testament to Jesus came to be called "typology." Its purpose was to disclose Old Testament "topoi" as prefigurations of Christ—which were, of course, unrecognizable before his appearance. At the time, however, typological readings of the Bible, which Jesus himself had recommended, were called "allegorical," for lack of a better name, though it was appropriate enough to the spirit of the times.

Church apologists long attempted to distinguish typology from allegory.[36] The latter was considered errant paganism that led to interpretive arbitrariness and frivolity, whereas typology had the completely different purpose of discovering Old Testament premonitions and analogues of Christ. Abraham's sacrifice of Isaac was taken to prefigure the sacrificial death of Christ at his father's bidding, just as the three days that Jonah spent in the belly of the whale mirrored the time between Christ's death and resurrection. This was undoubtedly a special kind of allegorical interpretation, though it was simply called allegory at the time. The first to speak of allegory expressis verbis was no less than St. Paul himself in his letter to the Galatians (4:21–25). There Paul produces a "typological" interpretation of the story of Abraham's two sons, one by the slave (Hagar), the other by the free woman (Sarah). This story, Paul informs us, is allegorically intended (allegoroumena). For the son born of the slave meant contemporary Jerusalem, which was bound by slavery, that is, by law. The other son, in contrast, is not a slave of the law (or the flesh) but free because he is the heir of spirit. Allegory, then, was the name given by the early Church to typological interpretation,[37] and thus the entirety of the Old Testament became an allegory of the New. The New Testament revealed the spirit by which the letter of the Old could be understood.

The most important theoretician of allegorical practice is Origen (c. 185–254). In the fourth book of his treatise On Principles he presented the

Western world's "first systematic discussion of the hermeneutic problem."[38] There, drawing on Philo,[39] he developed the famous doctrine of the three levels of scriptural meaning which laid the groundwork for the subsequent doctrine of four levels. Origen jusifies his doctrine by appeal to a verse of Solomon (Prov. 22:20) which, according to Origen's far-fetched reading, says that one must write Scripture "three times" in order to bear witness to its truth.[40] The three meanings of Scripture correspond to the body, the soul, and the spirit.[41] This tripartite division follows that described by Philo and in the New Testament.[42] Origen stresses the spiritual progression indicated by his doctrine. The corporeal or literal meaning, also called somatic and historical, is designed for simple, artless people. Such meaning is not to be despised, however, since the many believe aright because of it.[43] The second level of meaning—that of the soul—is addressed to those who have already made some progress in the faith, and whose souls can see that Scripture is susceptible of further meaning. And, finally, the spiritual sense—the ultimate mysteries of divine wisdom concealed by the letter—is disclosed only to good men made perfect.

Through the three levels of biblical meaning, God enables the Christian to progress from the visible to the invisible, from the material to the intelligible.[44] God wanted to avoid putting the mysteries at everyone's disposal, allowing them to be defiled by unholy feet. Thus the Holy Ghost (considered to be the author of Scripture) hid a deeper meaning under the veil of a common story (4.2.7). He scattered purposeful discords and contradictions in his narrative to alert the spirit of worthy and attentive readers to the need for surpassing the literal. Impeded by these obstacles to understanding, readers are stimulated to elicit a hidden, inner, spiritual, moral—in brief, a divine— meaning. To select one example among many, Origen mentions the nonsensicality of speaking in the creation story of a first, second, and third day, before the sun and night had been created. The Holy Spirit cannot err or teach something unworthy of God. Thus to move beyond literal meaning bespeaks not a lust to mystify or allegorize but rather an effort to preserve the coherence of Scripture and thereby save the letter as well[45]—a concern that Origen shares with Philo, though their interpretive practice may well have given the opposite impression.

Origen distinguishes himself from Philo in that his use of allegory is predominantly "typological." This is preeminently true of what is probably the most important hermeneutic challenge facing early Christendom: namely, christological interpretation of the Old Testament. Allegory was based on the specific way Christ was taken to have fulfilled messianic prophecy, for the advent could hardly be considered a fulfillment according to the letter. Indeed, for Origen, precisely the fact that the letter is not fulfilled signified that Scripture was to be interpreted spiritually.[46] The spiritual sense thus consisted in the discovery of correspondences between the Old and New Testaments, so that interpreting Scripture in effect involved two levels: the literal sense as well as the christological sense;[47] and Origen traced the latter everywhere, thereby universalizing the typological in the Old Testament.

Origen applied the allegorical-typological method of interpretation to the New Testament as well, since it too had its share of discordancies and mysteries (the book of Revelation comes immediately to mind). Like the Old, the New Testament is to be understood as foretelling what is to come, namely, the divine parousia—an expression of the early Church's faith in the Lord's second coming. Just as the Old Testament was believed to offer types of the New, so also the latter was viewed as a type of the "eternal gospel," according to the passage of Revelation (21:1) that Origen cites in his *De principiis*.[48] Thus Origen paved the way for Christendom to interpret the New Testament in an allegorical and symbolic way as the pledge of something other and higher to come. Origen overplayed his hand, however, when he exaggerated his thesis and suggested that *all* passages are to be interpreted spiritually (pneumatikon).[49] Everything in Scripture, Origen proclaimed, consists of mysteries, and thus he universalizes the typological dimension: if everything is designed for revealing mystery, then Scripture conceals a secret in every letter.

This thesis went much too far for early Christianity, especially since Origen's position was suspiciously indebted to heathens such as Philo and the language of orphic mysticism. His often arbitrary allegorizations brought his theology into disrepute, even though it had an unequaled impact on his successors. The later doctrine of the fourfold sense of Scripture, which might well be called the greatest accomplishment of hermeneutics in the Middle Ages, can be traced directly to Origen's theory of the three levels of meaning in the Bible. According to this medieval doctrine, which received its definitive formulation from Johannes Cassianus (c. 360–430/35), God intended Scripture to have four levels of meaning: the literal (that is, somatic or historical), allegorical, moral, and anagogical (which brings to light eschatological mysteries).[50] In the later Middle Ages, Augustine of Dacia gave this idea its most memorable formulation: litera gesta docet, quid credas allegoria, moralis quid agas, quo tendas anagogia (the literal teaches us what happened, the allegorical what to believe, the moral what we ought to do, and the ana-gogic what we are striving toward). As is evident from Thomas Aquinas's dis-cussion of this theory, there are in fact two possibilities of meaning, the lit-eral and the spiritual, the second of which unfolds in three horizons. Anagogic meaning, Thomas explains, is concerned with eternal dominion (quae sunt in aeterna gloria); and moral or tropological meaning deals with codes of behavior. Allegorical meaning emerges when Mosaic law contains typological premonitions of the Gospel (where, for example, Jerusalem, the holy city of the Jews, is taken as an image of the eternal Church).[51] The doc-trine of fourfold meaning was energetically rejected by Luther, but it lives on even today in the differentiation of literal from figurative or metaphorical meaning, as well as in the tension between the word and what is meant, from which the necessity for hermeneutics itself derives.

Even in his own time, Origen's universalization of typology raised suspi-cions about allegory, already distrusted because of its arbitrariness and hea-then roots. Against the universalization of allegory associated with the "Alexandrian school" (so called because Philo and Origen worked in Alexan-dria), opposition arose from the "school of Antioch," whose main represen-tatives were Diodore of Tarsus (d. before 394), Theodorus of Mopsuestia (c. 350–428), John Chrysostom (c. 349–407), and Theodoret of Cyrrhus (c. 393–466).[52] Their reaction against allegory, or at least its universalization, ushered in a new attention to the historical and literal level, as manifested in painstaking commentaries and editions.

6. Augustine: The Universality of the Inner Logos

With Augustine (354–430) we encounter for the first time in this study a philosopher who is highly influential among modern hermeneuticians, and that to a degree hitherto seldom noticed. This is no less true for Heidegger than for Gadamer. Devoting himself to the phenomenology of religion, Hei-degger indicated his interest in Augustine very early on. In the summer term of 1921 he gave a still unpublished lecture on Augustine and Neoplatonism,[53] and again in 1930 a likewise unprinted lecture by the title "Augustinus: Quid est tempus? Confessiones Lib. XI." The references to Augustine in *Being and Time* as well as in the published lectures are overwhelmingly positive in char-acter—which is especially notable, since Heidegger was by that time already committed to the critical destruction of Western ontology. According to Gadamer, Heidegger found in Augustine one source, if not the most important, for his conception of the enacted meaning [Vollzugsinn] of statements, a conception he deployed against the tradition of metaphysical idealism. To Augustine he traced the fundamental distinction between the actus signatus, the predicative statement, and its reenactment [Nachvollzug] in the actus exercitus. With this almost magical distinction, Gadamer recalls, Heidegger enchanted his audiences in Freiburg and Marburg—not least, Gadamer himself.[54]

Augustine exercised a deep and direct influence on Gadamer as well. In the preface I have already mentioned a conversation in which Gadamer ascribes the universal claim of hermeneutics to Augustine. In fact, a crucial chapter in the final section of *Truth and Method* is devoted to him. It is not too much to say "crucial," because Augustine shows Gadamer how to overcome the forgetfulness of language typical of Greek ontology, with its nominalistic and technical conception of language. Gadamer could show by means of Augustine—and this is what explains his immense significance— that the tradition had never completely forgotten language. Only in Augustine's deliberations on the verbum did the tradition do justice to the being of language.[55] In conceiving the word as a process whereby spirit, fully present in the Word and yet referring to Another, is incarnated, Augustine reveals that hermeneutics is universally bound to language.

As far as we can tell, Heidegger and Gadamer, too, were influenced primarily by the *Confessions* and *De trinitate*. It is also relevant to mention that Augustine wrote a major hermeneutic treatise, *On Christian Doctrine,* which, as G. Ebeling has rightly asserted, is "historically the most influential work of hermeneutics."[56] It becomes immediately evident that Heidegger learned a good deal from it when we look at the unfortunately very sketchy history of hermeneutics he offers at the beginning of his summer 1923 lecture on the hermeneutics of facticity. There he enthusiastically discusses the opening of book 3 of *On Christian Doctrine:* "Augustine presents the first 'hermeneutics' in the grand style: 'A man fearing God diligently seeks His will in the Holy Scriptures. And lest he should love controversy, he is made gentle in piety. He is prepared with a knowledge of languages lest he be impeded by unknown words and locutions. He is also prepared with an acquaintance with certain necessary things lest he be unaware of their force and nature when they are used for purposes of similitudes.'"[57]

Heidegger distinguishes this hermeneutics in the "grand style" from the later and, in his view, more formalistic hermeneutics of Schleiermacher: "Schleiermacher took the vital and comprehensive idea of hermeneutics and reduced it to a 'technique of understanding.'"[58] How appropriate is it to discern in Augustine the "vital and comprehensive idea of hermeneutics"? Heidegger was certainly impressed by the connection that Augustine makes in the proemium cited above between what is to be understood and the demeanor of the zealous interpreter whose sole concern is for the living truth. This tie lends Augustinian hermeneutics an unmistakably "existential" element that is to be found in all of his writing and long ago earned him the reputation of being a proto-existentialist. The desire to understand Scripture is no detached, purely epistemic process taking place between a subject and object. Rather, it testifies to the fundamentally anxious mode of being of a Dasein that is continually striving for meaning.

Augustine's text pertains to the issues at hand in other ways as well—especially since he focuses hermeneutic inquiry on the "dark passages" of Scripture (ad ambigua scripturarum). Augustine begins by assuming that Scripture is fundamentally clear, accessible even to children.[59] He thus notably distinguishes himself from those like Origen who considered everything in Scripture allegorical. For Augustine, explicit hermeneutical deliberation is necessitated only when dark passages present obstacles to understanding. In *De doctrina christiana* (especially book 3), his intent is only to offer instructions (praeceptae) for obviating obscurities. These instructions suggest Augustine is not only the father of existentialism but also in nuce of rule-based hermeneutics, but these matters cannot detain us here. A little aperçu must suffice.

Augustine reminds us that all knowledge of Scripture has three bases: faith, hope, and charity.[60] It must also be remembered that following the rules of interpretation does not itself suffice: the light needed to penetrate the obscure passages of Scripture must come from God. Thus everything depends on the spiritual disposition of the interpreter, especially on caritas. Whoever wants to embark on the study of Scripture with love and care must first read through all the canonical books, so that they at least are familiar, even if not wholly intelligible.[61] Moreover, the interpreter must acquaint himself with Scripture so that he can elucidate obscure passages by means of clear ones. Augustine offers this apparently banal piece of advice—clarify the obscure by paralleling it to the clear—on numerous occasions. Further, he recommends acquiring familiarity with the Hebrew and Greek languages, and he underscores the usefulness of various interpretations and translations for penetrating dark passages.[62] In this way his hermeneutics acquires a historical and critical aspect: the Christian who is a critical reader will always seek a meaning worthy of God and thus interpret the superstitious fables of Scripture in a nonliteral way. The historical context must also be taken into consideration, especially in dealing with the Old Testament. In order to understand it, one must bear in mind, for instance, that at certain times one man could live chastely with many women (as in the case of Abraham and Sarah, which St. Paul had already interpreted allegorically), whereas today a man can live a licentious life with just one.[63]

According to Augustine, confusing the proper and metaphorical senses constitutes the main ambiguity of Scripture,[64] the one that occasions the rise of hermeneutics (though not yet by that name). As a remedy for this confusion—beyond the rule of caritas that Augustine everywhere systematically invokes—the general rule that dark passages are to be elucidated by comparing them to clear ones is especially useful. Moreover, metaphorically intended passages should be distinguished from the literal. In order to see through the metaphors of Scripture to their spirit, Augustine recommends acquiring familiarity with rhetoric and mastering the various "tropes" and modes of discourse (from irony to catachresis).[65] He does not try to offer an exhaustive catalog of discursive figures, however, since they are so numerous that no one can comprehend them all. Augustine closes the third book of his treatise with a call to prayer, because it is only with the help of God that the spirit illumines the letter. This is what needed to be said, the last paragraph concludes, about the relationship of signs to the word and thought (de signis, quantum ad verba pertinet).[66]

The conclusion of the third book alludes to a relation between sign (signum) and word (verbum) that needs to be elaborated by reference to Augustine's *De trinitate,* especially since Gadamer refers to it in explaining his hermeneutics of language. Augustine conceptualizes this relation within a religious context: How can the son of God be understood as verbum or logos, without conceiving the verbum simply as the sensible utterance of God, and thus implying an anti-trinitarian subordination of son to father? In answering this question, Augustine recurs in the fifteenth and last book of *De trinitate* to the Stoic distinction between an inner (endiathetos) and an outer (prophorikos) logos or verbum. Original speaking and thinking, says Augustine, is inner: a language of the heart.[67] This inner speech does not yet have a sensible or material form; it is purely intellectual and universal—that is, it has not yet taken on the form of a particular sensible or historical language. When we hear a human word in a particular language, it is clear that we attempt to understand not its specific, accidental form but rather the verbum or reason that is embodied in it—incompletely embodied, of course, like every merely human incarnation of spirit. Thus it is necessary to transcend sensible, uttered language in order to reach the true human word (sed transeunda sunt haec, ut ad illud perveniatur hominis verbum).[68] What the listener strives to understand is the verbum, which no ear can hear; yet it dwells within every language and is prior to all the signs into which it can be "translated." If the soul or heart's inner word (verbum intimum) takes on the sensible form of a concrete language, it is not uttered as it genuinely is but rather in a form discernible by the body (nam quando per sonum dicitur, vel per aliquod corporale signum, non dicitur sicut est, sed sicut potest videri audirive per corpus).[69]

Augustine finds considerable theological significance in this doctrine, for the distinction applies by analogy to Christ, the Word of God, too. The Divine Word that entered the historical world at a particular time is not the same as the Verbum that was with God from eternity. This distinction allows Augustine to think through the difference as well as the similarity between God and the historically revealed Verbum. Just as an inner word precedes human utterance, so also with God prior to creation and the appearance of the earthly Christ was a Verbum which was traditionally understood as the sapientia or self-knowledge of God.[70] So that it could be communicated to humankind, this Verbum, too, had to take on sensible form at a particular time. Just as our language does not communicate an exact copy of our inner thoughts, the divine language also maintains a distinction between the sensorily apparent Verbum in its external, extrinsic form and the Verbum of God as it is in itself. However, the manifestation is one with God's sapientia, so that God is in fact fully present in the utterance of his word. This is true only of God.

For humankind, however, this identity of thought with the concrete word almost never occurs, and here Augustine locates the limits of the analogy between the divine and human word. For God's Verbum refers to the fullness of God's self-knowledge, whereas the human word does not manifest a comparable self-possession on the part of the speaker. Only seldom is our verbum a reflection of certain knowledge. Does our verbum derive only from what we know on the basis of demonstrative knowledge? Or, Augustine asks, isn't it the case, rather, that we say many things without having achieved ultimate clarity about them?[71] In contrast to God's Verbum, our own is informed by no absolute self-evidence. This is because our being does not dissolve into pure and true self-knowledge (quia non hoc est nobis esse, quod est nosse).

Our verbum always draws on implicit knowledge, a "je ne sais quoi" (quid-dam mentis nostrae),[72] to help its thought find expression. This je ne sais quoi (Augustine is here thinking about concrete language) has no fixed form, since it does not derive from a clear vision, but rather is infinitely formable (hoc formabile nondumque formatum). Thus Augustine contrasts human lan-guage with the divine self-presence manifested in the Son's Word.

For present purposes, we will need to confine our attention to the hermeneutic consequences of this insight as they have in part made their way into modern hermeneutics. First, Gadamer reminds us that the word that we are trying to understand does not consist of mere sounds. Rather, we try to understand what is designated by this sign—what is meant or thought, indeed the word of reason itself in its universality.[73] Now, what does this mean for present-day philosophy? Does it refer to a mental representation, thus threatening to relapse into mentalism, psychologism, or other such things? Along with Gadamer, we, too, must "turn our attention to the 'inner word' itself and ask what it may be."[74] We can begin with Augustine's remark that the signs by which we express our "mind" have something contingent or material about them. They manifest only one aspect of what one is trying to say, not the whole subject matter. The doctrine of the verbum cordis warns us against taking the verbal sign to be ultimate. It always presents an imper-fect translation (interpretatio) that anticipates something more still to be said in order to comprehend the matter fully: "The inner word is certainly not related to a particular language, nor does it have the character of vaguely imagined words summoned from the memory; rather, it is the subject mat-ter thought through to the end (forma excogitata). Since a process of think-ing through to the end is involved, we have to acknowledge a processual ele-ment in it."[75]

This processual element refers to the attempt to find the word and the understanding corresponding to it. Every expression formulates only a frag-ment of the dialogue in which languages live. The "subject matter thought through to the end," the actus exercitus or pragmatics [Nachvollzug] of speaking—which cannot be limited to the tangible actus signatus of actually uttered discourse—lives only in dialogue that asks to be understood. Gadamer learns from Augustine that meaning communicated by language "is not an abstractable logical sense like that of a statement, but the actual inter-play that occurs in it."[76] Western philosophy's obsession with propositions involves a truncation of the most important dimension of language: its embeddedness in dialogue. To concentrate on the logical content of propositions is an abstraction from the evident fact that words have the quality of answers—that is, they are dependent on what went before, namely, the question.[77] Moreover, words have the quality of questions that invite something further, and so are dependent on what follows. In this dialectic of question and answer lies the true universality of language, from which derives the claim to universality as it is raised in hermeneutics today. In Gadamer's essay "The Universality of the Hermeneutic Problem" (1966) it becomes unmistakable, though seldom understood, that this dialectic is the *"hermeneutic urphenomenon":* "no assertion is possible that cannot be understood as an answer to a question, and assertions can *only* be understood in this way."[78] This dialogical view echoes Augustine's doctrine of the verbum cordis, and through it Gadamer attempts to overcome Western forgetfulness of language—that is, abstraction from the event-character of meaning and consequently fixation on propositions as ultimates.

The truth of propositions lies not in themselves, in the signs chosen at a given moment, but rather in the whole that they disclose: "Words cannot be understood merely as signs directed at a determinate meaning; instead, one must, as it were, learn to hear everything that they bring along with them."[79] In his path-breaking essay "What Is Truth?" (1957), Gadamer had already tried to liberate the truth claim of language from its bondage to propositions: "No statement whose truth we are trying to grasp can be comprehended merely on the basis of the content it presents. Every statement has presuppositions that never get expressed."[80] Thus we see that the universality of language cannot be that of spoken language; it must be that of the "inner word," to put it in Augustine's rich if simple terms. This hardly implies any depreciation of concrete language. Quite the contrary, it brings this language back within its correct hermeneutic horizon. We cannot hear "spiritual" words, but we can certainly have them in view when we are understanding spoken language.

The universality of language is not qualified at all by pointing to prelinguistic experience, as J. Habermas does, or to the limits of language.[81] In fact, hermeneutics involves precisely thinking the limits of language to their end, for "the fact that words fail demonstrates their capacity to seek expression for everything."[82] A hermeneutics that stems from Augustine does not need to be reminded about the limits of spoken language. The universality it is concerned with is the universal drive to understand, either the attempt or the capacity to find expression for everything. Indeed, it is Gadamer's main thesis that every statement has limits *in principle,* which derive from our historical finitude and our being bound to the opacities of a preconstituted but still open language.

> From these examples we see the kind of limits that a statement has in principle. It can never say everything that is to be said. . . . Plato calls thought the inner dialogue of the soul with itself. Here the structure of the matter becomes completely apparent. It is called dialogue because it consists of question and answer, since one asks oneself just as one asks another, and says something to oneself just like saying it to someone else. Augustine long ago referred to this way of talking to oneself. Everyone is, as it were, a conversation with themselves. Even those in conversation with others must remain in conversation with themselves insofar as they continue to think. Language finds its paradigmatic example not in the statement, then, but rather in the conversation conceived as the unity of meaning that grows from the interchange of question and answer. It is only here that language is fully rounded out.[83]

With this Augustinian and Gadamerian insight into the universality of the inner logos we may close our brief overview of the history of pre-Reformation hermeneutics. From the highpoint of this universality we can certainly reaffirm Ebeling's judgment about the rest of the Middle Ages: "With respect to hermeneutics, the thousand years after Augustine did not come up with any fundamentally new kinds of inquiry or points of view."[84] It would certainly be inaccurate, however, to repeat the usual derogatory judgment about the "darkness" of the Middle Ages.[85] To avoid this common prejudice based on ignorance, one would do well to consult Henri de Lubac's excellent four-volume study of medieval hermeneutics, as well as Brinkmann's compendium.[86]

7. Luther: Sola Scriptura?

There is probably more secondary literature on Luther's hermeneutics than on any other classic of the hermeneutic tradition. This is undoubtedly due to Luther's enormous significance within church history and the history of ideas. Perhaps it is also due to the fact that the hermeneutic tradition was cultivated primarily by Protestants from Flacius to Schleiermacher, Dilthey, Bultmann, Ebeling, and perhaps also Gadamer.[87] For Dilthey, the first historian of hermeneutics, it seemed clear that the rise of hermeneutic science coincided with that of Protestantism.[88] Luther's reforming acts laid the basis for a hermeneutic revolution, to be sure, but one might modestly inquire whether

Luther himself really developed a hermeneutic *theory*. His "hermeneutics" is indivisible from his interpretive practice. His professorial lectures were concerned with exegesis alone, which was an innovation at the time.[89] Concentrating on the words of Scripture, Luther disdained the pursuit of philosophy and theory, which he was inclined to identify with empty scholasticism. Thus his conception of hermeneutics must be inferred exclusively from his methods of scriptural exegesis.[90]

Luther undoubtedly took the Reformation principle of "sola scriptura" as his starting point and wielded it against tradition and the Church's magisterial establishment. The reaffirmation of this principle certainly offered an affront to the neglect of the text then typical of the Church. Considered solely from a hermeneutic point of view, however, the principle was not entirely unfamiliar. The primacy of Scripture was widely accepted during the patristic period. Augustine always begins with the scriptura. Thus obscure passages are elucidated by comparing them with clearer ones. At the beginning of *De doctrina christiana* he first advises the reader to read Scripture completely through and thereby open himself to the clarifying light of the spirit. In contrast to the allegorizing tendencies of the Alexandrine school, Augustine begins with the premise of Scripture's fundamental intelligibility. That the Church of Luther's time had lost sight of this principle is not in dispute; but from a purely hermeneutic point of view it is of minimal importance, since the Reformation merely rediscovered the until then forgotten self-evidence of Scripture. Sola scriptura as well as the fundamental clarity of Scripture were in fact arrows already in the quiver of patristic hermeneutics, and Luther did not underestimate their power. In this respect, his repudiation of allegory and the fourfold meaning of Scripture in fact signifies a provocative renewal of patristic attitudes. More positively, Luther's rejection of allegoresis, which he still practiced in his youth, signified a decisive return to the sensus literalis.[91] Luther's basic intuition was this: the literal meaning, rightly understood, of itself contains its own proper spiritual significance. It is from the right understanding of the words themselves that the spirit of Scripture grows. The spirit is not to be found in some verbal Beyond; it is encountered in the word as fulfilled by faith. The word remains a dead letter unless the interpreter experiences the fulfillment, the spiritual regeneration, to which it refers—a conception reminiscent of Augustine's doctrine of the verbum. Luther's famous dictum that Scripture is sui ipsius interpres— that it is its own key—affirms just this: the word in which God presents himself waits upon the fulfillment that occurs when Scripture is understood through faith. That is, a word of Scripture is always tied to the fulfillment of the Verbum: to an interpretation resonating with the liberating whole of meaning revealed through God's grace. The word truly perceived—that is, according to its inner tendency—is already spirit. For Protestantism, this is the form of hermeneutic universality.

Luther, then, did not discover the principle of sola scriptura—that the word is its own interpres—or the corollary principles of the Verbum and the fundamental intelligibility of Scripture. It remains a question, moreover, whether Luther's implicit hermeneutics is sufficient to constitute a theory of interpretation, strictly speaking, in particular because it does not sufficiently address the ticklish dilemma of Scripture's obscurities (ambigua). It was for their sake that Augustine worked out the hermeneutic instructions presented in his *Doctrina christiana*. Scripture is clear and intelligible in principle, but not everywhere. Had Protestantism solved this problem? To many, the Protestant appeal to the Holy Spirit's inspiration and to a Scripture that was everywere unequivocally sui ipsius interpres seemed very unsatisfactory and in part naive, especially since it appeared unable to prevent antithetical interpretations and hence arbitrariness. For the Counter Reformation Council of Trent (1546), it was easy to demonstrate the inadequacy of Scripture per se and the consequent necessity of recourse to tradition. It was considered a compelling argument to say that any opposition between Scripture and tradition would be completely artificial, since they both stem from the *same* Holy Spirit. Catholicism capitalized on the considerable variations among Protestant interpretations themselves in showing that the notion of an absolutely clear and univocal Scripture was absurd. For understanding obscure passages, then, the testimony of tradition and the Church Fathers, whose knowledge of Hebrew and Greek was much better than Luther's, was unavoidably necessary.

The Counter Reformation drew attention to the Achilles' heel of early Protestant hermeneutics—or, more precisely, to its absence. Thus, developing an explicit hermeneutics became one of the most pressing desiderata of Protestantism. The evident absence of any such thing in Luther soon led to the development of a scholarly hermeneutics for Scripture. As with the Church Fathers, the problem centered on clarifying obscure passages, for which Protestantism (still) had no solution to offer. The first to find a key to Scripture was one of Luther's followers, Matthias Flacius Illyricus (1520–1575).

8. Flacius: The Universality of the Grammatical

In his *Clavis scripturae sacrae* (1567) Flacius presented the first paradigmatic hermeneutics of Scripture. This is the first book which can be described as a genuine Protestant theory of hermeneutics, even though the word hermeneutic is nowhere to be found in it. Its intention was to offer a key (clavis) for deciphering the obscure passages of the Bible. Flacius was splendidly equipped for such a task. He was educated in Venice by the humanist Johann Baptista Egnatius, and was blessed with an impressive knowledge of Hebrew. Melanchthon made him a professor of Hebrew at Wittenberg.[92]

Before entering on the difficult problem of obscure passages, Flacius's preface powerfully reaffirms the Lutheran principle of the general intelligibility of Scripture. If God has given us Scripture for our spiritual health, it is blasphemy to assert that it is dark and inadequate for the purpose of salvation.[93] The darkness of Scripture, Flacius says in reply to the Tridentine Council, is due not to its obscurity but to our own deficient knowledge of its language and grammar, a fault owing to the Catholic church. Part 1 of the *Clavis* presents a pure lexicon of the Bible, offering a detailed concordance of parallel passages. Nothing could more effectively underscore the importance that early Protestantism ascribed to grammatical knowledge. In that respect the *Clavis* came to have a decisive and systematic significance for Protestant theology.[94] Mastery of the letter, the gramma, was to provide the universal key to Scripture.

By means of this universal key Flacius explains at the beginning of book 2 that the difficulties of Scripture derive from purely linguistic or grammatical causes. All obstacles result from the darkness of language itself, for which the deficient education of its interpreters (that is, contemporary readers) is responsible. The reason is this: "Language is a sign or an image of things, like a pair of glasses through which we see the thing itself. Thus with effort we acquire through it knowledge of the subject matter itself."[95] Language here seems to be a vehicle for or means of imaging something else. This grammatical medium must be mastered if we are to break through to the spirit or subject matter of Scripture.

To allay the purely grammatical difficulty of Scripture Flacius proposes a number of remedies (remedia). In addition to the usual appeal to the Holy Spirit, Flacius always puts special emphasis on facility with language: "Herein lies what is probably the preeminent source of difficulty with Scripture, that theologians have almost never endeavored with sufficient care to become completely acquainted with the text of Holy Scripture or explain it to others."[96] The kind of explanation Flacius has in mind is a strictly immanent interpretation of Scripture based on the juxtaposition of parallel passages—which is, as it were, the concretion of Luther's intuition that Scripture is sui ipsius interpres. As with most other pieces of advice that Flacius gives, the principle of parallel passages is to be found as early as Augustine. Flacius frequently and explicitly appeals to the authority of Augustine and other Church Fathers—probably in an effort to demonstrate by reference to his predecessors that the apparent novelties of Protestantism are actually old and therefore legitimate.[97] Thus Flacius writes, "Augustine quite rightly says that a sentence cannot easily be found which is not clearly explained elsewhere."[98] The substantive references to the older ecclesiastical tradition, which Flacius is obviously deploying to criticize the Catholic church of his own day, make it seem that his own hermeneutics is not very original. There is hardly a hermeneutic rule in Flacius that is not to be met with among the Church Fathers—a fact that has not escaped historians of hermeneutics. Thus Dilthey observes, "Almost all of the fourth book of Augustine's *De doctrina* has been appropriated in detail. . . . This book [the *Clavis*] in fact derives from the fruits of all preceding exegesis."[99] This became the substance of the Catholics' charge against him. Richard Simon found it peculiar that Flacius had borrowed a great deal from the very Fathers whom he attacks in his foreword.[100] Nevertheless, the fact that the *Clavis* (1567) was still being discussed in 1685, the date of Simon's critique, demonstrates its broad and lasting influence. The utility of its lexicon as well as its summary of hermeneutic rules made this book one of the basic works of early Protestant hermeneutics.[101]

Flacius was deeply inspired not only by Augustine but also by the rhetorical tradition. His famous doctrine of the "scopus"—the importance of considering the view with respect to which a book was composed—is borrowed directly from rhetoric.[102] At this point the grammatical gives way to the intention underlying it. Flacius indicates the relative limits of the purely grammatical when he speaks of unlocking the text's scopus, its inexplicit logos—a notion connected to the older doctrine of the verbum interius with all its esoteric fascination. The influence of the allegorical tradition is probably also discernible in Flacius. In the *Clavis* we find esoteric elements that are thoroughly reminiscent of Origen. Since such allegorical elements are obviously difficult to reconcile with the Reformation principle of the universality of the grammatical, they are seldom emphasized. In order to correct this picture we need to cite the following, rather lengthy passages: "God has intentionally said much in a glass darkly, because it is not given to all to know the mysteries. . . . Much is hidden from the faithful so that they will inquire the more zealously into Scripture and strive to achieve clearer revelation."[103] The following description of the sensus literalis and spiritualis as two levels of wisdom also seems to echo Origen:

> In its own special way the Holy Scripture contains a double knowledge concerning the same things. The one is for simple people and children, and is metaphorically called milk. The other is for the mature and strong, and that is meat (I Cor. 3:2 and Heb. 5:13–14). The elementary catechism teaches the most important points briefly, generally, and simply. The more advanced includes the same things but in a much fuller and more detailed manner, since it inquires with care into the sources of things and reveals many concealed questions and mysteries. . . . One should take care to give beginners milk, the level first mentioned, and thereby satisfy them; the stronger, however, can be quickly introduced to the meat of more serious matters.[104]

To give the Reformation a universal key for clarifying obscure passages, Flacius presented a compendium that syncretized various strands from ancient hermeneutics; it emphasized the grammatical, and yet took over certain motifs from allegory as well. It would be worth inquiring to what extent this synthesis or mixture, preserving parts of the allegorical tradition, is reconcilable with Luther's repudiation of allegoresis. Whatever the case, the continuance of allegorical motifs in Flacius testifies to the impossibility of constructing a purely grammatical hermeneutics, and especially of exorcising the fascination exerted by the doctrine of allegory. For human understanding it is apparently difficult to construct a convincing case for the sufficiency of the letter. It is more natural to listen for a whole of meaning behind (or, better, by means of) the letter. That is indeed the purpose of hermeneutics, and its emergence by name could no longer be deferred.

II

Hermeneutics

between

Grammar

and

Critique

In the introduction I noted that there is good reason not to chart hermeneutic history in a teleological manner. We might better maintain a healthy skepticism toward the widespread idea that hermeneutics came into its own by
advancing from a loose collection of interpretive rules to the status of a universal problematic. In reviewing the course of its "prehistory"—called this
only because the word *hermeneutics* was not yet in use—we have seen that
such a teleological view is not borne out. At the same time, the various stages
of what came to be called hermeneutics (that is, theory of interpretation) laid
claim to universality. This claim—which took various forms in such authors
as Philo, Origen, Augustine, and Flacius—derives from a common insight
whose roots are already manifest in the words hermeneuein and hermeneia,
as the Greeks had discovered. This insight consists in the idea that the (verbal) word always embodies (in the truest sense of the term) the transference

or translation of something spiritual. Insofar as the utterance makes itself clear and evident, it requires no special effort of mediation on the part of the listener. The word mediates itself and is itself nothing but this mediation. Hermeneutic mediation first comes into question (and in Philo becomes a theory) when words fail to achieve this natural clarity. Among the responses to the disruption of the natural functioning of language, the initial solution was allegory: allegorical words refer to something spiritual that is concealed, as it were, and apparent only to initiates. Within the framework of religious language, it was only a short step to allegory, since the mysteries have nothing to do with earthly things. For Origen, the task of allegoresis took the specific form of typological interpretation of the Old and New Testaments. (Here we can see how problematical it would be to speak of progress from Philo to Origen, since the two give differing accounts of the universal function of the logos.) Augustine created not only the most widely recognized and influential hermeneutic theory in the ancient world, he subtly extended the fundamental meaning of the logos itself. By returning to the Stoic distinction between the inner and outer word, he was able to show that the verbum interius really dwells with the spoken logos. One could even speak of their identity in the case of God the father and the divine Word. For humankind, by contrast, this equivalence does not always occur, since a hermeneutic relation to the spoken word necessitates situating it within its correct horizon. What is said does not entirely reveal what is thought and intended, though it is meant to be nothing but the embodiment of the latter. We have seen that modern hermeneutics, exemplified by Gadamer, appropriated this conception, in order to do justice to human finitude as manifested in speaking. This applies no less to the Reformation's new understanding of the word. Its absorption in the word, along with the principle of a sola scriptura which was to be sui ipsius interpres, inevitably led to the rejection of allegoresis. Allegoresis has no function if the meaning of the words is already clear as a bell. Yet the principle of sola scriptura does not help much to solve the problem of obscure passages—which was the sole problem that hermeneutics in the Augustinian tradition was meant to address. Fundamentally, the experience of "dark" or objectionable passages was the reason for the Stoics' allegorical interpretation of myths. To meet this challenge, Flacius (the faithful disciple of Luther) soon offered the key to an immanent interpretation of Scripture, and thereby underlined the unavoidability of basic grammatical knowledge. Thus, genuine grammatical knowledge came to be recognized as the most fundamental and universal (if also least observed) precondition for penetrating the Word of God. This insight, crucial to the renovation of hermeneutics, conceived itself as the rebirth of the patristic understanding of the word and consequently the spirit.

It may seem that up to this point the universality of hermeneutics was limited to the domain of religious discourse. For the Middle Ages, of course, this was no limitation, since Scripture contained everything needful to be known. In this sense interpretation of Scripture was ascribed a universal value. Since the advent of modernity, the domain of what is worth reading and interpreting has broadened considerably, especially since the Renaissance, when study of the Greek and Latin classics again attained legitimacy. Studying and editing the ancient writers then came under the rubric of what was most frequently called the ars critica.[1] At that time other disciplines also concerned themselves with interpretation—notably jurisprudence, which was involved with interpreting laws, and medicine, whose task then (and now) consists in interpreting symptoms.

In this situation, as modernity was still seeking to define itself, the need arose for a new methodology that could comprehend all the sciences that were then springing up everywhere. A new organon of knowledge to complement or replace that of Aristotle became one of philosophy's most important desiderata. It found its most eloquent presentations, of course, in Bacon's *Novum Organum,* which was taken as the new propaedeutic of the sciences, and Descartes's *Discours de la méthode.* Exactly between Bacon and Descartes, the neologism hermeneutica was created, specifically in the attempt to supplement and renovate the former organon. This task fell to the Strasbourg theologian Johann Conrad Dannhauer (1603–1666).

1. Dannhauer: True Interpretation and Interpretive Truth

> *De solo sensu orationum, non autem de earum veritate laboramus.*
> *Spinoza,* Tractatus Theologico-politicus

Dannhauer has been long overlooked in the history of hermeneutics because he does not seem to fit in very well. Dilthey ascribes virtually no significance to him, and in *Truth and Method* Gadamer passes over him in silence.[2] Encyclopedia articles at most list Dannhauer among those who first use the word hermeneutics in the titles of their books: for example, his *Hermeneutica sacra sive methodus exponendarum sacrum litterarum* (1654). This fact would be insignificant enough if Dannhauer had merely seized on the word hermeneutics to denote the same thing that Flacius meant by the word clavis. The emergence of a word scarcely proves that the subject matter to which it refers had been unknown till then.

Dannhauer's significance, however, extends far beyond the accidental though innovative wording of his title. In a highly detailed and precise essay, H.-E. Hasso Jaeger[3] showed not only that Dannhauer had already created the neologism hermeneutica in 1629 but also that in a little-known piece of 1630, *The Idea of the Good Interpreter,*[4] he had already projected a *universal* hermeneutics under the express title of a hermeneutica generalis. This is of considerable interest for our nonteleological inquiry into the universal claim of hermeneutics.

The idea of such a hermeneutics arose in the process of searching for a new scientific methodology emancipated from scholasticism. Dannhauer undertakes to show that the vestibule of all the sciences (that is, the propaedeutic, for which philosophy is responsible) must contain a universal science of interpretation. Previously unheard of, the idea of such a universal science is introduced by way of a syllogism: everything knowable has a corresponding science; interpretive procedure is knowable; there must therefore be a science corresponding to it.[5] This "philosophical hermeneutics" is posited as universal in the sense that it finds application in all the sciences. There is only *one* hermeneutics, though its objects are of several kinds.[6] Dannhauer proposes a universal hermeneutics grounded in philosophy but enabling other disciplines (law, theology, medicine) to interpret written expressions according to their meaning.[7] At this time, the idea was beginning to flourish that all branches of knowledge had to do with interpretation, especially of texts. The notion that knowledge depended on interpretation and on texts was undoubtedly connected with the fundamental change brought about by the spread of printing.[8] The well-known Cartesian, Clauberg, was one of those who pursued Dannhauer's plan by working out a universal hermeneutics within his logic. He discovered that far more scholars were concerning themselves with the writings of famous authors than with research into things themselves.[9] By expanding the realm of books worth reading beyond the limits of the single holy book, the Renaissance necessarily brought about the appearance of a universal hermeneutics.

Given its universal scope, hermeneutics had to be a "propaedeutic" science, a position usually held by logic, according to the classical division of sciences. Dannhauer thus developed his hermeneutica generalis in a manner parallel and supplementary to the traditional logic epitomized in Aristotelian methodology (organon). The work most basic to the *Organon* was Aristotle's *Peri hermeneias*. In general, as we have seen, this work thematized the conceptual connections that are concretized in spoken discourse. The word hermeneia suggested a process of interpretation, a process which in Dannhauer's time was called "analytic," as prescribed by the tradition of medieval commentary on Aristotle. Logical analysis consisted in tracing statements back to their intended meaning (here analysis always means tracing complex things back to their constitutive elements).[10] We might recall the formula that Boethius employs in his commentary on *Peri hermeneias* to explain hermeneia: vox articulata per se ipsam significans. Statements are always the utterance of an intended meaning. In tracing statements back to their logical meaning, logic (the general theory of truth) understood its task to be distinguishing logical (that is, with respect to content) from illogical sentences.[11] Retracing was the basic idea of Dannhauer's universal hermeneutics, just as it had been the occasion for hermeneutic effort time out of mind. Like logic, hermeneutics is concerned with transmitting truth and combating falsehood. Whereas pure logical analysis sets itself the task of constituting the truth of intended meaning with respect to content by retracing it to the deepest foundations, hermeneutics contented itself with determining intended meaning as such, regardless of whether the meaning is true or false with respect to content. On the level of thought, of dianoia, an expression's intended meaning can appear obscure or muddled. Before it can be tested for logical or factual truth, its meaning needs to be determined by a universal and scientific hermeneutics. Admittedly, the distinction between sententia (truth of assertion) and sensus (meaning of the sense) was in circulation long before Dannhauer.[12] What is new is that he employs it to define the goals of a universalist hermeneutics. Clearly Dannhauer depends on the title *Peri hermeneias* for his usage of the word hermeneutica. He intends to extend Aristotle's treatise by adding "a new city," as he writes.[13] Indeed, he takes the original meaning of hermeneia, which signifies precisely the communication or utterance of meaning, and faithfully thinks it through to the end. Prior to determining truth, we need a hermeneutics whose task is to establish "hermeneutic truth"—that is, to clarify what an author wanted to say, without concern for whether it is strictly logical or factually correct. Thus Dannhauer defines the interpreter—the "good" interpreter, as the title of his book has it—as follows: he is the one who analyzes all discourses insofar as they are obscure yet "exponible" (that is, interpretable) in order to distinguish their true from their false meaning.[14] In this distinction, Dannhauer's hermeneutics introduces a whole series of instructions or media interpretationis—including, of course, paying attention to the scopus, what the author has in view.[15] The details of these hermeneutic rules, and their connection to older ones, need not detain us here.

Dannhauer's program of integrating a universal hermeneutics into logic found numerous successors among the rationalists of the seventeenth and eighteenth centuries—including Johann Clauberg, J. E. Pfeiffer,[16] J. M. Chladenius, and G. F. Meier. For this reason, hermeneutic historiography has unquestionably erred in taking Schleiermacher's well-known dictum as the first step in the universalization of hermeneutics: "At present hermeneutics exists only as various special hermeneutics and not yet as a theory of understanding in general."[17] Admittedly, the Enlightenment was hardly lacking in regional hermeneutics. Dannhauer himself contributed one under the title *Hermeneutica sacra,* where he appeals on page after page to Augustine as a forerunner.[18] More philosophically significant, however, was his programmatic attempt to produce a hermeneutica generalis that emerged in 1630, between Bacon's *Novum Organum* and Descartes's *Discours de la méthode,* and tried to broaden the logic and methodology of the sciences.

2. Chladenius: The Universality of the Pedagogical

Among the numerous universal hermeneutics produced in the sixteenth and seventeenth centuries, the *Einleitung zur richtigen Auslegung vernünftiger Reden und Schriften* (1742) by Johann Martin Chladenius (1710–1759) deserves special attention. Chladenius's "introduction to the correct interpretation of reasonable speeches and writings" opened up a new horizon of philosophical hermeneutics that points beyond Dannhauer's purely logical conception of the task. Chladenius thereby severed universal hermeneutics or theory of interpretation from logic, and thus established alongside logic a second great branch of human knowledge. In the preface to his theory of interpretation, Chladenius explains that scholars produce knowledge in two basic ways: on one hand, they increase knowledge by means of their own thoughts and discoveries; on the other, they occupy themselves with "useful or lovely things that others before us have thought of . . . and give directions for understanding those writings and monuments, that is, they interpret."[19] For the two kinds of knowledge, which each have their own advantages and attractions, there are two kinds of cognitive rules. The first teach us how to think correctly, and these constitute the "theory of reason," whereas the rules that help us interpret correctly comprise the general theory of interpretation. The latter rules are intended to improve interpretive capacities already in use. Within this general definition of purpose, we should pay special attention to the omnipresent pedagogical element of Chladenius's hermeneutics, so typical of the Enlightenment.

As usual in the hermeneutic tradition, the obscure sentences and passages are the special object of Chladenius's interpretive art. What is new here, however, is that Chladenius's hermeneutics is not concerned with *all* obscure passages, only with those of a particular kind. That is to say, there are obscurities that lie outside the competence of the interpreter. Chladenius establishes a strict division between four kinds of obscurity,[20] and this distinction has far-reaching consequences for reevaluating the place of hermeneutics and the other ancillary philological sciences in the eighteenth century.

1. Obscurity often results from textually corrupt passages. Rectifying them is the business of the criticus and its ars critica. Before finding new philosophical resonance in Kant's works, the word critique had since the Renaissance referred to the philological science concerned with editing, revising, and correcting ancient texts. This sense of the word critique was retained until late in the nineteenth century and assumed a prominent place among the ancillary philological and hermeneutic sciences. Lücke's 1838 edition of Schleiermacher's hermeneutics bore the time-honored title *Hermeneutik und Kritik,* and M. Frank has happily retained it in his new edition of 1977. Schleiermacher defines critique, the second philological art along with hermeneutics, as "the art of judging the genuineness of texts and correctness of passages, and of confirming them by means of sufficient evidence and data."[21] In his *Museum der Altertumswissenschaften,* which has a founding place in the history of classical philology, F. A. Wolf grouped grammar, hermeneutics, and critique together as ancillary sciences constituting the organon of classical knowledge.[22] August Böckh, too, based his *Enzyklopädie und Methodenlehre der philologischen Wissenschaften* on the distinction between hermeneutics and critique.[23]

Critique was apparently intended to be a purely factual science. Its task was first to determine the state of the text, before hermeneutics undertook to offer an interpretation. With only a few exceptions,[24] however, it went virtually unnoticed that editing a text—for example, recognizing that a particular passage was "corrupt"—represented a hermeneutic act of the first order. Nevertheless, if philology was to be established as a science, it first needed to rest upon a purely factual basis. The binary nineteenth-century distinction between hermeneutics and critique presupposed the trinary eighteenth-century distinction among grammar, hermeneutics, and critique, which is partly reflected in the title of the present chapter. All three functioned as formal or introductory sciences because they were concerned not with the concrete material of the philological sciences but with the rules (grammar, hermeneutics, and critique) with which everyone must be familiar in order to understand and explain written documents according to the rules of art. Dannhauer had already conceived hermeneutics as a propaedeutic, and so justified its claim to be universally applicable to the material sciences. Chladenius proceeded in a more philological than logical manner when he sought to demonstrate the universal function of interpretation by means of a scientific categorization of kinds of obscurity. For him, correcting corrupt passages was not what distinguished the genuine hermeneutician, for that is, rather, the business of a criticus.

2. Second, obscurity can derive "from insufficient insight into the language in which the book is composed."[25] This, too, does not necessitate the aid of the hermeneutician, because such obscurity is rectified rather by the "philologus" or language teacher. If the language has not been sufficiently mastered, there is in fact nothing to interpret. The only thing that can help is improved acquaintance with the language. Neither the obscurity of corrupt passages nor deficient familiarity with the language, then, falls within the hermeneutician's sphere of competence.

3. Finally, Chladenius mentions a third form of obscurity that, according to him, also falls beyond the reach of hermeneutics. It involves passages or words that are "ambiguous in themselves." The correction of such equivocal passages (like the two cases above) is assigned no special technique because ambiguities found in the text itself are not so much to be cleared up as accepted as such or censured. To dissolve them hermeneutically would obviously do violence to the text.

4. What kind of obscurity, then, does fall within the realm of hermeneutics? Have we not exhausted the entire field of obscurity? Basically that is the case for the various hermeneutics prior to Chladenius, since they sought to elucidate only the obscurities due to ambiguity or insufficient grammatical knowledge. What kind of obscurity could be left, especially when hermeneutics is conceived as universally, as in the case of Chladenius, who establishes the autonomy of a general theory of interpretation alongside a theory of reason? In his preface Chladenius describes the obscurity that belongs within the special province of hermeneutic competence in a way that may at first seem strange, but upon closer examination proves insightful:

It happens countless times, however, that one also meets with passages in which none of these [above-named] obscurities occurs and yet they cannot be understood: often readers can make no progress in a book of philosophy, for example, even though they are not lacking in acquaintance with the language; nor is the book written in an ambiguous manner, because it is well understood by those who have the proper training. One does frequently run into obstacles in reading ancient works, even though the authors and the manner of writing are not at fault in the slightest. Upon closer inspection one discovers that this obscurity results from the fact that mere words and sentences are not always capable of conveying to the reader the conception that the author attached to them, and that acquaintance with the language does not of itself put us in a position to understand everything in passages and books so composed.

The obscurity to which Chladenius here refers is that due to insufficient *background knowledge*. It is indeed often the case, especially with older texts, that the language seems completely clear, though the texts still remain unintelligible because we are lacking in historical or factual knowledge. In other words, we are unacquainted with the subject matter or with what the author really wanted to say. At first, as I noted above, this kind of obscurity may seem rather trivial. Yet Chladenius here touches on an absolutely fundamental phenomenon of language. Language always tries to express something literally, but this "something" often enough remains in the dark, because the words do not occasion the same meaning or effect in the receiver as intended by the speaker. Chladenius views this as a purely linguistic process, as he explains while introducing his idea of hermeneutics as a universal science: "A thought that is to be conveyed to the reader by words often presupposes other conceptions without which it is not conceivable: if a reader is not already in possession of these conceptions, therefore, the words cannot effect the same result in him as in another reader who is thoroughly knowledgeable about these conceptions."

Hermeneutics, then, has to do with passages that are obscure "for no other reason than because we are not equipped with the conceptions and knowledge required to understand them." The universality of this situation is immediately apparent: when does it happen that we wholly master the background knowledge necessary for insight into what is said? This situation is not limited to ancient authors, where we are lacking the necessary knowledge of context. Such background knowledge is necessary for understanding even our acquaintances' most trivial utterances. Who knows with any certainty what is happening in others' minds, when they utter this statement or that? In practice we must always assume that we do know it, but penetration into the verbum interius of the other can never be definitively confirmed. This impossibility encourages us to pose questions and discuss things further, but it also leads to misunderstandings.

Chladenius considers the latter to be a purely didactic problem. In this connection he appeals to the colloquial meaning of the word *auslegen*. Usually the word *interpretation* refers to the fact that those lacking sufficient insight into something are brought to understand it. They are informed of the concepts necessary to understand a passage. Thus Chladenius arrives at his emphatically pedagogical definition: "Interpreting is nothing but adducing the concepts necessary to the complete understanding of a passage." Only such a definition, Chladenius explains, is in a position to offer "a firm ground for a philosophical theory of interpretation." The emergence of the conception of a "philosophical hermeneutics" attracts our attention, of course, since Chladenius, who was the first to compose a hermeneutics in German, uses hermeneutics and the art of interpretation as synonyms.[26]

Chladenius's pedagogical conception of hermeneutics is in fact couched within a general philosophical framework modeled on the student-teacher relationship, as is evident from the particular examples that he cites. Interpreting thus appears to be a didactic process in which a teacher communicates the more comprehensive knowledge that enables the student to understand an author's thoughts correctly. This didactic model is anything but one-sided, for it also applies to the teacher's intercourse with the text, even with the language. Anyone who learns—and we never cease to be learners—must build up the necessary background knowledge in one way or another, by consulting lexicons, introductions, or other reference works.[27] Going beyond Chladenius, we can say that this applies to one's own speech as well. When we want to say something, we have recourse to dictionaries, synonyms, metaphors, and so forth, in order to say what we have "on our heart and mind." Physiologists, of course, are not likely to admit any such notions as heart and mind in the sense of spirit and soul; but how else can we describe the common experience of the inadequacy of our utterances to convey the depths of what we are trying to say? We, too, as students and speakers, remain dependent on teachers: on aid from others that we can also at times supply for ourselves.

The universality of this pedagogical hermeneutics is nowhere clearer than in Chladenius's theory of "viewpoint," a theory that virtually every historian of hermeneutics has highlighted because of its modernity. More important than the theory itself, however, is the place it occupies in Chladenius's didactic scheme. The word Sehepunkt (viewpoint) per se is nothing but the German translation of the Latin scopus, which had been a topic central to hermeneutics since Augustine and Flacius. Chladenius adds his own nuances, to be sure, and these prepare the way for the universal perspectivism of today's hermeneutics. First, he describes viewpoint in terms of one's personal situation: "The circumstances of our mind, body, and whole person that make or cause us to imagine something in this way rather than that, are what we call viewpoint."[28] Without referring to the doctrine of scopus, Chladenius suggests that it was Leibniz who first formulated the notion of viewpoint. Leibniz pointed out the insuperable perspectivism of monads with no window to give them a direct glimpse of what lies without. Thus each monad constructs for itself perspectives or images of what is occurring in the outer world, and these are thoroughly conditioned by its subjective viewpoint. Chladenius incorporates his theory of perspectives within the framework of his didactic philosophical hermeneutics. Viewpoint, he argues, is "unavoidable if one is to do justice to the countless ways people conceive things."[29] It follows that for Chladenius perspectivity presents no danger to "objectivity," in the way that some fear today. Quite the contrary, it is designed above all to make adequate and superior knowledge possible. Only when viewpoint is taken into account can one do justice to the individualized "ways people conceive things." What is involved, then, is coming to a correct understanding of language by tracing it back to the viewpoint that underlies it. An objectivist theory of language that tried to ignore viewpoint would completely miss the point. And this is the fundamental doctrine of universal hermeneutics. The hermeneutical concept of viewpoint, then, is motivated by a pedagogical impulse and the demand for fairness as well. It, too, serves to "bring into play" the concepts (in the broadest sense) needed to understand a passage. Chladenius felt it appropriate to recommend to his age, the Age of Enlightenment, a universal hermeneutics that takes viewpoint into consideration. This may still be good advice for present-day enlightenment as well.

3. Meier: The Universality of Signs

The final stage of universal hermeneutics in the Enlightenment to claim our special attention is the *Versuch einer allgemeinen Auslegungskunst* (1757) by Georg Friedrich Meier (1718–1777).[30] It represents not only the last instance of rationalist hermeneutics but also a fundamentally new form, one that surpasses even the universal claim that we encountered in the propaedeutic works of Dannhauer and Chladenius. The new impulse toward universalization, highly characteristic of its age, consists in the fact that Meier's interpretation theory finds application far beyond the horizon of the verbal. It comprehends the totality of all signs, even the natural. The fact that Chladenius's hermeneutics was "limited" to verbal objects appears from the title of his book: *Introduction to the Correct Interpretation of Reasonable Speeches and Writings*. In Meier's title, *Versuch einer allgemeinen Auslegungskunst,* the word "allgemeinen" (universal) indicates that now all the signs of the world fall within its domain. The hermeneutics of human discourse, then, is merely part of the universal hermeneutics that includes signs of all kinds. The very first sentence of Meier's *Versuch* expresses this clearly: "Hermeneutics in the broad sense (hermeneutica significatu latiori) is the science of rules the observance of which enables meanings to be known from their signs; in the narrower sense (hermeneutica significatu strictiori) hermeneutics is the science of the rules that must be observed in order to know the sense of something said and convey it to others."[31] The interpretation of verbal objects constitutes only one sphere within the universal art of interpretation that is applicable to all signs, natural as well as artificial. Behind this conception lies a universal theory of signs or semiotics like that which Leibniz projected under the rubric of a "characteristica universalis." Here *universalis* means that everything in this world is a sign and relates back to the universal semiotic nexus [Zusammenhang: also, connection and context] designed by the divine creator of all signs. Thus hermeneutics was integrated into the universal "characteristic" of all things or signs: "Characteristic is the science of signs. Since interpretation theory concerns signs, it is part of characteristic and derives its axioms from universal characteristic."[32] Signs, however, are not specifically verbal. Each thing in the world is a sign, a signum or a character, insofar as it is a means whereby the reality of something else can be known. Interpreting in the broad sense thus denotes knowing the meaning from the sign— more exactly, it assigns each thing its place in the universal characteristic.

With Meier's semiotic hermeneutics begins the notion that understanding something consists in integrating it into a semiotic whole. Behind the sign stands nothing like a meaning or spirit, just a general, coherent horizon of signs. What is known or understood is not so much a meaning as a clear relation between the particular sign and the whole world of signs: "An interpreter in the broad sense knows clearly how the sign is connected with its meaning. Thus interpreting in the broad sense means nothing less than seeing the connection between the things signified and their signs."[33] Moreover, there are various degrees of insight into the semiotic context, as we recall from Leibniz's epistemology: when an interpretation is *clear* (that is, according to Leibniz,[34] when it is sufficient to differentiate the subject matter from all others), then it is a *rational* interpretation. It is even a logical interpretation (interpretatio logica erudita, philosophica)[35] if it occurs in its perfect form. An unclear interpretation must be termed sensory or aesthetic.

A more comprehensive hermeneutics can hardly be conceived: as a universal theory of interpretation, it covers all signs whatsoever. Everything in the world is now a sign. Each sign, moreover, can be related to every other because in this world optimal integration rules. Leibniz's doctrine of the best of all worlds obtains in semiotics as in all other respects: "This world, because it is the best, exhibits the most comprehensive, universal semiotic connection that is possible in a world. Consequently every actual part of the world can be an immediate or mediate, distant, or proximate natural sign of every other actual part of the world."[36]

We need to keep in mind that Meier's universal hermeneutics attempts to illuminate the semiotic whole alone. For the interpretation of discourse, this implies that his hermeneutics, like that of Dannhauer, is concerned with a strictly hermeneutic rather than logical or metaphysical truth. Since finite human beings can be mistaken, we need to distinguish between hermeneutic and factual truth in interpreting what they say.[37] What is meant by hermeneutic truth is exclusively the author's viewpoint, typically called the mens auctoris.[38] Thus authorial self-interpretation—Meier calls it "authentic explanation"—enjoys special privilege, as long as it cannot be shown that the author has altered his viewpoint.[39] No finite interpreter can know the author's intent and purpose with as much certainty as the author himself. Every author is therefore himself the best interpreter of his own words.[40]

Furthermore, Meier's principle of hermeneutic equity (aequitas hermeneutica) is of great hermeneutic significance. By this principle he means "the interpreter's tendency to consider hermeneutically true the meanings that best accord with the perfection of the originator's signs, until the contrary is proved."[41] In practice this principle means that interpretation must begin with the assumption of maximum semiotic integration. Applied to natural signs, it of course takes the form of a "hermeneutic reverence for God" (reverentia erga deum hermeneutica), and expectation that the natural signs will be maximally perfect, because they are in maximal accord with the perfections of God and his omniscient will. With reference to finite beings and their texts, the presumption of equity implies that the interpreted discourse is held to be true as long as the opposite has not been demonstrated. This principle expresses the reader's expectation that there is always something to be learned from what is worth interpreting. In other words, the signs to be interpreted, however connected to still other signs, are nevertheless trying to convey something true—and this is considered self-evident in every just ("equitable") interpretation. As the means of discovering this hermeneutic truth or mens auctoris, Meier offers textual critique ("the science of rules that must be employed to determine whether the discourse in all its parts is the discourse that the author to be interpreted in fact used").[42] Critique includes authentic (that is, authorial) interpretation, mastering language and grammar, collecting parallel passages, and acquainting oneself with the purpose that the author had set for himself.

These principles of universal interpretation theory are meant to be concretized in the practical branches of hermeneutics—that is, applied to the several objects of hermeneutics.[43] The art of practical interpretation that applies general hermeneutic rules to Scripture is called the art of sacred or theological interpretation (hermeneutica sacra). Its first rule, of course, is equity or hermeneutic reverence for God.[44] Among the other spheres of applied hermeneutics, Meier recognizes the legal (juris or legalis), the diplomatic (which examines documents), the moral, and even the mantic (which interprets natural signs) and hieroglyphic (for arbitrary signs). In mantic interpretation we hear, as it were, an echo of the Greek hermeneutike that is found as early as Plato. Its appearance in the age of enlightenment and reason should hardly be surprising. In a world where everything can be a sign of anything else, signs and portents of the future must certainly exist, for nothing is totally without (semiotic) relation to other things. There must therefore be an art of mantic interpretation[45] representing the application of universal hermeneutics, just as that in turn belongs to the characteristica universalis.

The influence of Leibniz is unmistakable here. Nothing is more rational than a world in which everything points to something else as its own ground, which in turn is a sign of something still further, and so on until we arrive at the original creator of all signs. The universality of hermeneutics seems to go hand in hand with universal semiotic or characteristic. To a man of Leibniz's universal genius the expression hermeneutica was of course well known,[46] but he seems not to have conceptualized its significance in such a comprehensive way. Perhaps the universal semiotic context was so transparently obvious to him that a special art of hermeneutics seemed superfluous. However that may be, his thought gave rise to the eighteenth century's two most significant forms of the hermeneutic claim to universality. On one hand, he introduced the concept of viewpoint that Chladenius employed to pedagogical ends. On the other, Leibniz's universal characteristic prepared the way for Meier's universalization of the concept of sign beyond the limits of language. Thereby Leibniz doubtless sketched out two fronts of present-day hermeneutics: first, he anticipated the challenging ubiquity of perspectivism (which, for nineteenth-century scientism, came to be equated with certain kinds of relativism); and second, he anticipated the semiotic branch of hermeneutic thought within structural linguistics and deconstruction, for which every word signals the interplay of signs. The universalism of contemporary hermeneutics, and its present-day semiotic avatars, is anything but new. It was already highly developed in the Enlightenment, and perhaps we still have something to learn from its innocence about relativism and semiotics.

4. Pietism: The Universality of the Affective

Meier's attempt to produce a universal art of interpretation in 1757 represents the highpoint of universal hermeneutics in the Enlightenment. His project, however, virtually fell on deaf ears.[47] The classic theoreticians of hermeneutics at the beginning of the nineteenth century (Ast and Schleiermacher, among others) knew nothing of him. Thus occurred a disintegration of universal hermeneutics, so to speak, in the time immediately following Meier. This process had already begun in the eighteenth century. As we had occasion to suppose in the case of Leibniz, the idea of a special art of deriving knowledge from written (or natural) signs may have seemed somewhat strange to the Enlightenment. Rationalism placed much more value on the confirmation of one's own reason than on studying ancient writers whose susceptibility to prejudice had been exposed with increasing frequency. This relative distrust of hermeneutics during the Enlightenment is eloquently described by no less important an advocate than Chladenius: "We no longer need the art of interpretation so much in philosophy, when each needs only to exercise his own power of thought; and the precept wrung from a philosophical text only by interpreting it deeply cannot do us much good because we must first address the question whether it is true—and that constitutes the real art of philosophy."[48] The contrary notion that one's own thought is not autonomous but rather is dependent on the previous achievements of tradition is a pre-Enlightenment insight. Romanticism merely rediscovered it.

The eighteenth century saw the blossoming of not just universal but special hermeneutics, particularly the theological and jurisprudential. Because our topic is limited, we must forgo discussion of these special areas, especially because they are treated in numerous reference books. If I might be permitted a small exception, however, it would be useful to refer briefly to the pietistic contribution to hermeneutica sacra—because (inter alia) it has found a systematic place in present-day hermeneutics[49] and represents the threshold between Schleiermacher and the older Protestant hermeneutics that preceded him.[50]

Pietism discloses another important element of the hermeneutic claim to universality, one that can be called the universality of affect. The father of pietistic hermeneutics, August Hermann Francke, teaches that an "affect" dwells within *every* word that is uttered in human discourse and that emerges from the inwardness of the soul.[51] If the Word of God is to be interpreted, and hermeneutica sacra has no other purpose, we must have at our disposal a sufficient theory of affects or "pathology" of Scripture. From this assertion we can see the extent to which the pietistic vision helps guard against the naive verbal objectivism discernible in Protestant orthodoxy. Behind every word is to be found something inward, namely, an affective condition of the soul impelled toward expression. Thus, in its own special way pietism encourages a return from the logos prophorikos to the logos endiathetos, conceived as the soul of the former. To understand Scripture appropriately, it is necessary to go back to the condition of the soul that it expresses.[52] What does interpreting mean, if not deriving the soul's full meaning from the letter— that is, recreating what the word bears within it? For this reason it is understandable that pietism successfully opposed the sterile fetishization of the word typical of Protestant orthodoxy and returned the affective aspect of language to the foreground.

As the key to (theological) hermeneutics, the universality of affect and the expressive nature of language became the foundation of Rambach's influential *Institutiones hermeneuticae sacrae.* Rambach forcefully argued that "the words of an auctoris cannot be completely understood and interpreted without knowing from which affect they have flowed." For "our discourse is an expression of our thoughts. Our thoughts are almost always coupled with secret affects. . . . Therefore by means of speech we enable another to understand not only our thoughts but also the affects coupled thereto. From this derives the following consectarium, that it is impossible to interpret and see deeply into the words of a scriptoris, when one does not know what kind of affects are bound up in his mind with his having spoken them."[53] Affect, then, is not merely an ancillary phenomenon; it is also "anima sermonis," the soul of speech.[54] It is what is to be communicated to the reader of Scripture.

This notion received its most influential form in the pietistic doctrine of the "subtilitas applicandi." To understand (intelligere) or explain (explicare) Scripture's affect is obviously not enough;[55] it must also touch the soul of the listener. Thus, to the subtilitas intelligendi and explicandi, which have traditionally been taken to comprehend the whole task of hermeneutics, must be added a third characteristic: the "subtilitas applicandi"—the capacity to inscribe the affect of Scripture, as it were, upon the affect of the listener. The preacher is the most self-evident bearer of this subtilitas. In preaching, the task is to translate (hermeneuein!) the meaning of Scripture into the souls of the congregation. Later, Gadamer's hermeneutics infers from this doctrine that the meaning so understood must always be applied to us and embody a significance for us. The application to the interpreter is no supplement to intelligere; it constitutes the very essence of successful understanding.

However new the pietist subtilitas of application may seem, it nevertheless represents a revised version of the *sensus tropologicus,* familiar from the theory of the fourfold meaning—that is, the meaning that pertains to the believer's moral transformation.[56] Augustine's doctrine of the word must also be mentioned here, which presented God's Son as the Word that could encounter us only in the form of a gospel relevant to us. Thus Gadamer writes, "In this respect the theological conception of the verbum remains very fruitful, since 'the Word' comprises the whole of the divine message, and yet it exists only within the significance of the *pro me.*"[57] Only the nineteenth century, drunk with positivism, could disfigure this *pro me* into a relativism of worldviews.

In the pietist concept of subtilitas applicandi emerges a genuinely hermeneutical, universalizable conception of the word. It can hardly surprise us that pietist hermeneutics enjoyed much broader influence than the philosophical, highly schematized, universal hermeneutics of Dannhauer, Meier, or even Chladenius. In opposition to the rigid semiotic world of the characteristica universalis, it finally came to be realized that the word is to be viewed as the expression of a soul (and for the soul) and only in that way. From this intuition, and in almost complete oblivion to the preparatory work performed by their Rationalist forebears, the Romantics charted a new course for hermeneutic universality.

III

Romantic Hermeneutics and Schleiermacher

*I am teaching hermeneutics, and trying
to raise what has been till now only a
collection of unrelated and in part
highly unsatisfactory observations to the
status of a science that comprehends
the entirety of language as an intuition
and strives to penetrate its innermost
depths from without.*

Schleiermacher, letter to Ehrenfried von
Willich, June 13, 1805

1. The Post-Kantian Transition from the Enlightenment to Romanticism: Ast and Schlegel

If Romanticism means simply an unsatisfiable longing for completeness, nine-teenth-century hermeneutic theory was certainly Romantic. It was distinguished in fact by an unprecedented reticence about finally bringing work to publication. Hardly any authors of the great hermeneutic classics, from Schlegel to Schleiermacher, Böckh, Droysen, and Dilthey, risked allowing their hermeneutic works even to go into print. It is only thanks to their students that their inquiries were transmitted to posterity.

The transition from the Enlightenment to Romanticism is characterized, above all, by a great discontinuity. Even at first glance this is already manifested by the fact that Schleiermacher seems oblivious to the numerous examples of universal hermeneutics that had been developed over the centuries. He is acquainted only with the "many special hermeneutics" (preeminently the theological) that had been leading an innocuous existence as unsystematic ancillary disciplines on the margins of the real sciences.[1] Schleiermacher envisioned the development of a universal hermeneutics or art of understanding—and here hermeneutic histories concurred with him—as a perfectly new desideratum, one which it was his vocation to be the first to fulfill. A vast abyss separates Enlightenment Rationalism from the nineteenth century. Peter Szondi, who has investigated this later period thoroughly, has rightly remarked that "the half century between Meier and Schleiermacher represents one of the most remarkable caesuras in all intellectual history."[2] What could explain this break?

In a word, Kant. The influence of Kantian critique was many-faceted, but in one respect especially it had an unmistakable historic impact: it dissolved the rationalism to which Dannhauer, Spinoza, Chladenius, and Meier owed their allegiance.[3] However highly Kant celebrates the capacities of pure understanding whose accomplishment was the constitution of nature, the critique of pure reason nevertheless also had the effect of reducing the status of pure reason. The fundamental presupposition of Rationalism was that the human mind, though finite, could by means of thought come to penetrate the logical and regular construction of the world. Thinking was guided by the principle of reason (nihil est sine ratione) that is inscribed in our mind. From this proposition, that nothing is without a reason, derive the a priori truths of reason (vérités de raison, as Leibniz called them), that is, these truths are deduced from the principles of our reason. Because the Satz vom Grund stems from *our* reason, Kant concludes that the order it produces or discovers is valid only for the world of phenomena, things as they appear to us and are framed by us. Thus the world of things in themselves disappears into pure unintelligibility. In the distinction between phenomena and things in themselves lies one of the secret roots of Romanticism and the emergence of hermeneutics. If every approach to the world (or, say, to a text) involves a subjective interpretation or viewpoint, a philosophical investigation trying to be fundamental must begin with the interpreting subject. It is on this level, for example, that such an investigation will need to raise the question how and whether objectivity can be achieved in scientific or hermeneutic endeavor. Schleiermacher's definition of hermeneutics as the theory of *understanding* certainly does represent something new, then, since it presupposes a break with belief in unproblematical, purely rational access to the world.

In this situation, as the subject was becoming increasingly worldless, the

exemplariness of the Greek mind came to possess an almost magical fascination for such figures as Goethe, Schiller, and Winckelmann.⁴ When the
autarchy of human reason was reduced by Kant's dialectic, the apparently
beneficent, life-giving spirit of Greece experienced a reawakening. In this context (which was no longer connected to Kant, of course), "idealistic" hermeneutics set itself the task of revitalizing the Greek spirit. This is probably the common denominator among the various strands of early Romanticism. It is
discernible in the authors—as different as Friedrich Ast and Friedrich
Schlegel—whose work was to prove influential on Friedrich Schleiermacher.

In 1808, Ast, the student of Schelling, brought out a book titled *Grundlinien der Grammatik, Hermeneutik und Kritik*. Its aim was to rediscover, through
intuition, the undivided unity of the spirit that expressed itself not only in
antiquity but, through "intuition," in all history. For the Enlightenment such
an ambitious task simply could not be conceived under the rubric of
hermeneutics. Ast begins with the conclusion reached by identity philosophy
that all understanding would be impossible were it not for the originary unity
of all-cognizing spirit, and to this spirit nothing is alien.⁵ The knowledge of
antiquity, however, is the starting place for the hermeneutic comprehension
of this spirit. Thus Ast explains, "*Hermeneutics* or *Exegetics* (called hermeneutike, exegetike, also historike: ennaratio auctorum, in Quintil. *Inst. Orat.* 1:9.1)
therefore presupposes the *understanding* of antiquity in all its inner and outer
aspects, and upon it is based the *explication* of the written works of antiquity."⁶

Naturally, Ast's project is universal in scope because its object is the
hermeneutic self-understanding of a single, self-identical spirit in all its man-
ifestations, beginning in antiquity. In this connection the doctrine of the
scopus, according to which each passage is to be elucidated by reference to
its intention and context, acquired new significance: now, every individual
utterance must be conceived by appeal to the whole of spirit. Thus the
"hermeneutic circle," as it later came to be called, received perhaps its first
and at the same time most universal formulation: "The fundamental law of
all understanding and knowing is to discover the spirit of the whole in the
individual and to grasp the individual in terms of the whole."⁷ This "fundamental law" served to open up a general problem for future hermeneutics,
since it left unclear *how* the whole was to be discerned in the parts and
whether the premonition of the whole does not distort comprehension of the
parts. For Ast, however, this law is still purely descriptive in character: the
whole is to be understood from the individual, and vice versa. Neither is prior
to the other; each mutually conditions the other, and together they consti-

tute "one harmonious life."[8] Once this harmony was problematized, the formerly comprehensible theory of the hermeneutic circle came to be a decisive point of contention for subsequent hermeneutics. For Ast it merely referred to the obvious fact that everything literal had to be traced back to a superordinate spirit.

Schlegel's understanding of hermeneutics remained undocumented for a long time. His main hermeneutical considerations are concentrated in his notebooks on philology composed between 1796 and 1797, though first published in 1928 and appearing again in 1981 in the new edition. Generally unknown in the nineteenth century, they deserve mention here because it is more than probable that Schleiermacher was acquainted with them.[9] At the time of their composition, Schleiermacher and Schlegel lived in the same house and had planned to undertake a joint translation of Plato, though Schleiermacher later completed it alone.

As the starting point of his meditations, Schlegel sought to devise a philosophy of philology or a philology of philology. Given the self-destruction of philosophical reason resulting from Kant's critique of metaphysics, it seemed to follow that only a new self-conception of philology could bring about a revitalization of philosophy. Schlegel took his orientation from the classical division of philology into grammar, (textual) criticism, and hermeneutics. Grammar was taken to be foundational. The relation between criticism and hermeneutics revealed a certain antinomy, one we have underlined above: In order to understand a text correctly, the interpreter needs a reliable critical edition, but in order to edit the text, critique needs the aid of hermeneutics.

Such vacillation and antinomic thinking were not uncharacteristic of Romanticism, and certainly not of Schlegel. It is clear that the image of antiquity dominated philology's conception of its method. "Criticism and hermeneutics presuppose a historical aim." If hermeneutics were ever to come to fruition, then historical knowledge of antiquity would be necessary.[10] But specifically in what way does hermeneutics relate to classical philology? It is difficult to distill a concrete program out of Schlegel's vague though suggestive sketches. He envisioned a "philosophical hermeneutics" that could produce a skill modeled on the exemplary classicality of the ancients.[11] Its aim would be to transform what to them was intuitive know-how into a systematic and self-conscious methodology for philology. He wanted to arrive, as it were, at a self-understanding of understanding that would derive a theory or art from exemplary practices of the ancients, for "antiquity is the arena of philological art."[12]

If this is correct, it implies that Schlegel may well represent a universal function of post-Kantian hermeneutic theory. For in response to the pressing need for an art of understanding he points back to the "enduring" model of antiquity. The hermeneutic subject, increasingly worldless and unsure of itself, becomes Romantic: it gropes toward antiquity to discover the artful rules governing its activity. Basic to this Romantic view is the fundamental uncertainty of the subject implied by its dependence on tradition. The primary element of Schlegel's world is the state of mutual unintelligibility to which finite subjects are permanently consigned. Understanding is always at the same time non-understanding, for retranslating an expression back into intelligibility always involves a certain amount of wrenching.[13] Genius, in fact, can never be understood (and this is the real question for Schlegel) if understanding means explaining things in terms of the familiar and common.

Schlegel likewise anticipates and represents Romantic hermeneutics in that his views on hermeneutics were never brought to systematic fruition and publication—a failure immanent, as it were, in his own conception of the insecurity of knowledge. Deeply influenced by the Romantic foundations laid by Schlegel, Schleiermacher (1768–1834) undertook to incorporate the subject's fundamental uncertainty into a universal art of understanding.

2. Schleiermacher's Universalization of Misunderstanding

From the very beginning of his tenure as a teacher at Halle in 1805 to his death in 1834, Friedrich Schleiermacher focused his attention on the questions of hermeneutics. Nevertheless, the renowned professor of theology and translator of Plato, who received a chair in Berlin in 1809, never did allow a mature, fully developed presentation of his hermeneutic theory to be published. His highly polished, albeit somewhat idiosyncratic Academy lectures delivered in 1829, "On the Concept of Hermeneutics with Reference to F. A. Wolf's Remarks and Ast's Handbook," was the only piece he considered worth publishing. (There he took issue with his philological teachers, who nevertheless exercised a minor influence on his hermeneutics.) The impact of Schleiermacher's hermeneutics is due entirely to the work of his student Friedrich Lücke, whose carefully crafted edition, *Hermeneutik und Kritik, mit besonderer Beziehung auf das Neue Testament,* is assembled from handwritten manuscripts and lecture notes. Though not personally in attendance at Schleiermacher's lectures,[14] Lücke had a broad fund of materials for putting together his compendium, because Schleiermacher held nine lectures on hermeneutics between 1805 and 1832. In 1805, he began teaching a course entitled "Hermeneutica sacra" modeled on J. A. Ernesti's pietist textbook. By 1809–1810 he was already lecturing about "universal hermeneutics."[15] Paralleling his lectures, his notebooks contain a few sketches of hermeneutics that he wrote down apparently with a view to publication. Though his publication plans seem to have been set as early as 1805, they never came to fruition.[16]

It is not easy to say why Schleiermacher was so reticent about publication. The reason is certainly not that he assigned hermeneutics a secondary importance compared, say, to his theological studies. His continual work on the question and his hermeneutic sketches prove just the opposite. To be sure, one might say that Schleiermacher's "unexpectedly early death"[17] (though he was sixty-six years old) was responsible for his failure to complete his work. More plausible, perhaps, is the suggestion that Schleiermacher was a real Romantic (and hermeneut!) in being never fully satisfied with his sketches in substance or form. Though his overall conception remained essentially the same, his dissatisfaction is manifest in the continual vacillation of his terminology and points of focus, which has given no little trouble to scholars of Schleiermacher and of hermeneutics. For the purposes of the present introduction, however, we can only be concerned with Schleiermacher's overall conception (which is quite coherent throughout his career) and the new beginning which it represents for hermeneutics.

Any talk of Schleiermacher's "new beginning" is itself somewhat deceptive and in part false,[18] for he is basically duplicating old hermeneutics when he states in the opening of his hermeneutics that "every act of understanding is the inverse of an act of speech, in that the thought underlying the speech must enter consciousness."[19] So, given the premise that "all speech depends on an earlier thought,"[20] the basic task of understanding undoubtedly consists solely in tracing an expression back to the intent that animates it: "What we are looking for is the very thought that the speaker wanted to express."[21]

What the interpreter is trying to understand is the meaning of an utterance, that is, another person's expression or thought.[22] Understanding therefore has no other object than language. In a motto made famous by Gadamer's adopting it as the epigraph for the third part of *Truth and Method*, Schleiermacher writes, "Everything presupposed in hermeneutics is but language."[23] For Schleiermacher this foundational presupposition has a specific, architectonic sense. Language can be viewed in two ways. On one hand, any given utterance to be understood is an instance of the overall usage of a given language community. That is, every expression follows a prescribed syntax or pattern of usage and is to that extent supra-individual. The aspect of hermeneutics concerned with this aspect of language Schleiermacher calls "the grammatical side" of interpretation.[24] Its task is to elucidate an expression by reference to the total context constituted by the possibilities of a language. Yet an expression is not merely the anonymous vehicle of a fundamentally supra-individual language; it is also the manifestation of an individual mind. People do not always mean the same thing by the same words. If they did, there would be "only grammar."[25] Contrary to the tendency to dissolve understanding into grammar associated with structuralism during the 1960s, hermeneutics must also pay attention to the other side of interpretation: the individual. "Technical" interpretation is the term Schleiermacher gives to this second aspect of understanding. Apparently, *technical* here refers to the fact that the interpreter is trying to understand the *special* art (technē) that an author employed in one of his works. Clearly, in order to do so, the purely syntactic view of language must be superseded by what the utterance really is trying to say. The end and purpose is to understand a mind that discloses itself, a soul that manifests itself through the language it brings forth from within it. Thus Schleiermacher later came to call this side of interpretation "psychological."[26]

Schleiermacher's universal hermeneutics took on two tasks and consequently two forms: the grammatical and the technical (or psychological). The grammatical concerned itself with language in respect to the totality of usage; the technical-psychological conceived of language as the expression of inwardness. The ambition of hermeneutics, moreover, is to be a "methodology" (Kunstlehre)—a term that acquired new connotations under Schleiermacher's hand, for hermeneutics was increasingly assigned the task of regulating the act of understanding "methodologically" (kunstmäßig), which reminds one a good deal of Schlegel. Most significant in this regard is Schleiermacher's distinction between a *stricter* and a *laxer* practice of interpretation, which in turn reflects two fundamentally different hermeneutic purposes. The laxer practice (the one most common in the history of hermeneutics) begins from the fact that "understanding occurs of its own accord and that its goal is expressed in the negative: the avoidance of misunderstanding." There is no doubt that Schleiermacher meant here to be describing classical hermeneutics that limited itself to specific passages, since it offered occasional directions for shedding light on obscurities. By contrast, Schleiermacher himself aimed to employ the stricter practice that begins with the fact that "misunderstanding occurs of its own accord and that understanding must be consciously sought at every point."[27]

The genuine originality of Schleiermacher's hermeneutic initiatives manifests itself in that distinction. From this point on, what he called the laxer practice was equated with artless, intuitive understanding.[28] Of course, understanding is normally artless—that is, unproblematical for itself. Traditional hermeneutics held that people generally understand things quickly and easily, unless they come up against some obstacle or contradiction.[29] That is, hermeneutics becomes necessary only when someone does not understand (any longer). Formerly, the state of understanding was considered normal and natural; non-understanding is therefore an exception, and to deal with it special hermeneutic assistance was needed. Schleiermacher took this "naive," provincial perspective and stood it on its head when he premised that misunderstanding was in fact the normal state. From the outset, then, the interpreter must be on guard against possible misunderstanding, and for just that reason understanding needs to proceed 'by the book' (kunstgemäß) at every step. "The business of hermeneutics cannot begin merely when the faculty of understanding becomes uncertain of itself; rather, it is involved from the very beginning in the endeavor to understand something said."[30]

Schleiermacher's hermeneutics is intended to encourage this stricter practice. Thus he universalizes misunderstanding as the situation and occasion of interpretation. This universalization is penetrated through and through by a notion of radical subjectivity, just as it was for Schlegel. Post-Kantian reason, with its cognitive claims now problematized, has become fundamentally unstable because it has become aware of the limited, perspectival, hypothetical character of its endeavors to understand. Henceforward it must take the universal primacy of misunderstanding as its starting point. And this element of understanding is indeed susceptible of being universalized: can one ever really claim to have thought something through to the very end? In every attempt at understanding—even one that appears to have succeeded—the possibility of some last vestige of misunderstanding cannot be ruled out. It is by universalizing this all too human experience that Schleiermacher can write in 1829, "non-understanding is never completely eliminated."[31]

Schleiermacher thus conceptualizes the fundamental operation of hermeneutics (that is, of understanding—for the first time the two terms can be strictly equated) as an act of reconstruction. In order really to understand something said (that is, to anticipate the ever-present danger of misunderstanding), I must be able to reconstruct every part from the ground up, just as if I were the author. The end of understanding is not the meaning that I find in the subject matter but rather the meaning that appears in the reconstructed viewpoint of the author. Since the task of hermeneutics consists in doing justice to this viewpoint, Schleiermacher comes to formulate the task of hermeneutics as "understanding the discourse first as well as and then better than its author," a maxim (first devised by Kant) that Schleiermacher inserts in all his works on hermeneutics.[32] The aim of understanding better can only be conceived as an ideal, for so stated, it involves an "infinite task," as Schleiermacher often emphasizes. Yet, though the task seems overwhelming, the imperative to understand an author better than he understood himself can be read in more modest fashion: given the universal potential for misunderstanding, the maxim is an open invitation to ever deeper interpretation.[33] Since we can never be completely certain of our own understandings, we cannot cease trying to penetrate the matter anew. The goal of understanding better, conceived in terms of an unreachable telos and the impossibility of complete understanding, bears witness to the fact that the endeavor to interpret more deeply is always worthwhile.

This raises the question, of course, whether a formal "methodology" whose ambition is to produce a strict reconstruction of interpretive practice can really do justice to it. Schleiermacher himself presents a few canons and rules, particularly for the grammatical part of hermeneutics. Yet he remained aware that for the application of hermeneutic rules themselves there is no rule.[34] Schleiermacher does offer general "methods" of interpretation, which in substance reintroduce the rules found in ancient hermeneutics—for example, the requirement that passages be elucidated in terms of their context—but he consistently refrains from specifying applications for rules and from assigning them any decisive importance. In fact, with respect to "technical-psychological" interpretation, which treats discourse as a manifestation of an individual, Schleiermacher says that interpretive "divination" is unavoidable. By this term he refers not to a sacred gift but merely the process of guessing (divinare).[35] At the point when the fundamentally comparative means of grammatical interpretation leave us at a loss—that is, when it is not the commonness but the uniqueness of a particular style that is to be elucidated— then often enough we simply have to guess what the author was trying to say.

Schleiermacher always supposes, and rightly so, that behind every spoken or written word stands something else, something thought, which constitutes the real target of interpretation. What is thought presents itself only in words however, and so finally it can only be guessed. Schleiermacher therefore puts increasing emphasis on the divinatory aspect of hermeneutics. For this reason he may well have "misunderstood" his own hermeneutic program, insofar as he conceived of it as belonging to a rule-governed methodology. Like scarcely anyone else, he possessed an acute sense of the limits of methodizability and the necessity for tactful divination in the sphere of interpretation. Was it perhaps for this reason that he refrained from publishing his hermeneutics in the form of a methodology?

3. Limiting Hermeneutics to Psychology?

Since the textual sources remain incomplete, it is still risky to speculate about the development of Schleiermacher's hermeneutics. As far as we can tell, however, Schleiermacher scholars and others who point to the fact that technical interpretation later came to be called psychological[36] seem to have good reason for detecting an increasing emphasis on the psychological in Schleiermacher's later work. More and more, Schleiermacher affirmed that purely grammatical interpretation can bear only very modest fruit. For this Romantic, the ultimate goal of interpretation is to penetrate behind utterance to reach the inward recesses of thought. The fact is that passages are usually unproblematical on a purely verbal or grammatical level. What remains to be understood, and is always being misunderstood, is precisely what the author wanted to say. For that reason, we want to and indeed must "interpret"—that is, we need to make sense of discourse by tracing it back to an impulse to utterance, the desire to say something. The Academy lectures of 1829 make it clear in every way that "outward" speech must be made understandable by being related back to the author's inward thought.[37] The fact is that the whole history of hermeneutics to that point really never had any other aim.

Recent hermeneuts, however, have faulted Schleiermacher on this score: for having dissolved the tie to sense and subject matter typical of the older hermeneutics. For Schleiermacher, they argue, the point of interpreting is to understand an author or creative act, instead of mediating sense or truth. As Gadamer's well-known accusation phrases it, Schleiermacher encouraged the interpreter to consider "the texts, independently of their claim to truth, as purely expressive phenomena."[38] Many Schleiermacher specialists, especially M. Frank, have taken exception to this charge; but they did so in order to acquit Schleiermacher of "psychologizing" hermeneutics in the manner associated with Dilthey, widely held to be unacceptable. According to Frank, it was Dilthey, not Schleiermacher, who spoke of the interpreter's transposing himself into the soul of the author. It is indeed true that Dilthey understood Schleiermacher in a predominantly psychological way. Schleiermacher's "seminal thought," he believed, was the conception of interpretation as the reconstruction of the living act of the author, which implied that the task of hermeneutic theory was "to base this reconstruction scientifically on the nature of the productive act."[39] Nevertheless, we should not interpret Schleiermacher as if he had never written that "the task of hermeneutics consists in reproducing, as completely as possible, the entire inner course of the writer's activity in composing."[40] At issue is only one thing: whether it is appropriate to view speaking as the utterance of an inner thought. It is entirely pointless to try to reconstruct the unconscious process of thought production that occurs in composition. This is of interest to no one. But is it really a mistake to inquire into the subject matter and intended truth that lie behind speech? As far as we can tell, it is only the reconstruction of this inward content that Schleiermacher has in mind. Can this be fairly described as "psychologizing"? It hardly implies ignoring the truth content of discourse. Quite the opposite, the truth claim is restricted because it overlooks the inner thought that everything said bears within it. The interpreter becomes open to the truth only by adopting this hermeneutic orientation—that is, by being prepared to burst through the purely grammatical level and enter into the spirit of the word.

4. The Dialectical Ground of Hermeneutics

Schleiermacher can be charged with psychologizing and overlooking the subject matter to be understood only by someone who fails to take into consideration the dialectical—or, more precisely, the dialogical—horizon of his hermeneutics. For Schleiermacher, dialectic (in his view the highest philosophical science and the one to which hermeneutics is subordinate) means the art of mutual understanding. The need for it stems from the fact that "perfect knowledge" cannot ultimately be achieved and that there is no Archimedean fulcrum for humankind. Given our finitude, Schleiermacher believes, we must accept the fact that the sphere of thought presents endless matter of debate, as the history of the sciences shows clearly enough.[41] Thus we always remain dependent on conversations with one another—and with ourselves, Schleiermacher emphasizes—in order to arrive at sharable truths that for the moment are no longer the object of debate. This dialectical impulse, which arises once the attempt to find ultimate foundations has been abandoned, goes hand in hand with the universalization of misunderstanding that gives Schleiermacher's hermeneutics its special thrust: the individual, intrinsically disposed to error, achieves knowledge only through conversation and sharing thoughts with others.

Hermeneutics, conceived as "the art of rightly understanding the discourse, and especially the writing, of another," participates in this dialogical search for knowledge.[44] In order to understand a text, one must enter into conversation with it and thereby get behind what the words say on the surface: "Who is it that in their intercourse with especially gifted people does not make the effort to listen between the words, just as we read between the lines of rich and complex texts; who would not deem a meaningful conversation worthy of interpretation (a conversation which in many respects can easily also be a meaningful deed) that does not think it all the more important to pluck out the heart of the matter, grasp its inner connection, follow out all the faint hints."[43] Hermeneutics rests upon dialogical foundations: To interpret a text means to enter into a conversation with it, direct questions to it, and allow oneself to be questioned by it.[44] Again and again interpretation must, lest it become superfluous, supersede what is written as such and "read between the lines," in Schleiermacher's happy phrase. This art resembles that of conversation. Every written word is in itself an invitation to the dialogue which the text can lead with another mind. Thus Schleiermacher urges the interpreter of written works "to practice interpreting significant conversation."[45] That the art of dialogue really amounts to bad psychologizing is not obvious at all.

Schleiermacher's conception of the hermeneutic circle is framed within this dialogical context. In considering Friedrich Ast we saw that every individual utterance of mind must be understood by appeal to its total context, the whole to which it belongs. For Ast this whole ultimately consisted of the all-encompassing unity of spirit as it spins itself out over the course of epochs. For Schleiermacher, however, this idealistic whole is too grand. In his view the whole can be more modestly defined by reference to two sides, corresponding to his bipartite conception of hermeneutics. From the viewpoint of the grammatical side (now called objective), the whole that elucidates the part is the literary genre to which it belongs. From the psychological or subjective side, on the other hand, the part (whether passage or work) is viewed as the "act of the producer" and thus explained by reference to "the whole of his life."[46] Thus Schleiermacher conceives the individuum as the asymptote which interpretation is always approaching without ever reaching. In this way he notably distances himself from his teacher Ast's aspiration to "once again reanimate" the circle and conceive individual creations as part of a still higher whole, whether idealistic or historical.[47] Schleiermacher limits the circle to the totality of an individual life, a limitation that follows from his attempt to understand the spoken as an emanation of inner thought: as one soul's attempt to communicate with another. In interpreting the circle historically, however, Ast (perhaps contrary to his own idealist aspirations to universal history) had anticipated the prospect of historicist relativism that interprets everything as the expression of its age. We turn now to the universal claim that this new way of seeing things opened up for hermeneutics.

IV

The Problems
of Historicism

*History is the gnothi sauton of
humanity.*

Droysen, Historik

1. Böckh and the Dawn of Historical Awareness

Schleiermacher wanted to limit the theory of the hermeneutic circle to written texts and to the author's individuality. His purpose was to keep in check the arbitrariness of circle, the power of which, Ast suggested, could no longer be circumscribed. Although the idea of a circle summons up the idea of a fallacy to be avoided, at bottom it rests upon a logical basis: the demand for coherence, that is, for understanding the particular only in the context [Zusammenhang] of the whole to which it belongs. For the nineteenth century, this coherent whole was concretized in the historical context of a given epoch. The basic doctrine here—since then called historicism and sometimes relativism—is that every particular phenomenon must be conceptualized within the context of its age. The point is to avoid judging other times by the standards of our own, and instead to interpret historical events immanently, as expressive of *their* time. To be sure, this historicism, practiced thereafter by every scholar, bespeaks a basic desire to be fair to historical phenomena. It raises a striking epistemological problem, however: if every age is to be explained by reference to itself, this same principle must hold true of our own age. Our view of earlier ages must itself be produced by reference to our present, and it is thereby relativized. Our time merely represents one age among many. How, then, is any kind of strict science of history possible? In other words, how is it possible under the auspices of historicism, now generally recognized, to formulate the idea of a binding and yet nonrelativistic truth? Doesn't everything dissolve into present-day perspectives and temporal conditionedness? How, if at all, is it possible to escape from the hermeneutic circle of our historicity? These are the basic problems of historicism.

It is easy to see why hermeneutics, the art of understanding, became entangled in them. No doubt it started with the Romantic insight into the ineluctable uncertainty of understanding between individuals, which Schleiermacher had pushed to the point of universalizing misunderstanding. As far as we can tell, Schleiermacher did not yet conceive of this uncertainty as deriving primarily from the fact that understanding is conditioned by its time. The problems of historicism, as we are familiar with them, hardly occupied him. He was instead concerned with the metaphysical or monadic isolation of the subject threatened with the danger of constant misunderstanding, rather than with the view (which he indeed rejected) that every particular phenomenon needs to be reconstructed out of the context of its age. The emergence of historicism involved a different kind of experience than monadic isolation.

The nineteenth century was not just the Age of Romanticism; it also witnessed the triumph of science and methodology (by which we refer here to philosophical reflection on the foundations of science, and even the reduction of philosophy to that reflection). The victory of the modern, mathematical and physical sciences, which emancipated themselves from the guardianship of philosophy precisely during the nineteenth century, seemed to justify the belief that strict science and absolute truth were still possible. This was the case at least for the natural sciences, whose grounds were elucidated by Kant's *Critique of Pure Reason*. After Kant, the only task remaining for nineteenth-century methodological reflection was to find a link to the new problems of historicism, and so conjure up "a critique of historical reason" for the historical world. In such methodological dress, inquiry into the conditions of the objectivity of historical knowledge offered the prospect of eluding the hermeneutic circle of our historicity.

Schleiermacher concerned himself very little with this issue. The burden of developing its methodological implications fell, rather, to August Böckh (1785–1867) in his *Enzyklopädie und Methodenlehre der philologischen Wissenschaften,* which is a collection of lectures based on a notebook written by the classicist Böckh in 1809 and delivered from 1809 to 1865 in the course of twenty-six semesters in Berlin. It is virtually certain that they were not significantly influenced by Lücke's edition of Schleiermacher's hermeneutics. Böckh himself confirms this: "In my presentation, Schleiermacher's ideas are borrowed not from this work but from earlier communications, so much so that I am no longer able to distinguish mine from thine."[1] As is well known, Böckh deepens Schleiermacher's basic intuition in that he understands the real task of philology to be "the knowledge of the productions of the human spirit, i.e., what is already known."[2] Unlike philosophy, philology is not productive but, rather, reproductive and reconstructive. Knowing the known, in Böckh's terminology, is "understanding." What is understood is always something already known—or, more exactly, the expression of knowledge in a certain hermeneia or utterance whereby "human thought takes on form."[3] Thus, the task of hermeneutics is to understand this hermeneia as the result of an act of knowing, which it is its job to reconstruct.

What is especially insightful in Böckh's formulation of hermeneutics as re-knowing what is already known is its standing invitation to further research, to the deeper penetration into the word that constitutes the soul of every hermeneutics: "Investigation of the spoken or written word is the most fundamental philological impulse."[4] This suggests that the communication encoded in signs and symbols is only a part or end product of what is known by the author. So it comes as no surprise that Böckh adopts Schleiermacher's formula about understanding an author better than he understood himself. Authors produce their work unconsciously for the most part, whereas interpreters cannot avoid reflecting about the knowledge deposited in the expression if they are to elucidate its unexpressed content. Generally speaking, Böckh takes over a good deal from Schleiermacher, especially from his conversations with him. Compared to Schleiermacher's, Böckh's "Theory of Hermeneutics" is relatively unoriginal. Within the sphere of historicism, however, it is important to note that to grammatical, personal, and generic interpretation he adds historical interpretation, for the process of understanding needs to be completed by situating the meaning to be understood among its "real [that is, historical] relationships."

Even if Böckh boasts of offering a "scientific elaboration of the laws of understanding," his hermeneutics remains more descriptive than prescriptive.[5] What he gives us is in fact less a methodology than an "encyclopedia" that displays the "interconnectedness of science."[6] Böckh wants to prevent his discipline from seeming so rhapsodic and to develop its organic integrity. At the beginning of the nineteenth century (Böckh's projects date as far back as 1809), no one yet felt any burning need for a pure methodology. But by the end of the century, when Böckh's lectures of 1877 were first edited by his student Bratuschek, the perceived need for methodology had become the main focus of philosophy.

2. Droysen's Universal Historiology: Understanding as Research in the Moral World

The methodological problem of historicism was first fully grasped by Johann Gustav Droysen (1808–1884), who had studied with Böckh in Berlin. Droysen was undoubtedly modeling himself on his teacher when he titled his lectures on methodology "Enzyklopädie und Methodologie der Geschichte." He, too, recoiled from publishing his lectures; they did not appear until R. Hübner's extensive edition in 1937. In 1868, however, appeared the important though sketchy *Grundriß der Historik,* on which Droysen's extensive influence is based.

It should be noted, though, that Droysen virtually never mentions hermeneutics. Except for the hapax legomenon of the Greek adjective hermeneutike, there is not a single instance of the word hermeneutics in the whole *Historik.*[7] Droysen thematizes "interpretation," of course, but not until a relatively late part of the *Historik,* in a subsection on method concerned with interpreting sources (after that on critique!). What connects Droysen's view of interpretation to Böckh and Romantic hermeneutics (Schleiermacher is almost never cited in this context) is the concept of understanding, which had come to assume a central significance in methodology. Understanding now comes to be viewed as a specific procedure for the historical sciences, and the *Historik* promised to deliver its methodology.

Our time, Droysen remarks, is the age of science, and the mathematically based natural sciences provide its paradigm. What explains their indubitable success? According to Droysen, it depends on the fact that "they have made their tasks, their means, and their methods fully conscious and that they observe the objects that lie within the sphere of their research from the viewpoints on which their method is based, and only from them."[8] Clarity of methodological consciousness, then, explains the natural sciences' success. If historical knowledge is ever to claim the title of science and historiography is to resist the incursion of a methodology appropriate to mathematics and physics, Droysen concludes, the historical sciences will need to develop their own methods. The problem of legitimizing the historical sciences, then, arises as a direct consequence of the victorious course of methodology in the wake of the exact natural sciences. "At the point when the natural sciences, fully conscious of their way, grounded their methods with certainty and thereby achieved a new beginning, the idea first emerged of giving the amethodos hyle of history a methodical side as well."[9]

In order to sharpen the methodological self-understanding of historiography, Droysen avoids following two specious patterns: on one hand, the positivist pattern that tries to subordinate history to the mathematical model of natural science and suggests searching for something like the statistical laws governing history; and on the other, the view of historiography that considers it a merely narrative, chatty, and in brief a dilettantish art-form. Given the latter, history would enjoy no right to call itself a science. Yet history is not the same kind of thing as natural science. The purpose of historiology (or theory of historiography), therefore, is to legitimate the meaning and procedure proper to historical study. As Droysen's 1867 essay "Kunst und Methode" concisely states it, the task of historiology is "[to show how] all the methods that are applicable to the sphere of historical study can be resolved into the common thought that joins them, to develop their system, their theory, and thus to determine not the laws of history but the laws governing historical research and knowledge."[10] Although the notion of a critique of historical reason stems from Dilthey, it is equally applicable to Droysen, who assimilated his methodological endeavors to those of Kant: "We need a Kant to provide [not merely a model for gathering] historical materials but a critical paradigm for theory and practice toward and in history."[11]

Droysen also follows Kant's example in erecting his *Historik* upon anthropological and gnoseological grounds. Consequently he employs two basic ways of conceiving of spirit: nature and history (or, expressed in a more Kantian way, space and time). Our mind is not satisfied with collecting empirical facts; it must subsume what is comprehended under concepts and categories, of which the most general are space and time: in space or nature what predominates is the static, what is always the same, and sensorily perceptible; in history and time, what changes come to the fore. These dual approaches to the world are connected with the duality of human nature, which is at once both intellectual and sensory. This as it were a priori duality makes possible two ways of observing existing things, as well as two kinds of experience, and these find their respective expressions in the natural and human sciences. Whereas the method of the natural sciences consists in discovering the normative laws of observed phenomena,[12] the essence of historical science consists in "forschend zu verstehen," understanding through research.[13] However new its methodological horizon, the concept of understanding brought into play here cannot be entirely divorced from earlier hermeneutics: understanding means, as it always has, "tracing back [utterances] to what is trying to come to expression in them."[14] In such phrases Droysen emphasizes that historical understanding is built up by the interpreter's recurring to the power, the might, the inwardness that manifests itself in historical expressions.

In this process what we are trying to understand is not the past itself— which is, of course, no longer present—but instead what is still retained in present-day materials and sources.[15] Historical understanding concerns itself with the vestiges of the past handed down to us. Droysen denounces as chimerical the notion that historians deal in objective discoveries about the past: "It would be completely to mistake the nature of the things with which our science is occupied, if one thought it had to do with objective facts. Objective facts in their reality never emerge in our research."[16] The historian's subject matter is, rather, enduring witnesses—that is, previous interpretations of the past—which need to be given new life so that the past that is not given as such can be reconstructed. In that it interrogates its sources critically, historical science "does not merely repeat what has been handed down as history; instead, it must penetrate more deeply; it tries as far as possible to find whatever of the past is still left to be discovered; in the spirit of letting things come to life again and understanding them, it tries to create new sources, as it were."[17] Critically reenacting the event in understanding is a consequence of attempting to understand history better than the way it has been handed down to us. What we achieve thereby is, of course, "not a picture of what happened as such but rather our own construal and intellectual reworking of it."[18] By inquiring into what lies behind traditional comprehensions of a given subject matter we can achieve a better perspective on it, but nothing more—that is, such a perspective is only the reinterpretation of something understood that always needs to be interpreted yet again.

When the historian investigates what lies behind historical utterances, by examining what exists within them all, he strives to reconstruct the individual on the basis of the whole from which it emerged, and the whole from the particulars in which it expresses itself.[19] To be sure, history remains an empirical science that relies on evidence and witnesses, but inquiry becomes science only when a recognizable universal advenes to the particulars that are experienced.[20] But how can we define the universal, the "inside" that is sought by the historian? This is the question, in Droysen's words, of how events are turned into history [Wie wird aus den Geschäften Geschichte?].[21] The universality and necessity supposedly uniting the various single facts together, according to Droysen, lie in the "continuity of progressive historical work and production"—in the epidosis eis auto, the immanent growth of the historical world.[22] The nature of the increasing continuity of history can only be ideal and moral. The course of history, as we strive to understand it though research, is characterized by the (alleged) increasing continuity and progress of the moral world. Any given event may be isolated and regressive but "regressive only to spring forward again with redoubled integrative power."[23] It is in this way that the object of historical research can be outlined: in essence, to understand history is to understand the progressively developing moral powers. As Droysen writes again and again, the moral powers (family, language, religion, law, science, and so on) give the historian the *series of questions* with which to interpret the moral content of the historical material. The objective of historical research is thus defined more sharply. Understanding the particular means relating it back to the entirety of its historical-moral development, conceived as its inside, its law or meaning. For "humanity is only the integrated totality of all these moral powers and forms, and every individual [exists] only in the continuity and community of these moral powers."[24]

In this connection Droysen talks with good reason of *forschenden* Verstehen, understanding through research, in order to distinguish the "method" of historical study from its alternatives. By contrast to the century's most familiar positivistic frameworks, research does not here mean the bee-like business of gathering facts. Gadamer suggests the possibility of a religious undertone in the phrase "understanding through research," something like "searching one's conscience."[25] What connects the two is the notion of an ongoing search which never reaches a definitive end. Droysen speaks of (re)searching because the whole of history that is the concern of understanding is never given as such. Indeed, understanding means searching through given documents and signs for what is not immediately given.

This connotation of the word (re)search becomes especially clear when

Droysen broaches the topic of the end of history. The interpretive historian presupposes that history progresses toward moral ends. Of course, the "purpose of purposes," the goal of history, cannot be empirically discerned. The only thing we can say is that our understanding and expression of this purpose of purposes rise and deepen at every stage of the way. In fact, just this— the broadening and refinement of our understanding of the goal of all goals—is precisely what needs to be viewed as the progress of humanity proper. Thus conceived, history is nothing other than humanity's steadily increasing consciousness and awareness of itself: "Over the course of the stages it traverses, humanity increasingly comes to express the purpose of purposes, its longing for it, and the way toward it. The fact that with every step this expression broadens, rises, and deepens—*this and only this* can be considered human progress."[26] Thus the epochs of history become stages in the progress of human self-knowledge—indeed, knowledge of God, Droysen ventures.[27] Since history still remains unfinished, historical understanding is likewise unfinished—that is, it continues merely searching and researching. It is in this context that the notion of interpretive research manifests its special significance. Such "(re)searching" occurs only when we are precluded from achieving definitive knowledge, where the meaning behind historical phenomena can only be conjectured: "To the finite eye, the beginning and ending are concealed. But by *searching and researching* it can discern the direction of the moving current."[28]

For finite beings, all understanding basically amounts to tentative searching. They are therefore always obliged to point to a meaning, situated behind what is immediately given, that is not determinate or determinable. Only by searching and researching—by conjecture and supposition—do we come to know our historical world. This conception of interpretive research echoes Böckh's astute formulation of understanding as knowing the known: our understanding strives unceasingly to get behind what is already known in order to discover or devise the meaning that surpasses the literal.

The procedure of interpretive research into the moral world, according to Droysen, brings a certain order to the amethodos hyle of history and stakes out the framework of historical science, the theoretical legitimation of which was the objective of Historik, or theory of historiography. It is highly dubious and finally pointless, however, to assert that "interpretive research" offers a degree of methodological certainty comparable to that of the natural sciences. What Droysen ultimately succeeded in legitimizing was far less the *methodology* than the hermeneutic autonomy of the interpretive sciences in the face of the scientistic attempt to subordinate the way they go about their business to the exact, mathematical sciences. Research and understanding are possible even in spheres neither governed by mathematical patterns nor expressible in mathematical terms. Because the procedure of scientific experiment is not available to us here, writes Droysen at the end of his lecture, what is left is (re)search, and only (re)search.[29] Understanding erects its edifice by researching what has been already understood, which in its turn is based upon deeper understandings still. Droysen's somewhat grandiose promise to construct a methodology of historiography is finally a concession to the positivist spirit of his times: historicism's self-misunderstanding, as it were, in its struggle with itself.

3. Dilthey: On the Way to Hermeneutics

Wilhelm Dilthey (1833–1911) likewise made the methodological challenges of historicism his starting point. From the very first blossoming of his philosophical endeavors in the 1860s to his final jottings, he envisioned his whole life's work as belonging to a Critique of Historical Reason,[30] the task of which was to provide the epistemological legitimation of the human sciences as sciences. His impassioned investigations in this direction came to no conclusion that he found satisfying. So he refrained from distinguishing any of his writings with the pregnant title, Critique of Historical Reason, and renounced publication of the second, systematically oriented volume of his *Introduction to the Human Sciences,* even though he already had important materials and preliminary work at his disposal, as we can see from the posthumous writings that have since been made available.

Dilthey considered himself to be the methodologist of the historical school. Like Droysen, whom he mentions remarkably seldom, Dilthey aims to conceptualize the human sciences as autonomous sciences and defend them from the encroachments of natural science and its methodology; and to do so, he attempts to place them upon universally valid, gnoseological foundations and so legitimize them philosophically. Thus, in the preface to his *Introduction,* his incomplete magnum opus, he inquires into the "solid foundation" common to all assertions in the human sciences that lay claim to certainty.[31] Dilthey is clearly intent on emancipating the human sciences from their subordination to the natural sciences, as was the case for Mill and Buckle; nevertheless, his talk about seeking unshakable foundations still bears witness to his fascination with the scientistic paradigm. That is, it seems that the sciences of man that deal, after all, with mutable, sublunary things also need something like an Archimedean fixed point in order to maintain their claim to scientific respectability.

Dilthey first locates the solid foundation of social-scientific research in inner experience, or the "facts of consciousness." All science is empirical, experiential science, Dilthey argues, but experience derives its coherence and validity from the structuring apriori of our consciousness.[32] Thus it seems likely that the human sciences' conditions of validity and objectivity are to be found in inner experience, just as the foundations of pure natural science, as Kant showed, derive from the principles of pure understanding. In 1880 and the years that followed, methodological research into the human sciences had to be guided by the universal "principle of phenomenality" in consequence of which all reality (that is, all external facts, things as well as persons) is governed by the conditions of consciousness.[33] From this fact Dilthey draws the conclusion that only reflection on the psychological foundations of the human sciences would be capable of grounding the objectivity of their knowledge. Beginning in 1875 with his essay "On the Study of the History of the Sciences of Man, Society, and the State," through the programmatic and historical first volume of the *Introduction,* and up to his "Ideas Concerning Descriptive and Analytic Psychology" in 1895, Dilthey used one approach after another in the task of laying the psychological foundations of the human sciences. In so doing he envisioned a new kind of psychology that would proceed by way of "understanding" rather than "explanation." Dilthey elucidates this distinction (reminiscent of Droysen, though he is never mentioned) in his important study of 1895. This work has special significance because there, for the first and virtually the last time, Dilthey published materials from the second volume of the *Introduction,* his unwritten Critique of Historical Reason.[34] After the historical archaeology of the human sciences had been traced out in the first volume, the second was to provide what he always calls an epistemological-logical-methodological foundation for these sciences.[35] With high hopes and lavish claims Dilthey presents a preliminary version of his project in the "Ideas" essay of 1895. The devastating critique it received, especially from H. Ebbinghaus,[36] seems to have made a deep impression on Dilthey and deterred him from carrying out his program in public, though he continued to work on it (along with his numerous historical studies, including that on Schleiermacher) until the time of his death.

By "explanatory psychology" Dilthey meant a purely casual explication of psychic phenomena, one that tried to trace all mental life back to a limited number of univocally defined factors. Like a chemist, the explanatory psychologist attempts to conceptualize mental functioning by hypothesizing the interaction of a few simple elements. Such hypothetic constructs, Dilthey shows, cannot be definitively verified in the sphere of psychology as they can in the sciences of nature. Thus in place of explanatory psychology and its extrinsic constructs, he introduces the idea of an *interpretive* psychology whose starting point is the wholeness of a person's life context as it is given in their experience. Instead of explaining mental phenomena—that is, tracing them back to basic psychological or even physiological elements—it tries to describe aspects of mental life by reference to their intrinsic structure, or (since that amounts to conceiving the parts in terms of the whole) it simply tries to "understand." As Dilthey's guiding maxim puts it, "We explain nature, we understand mental life."[37]

Is a purely descriptive psychology possible, however? Dilthey replies that it is, for mental phenomena have an advantage over externals: they are immediately intelligible by means of inner experience. They can be conceived just as they are, that is, without the mediation of the senses, which are unavoidable in perceiving the external world. Through direct awareness of our inner experiences, a "fixed structure [is] immediately and objectively given," Dilthey asserts, and this provides the "indubitable, universal foundation" of descriptive psychology.[38] Because it is based on certain grounds, psychology acquires methodological significance. It becomes the foundation of the human sciences, as mathematics is of the natural sciences.[39]

The unsatisfactoriness of Dilthey's psychology of lived experience, thus methodologically presented, did not escape his contemporaries, and soon perhaps Dilthey himself perceived it. Two deficiencies are especially evident. First, it is doubtful that merely descriptive psychology (which in certain respects predates Husserl's idea of a phenomenology of inner experiences) really offers direct, hypothesis-free access to the coherent mental structures whose self-evidence to inner perception has been postulated. If these structures were in fact so self-evidently given, there would be no dissent about them within psychology. Second, Dilthey did not succeed in proposing a plausible connection between his new psychology and the concrete human sciences whose foundation he was supposed to be elucidating. Nowhere does he show how interpretive psychology could validate the objectivity of propositions in the human sciences. In these respects, too, Dilthey's project could not get beyond the merely programmatic stage.

We need to consider another fact about this psychology and the insight it offers into the system Dilthey had in mind, namely, the relative absence of hermeneutics. By name at least, hermeneutics does not emerge even once in the work of 1895. It is virtually absent from the four-hundred-page collection of preliminaries for the second volume of the *Introduction* that now appears in volume 19 of the collected works.[40] To all appearances hermeneutics seems at first to have no role to play in Dilthey's methodological ventures. This "abandonment" of hermeneutics stands in marked contrast to Dilthey's intense preoccupation with the history of hermeneutics when he was a young man and to the role that would seem appropriate for it in the later work. An interpretation of this later work faces major obstacles, not least because Dilthey shied away from making his systematic work available to the public, especially after 1895. It is primarily the collection of his final manuscripts in volume 7, titled *The Construction of the Historical World in the Human Sciences,* that gives us a glimpse into Dilthey's workshop, and it is on this collection that Dilthey's reputation as a hermeneutic thinker depends. The starting point of the later work lies in the concepts of "lived experience" [Erlebnis] and "understanding" that he had been employing at least since 1895. "Lived experience" especially seems to have become a key term. In it, however, resonances of his earlier ideas about the facts of consciousness are still to be heard. As always, these facts are taken to be "the ultimate data" and "foundation" of the "coherence of mental life," combining our perceptions and values.[41] Following out this logic, Dilthey formulates the "principle of experience" thus: "everything that exists for us is given as such in the present"—which in effect replaces the "principle of phenomenality."[42]

The concept of understanding also enables Dilthey to bring together the foundational notion of lived experience with the concrete work done in the humanities. The human and natural sciences are distinguished not by their objects (nature/spirit, universal/individual, physical/psychical) but rather by their different approaches to their objects. Specifically, the human sciences have a marked tendency to consign the physical side of events to the role of mere means of understanding. The intention of these sciences is to delve behind the external expression to its inside—a process that Dilthey considers a movement of coming to the inner "self-awareness," which, as it were, is already crystallized in the objective side: "It is orientation to self-awareness; it is the course of understanding that proceeds from the outside to the inside. This impulse cherishes every manifestation of life for expressing the inwardness from which it stems."[43] Understanding in the human sciences consists in a return from outwardness to the inwardness—more precisely, the self-awareness—that makes itself known in the expression. Every expression orig-inates in a process of self-deliberation that understanding then tries to reex-perience. But the thing understood is nothing psychological, Dilthey now emphasizes; rather, it is a form of spirit.[44] This is what we mean by the "spirit" of Roman law, and this way of talking does not imply that what is compre-hended is a particular psyche. From now on, the triad of life (or experience, Erlebnis), understanding, and expression functions as the foundation for the human sciences, because sciences such as literature or poetics, for example, "have only to do only with the relation [of a] meaningful connection of the words to that which is expressed through them."[45] Research into the emer-gence of the inner word that lies behind the expression, which had been the goal of the entire hermeneutic tradition from the Stoa to Schleiermacher, now becomes the central task of all the human sciences whose end is to understand. What is common to all is the "orientation to self-awareness," to the inner conversation that every expression bears within it.

It is therefore hardly surprising that beginning in 1900 hermeneutics once again becomes the focus of Dilthey's thought. The fragmentariness of the later works permits no more than suppositions about the role it really plays, however. According to the standard interpretation offered by Misch and Boll-now, hermeneutics *displaced* psychology as the methodological foundation of the human sciences.[46] This changing of the guard, they argue, necessarily fol-lows from the fact that a purely psychological access to the life of the mind and soul is not entirely possible, and can only be brought about by under-standing its expressions—that is, hermeneutically. Against this plausible expli-cation, we need to remember that for Dilthey psychology still retained its foundational function.[47] The fact is that he himself never spoke of the dis-solution of psychology by hermeneutics, and it cannot be said that volume 7—despite all the emphasis on the triad of life, expression, and understand-ing—raises hermeneutics to the level of establishing a new methodology. In fact, references to hermeneutics are rare in the later work, though they deserve careful consideration.

The essay of 1900 on the rise of hermeneutics, of course, invites our spe-cial attention. Admittedly, it can be called a "later work" only in a qualified sense, for its historical section clearly derives from the prize-winning though unpublished essay of 1860 on the history of Protestant hermeneutics. It is as if Dilthey had rescued a forty-year-old manuscript from his files in order to make a lecture out of it in 1900. The points this piece makes about his sys-tem are therefore all the more significant. Characteristic of Dilthey's research at that time and his increasing focus on prior hermeneutics is his description of understanding as a "process whereby we discern something inward by means of signs outwardly given to the senses."[48] Likewise reminiscent of Schleiermacher's conception of an art of understanding is Dilthey's idea that explication and interpretation need to be conceived as the *artful* understanding of the enduring expressions of life. Thus hermeneutics itself must offer "an art for understanding the expressions of life fixed in writing." Moreover, the new threat of historical relativism is more acute than in Schleiermacher. Dilthey expects hermeneutics to allay doubts about the individual's capacity for "scientific knowledge"—that is, to offer universally valid rules protecting understanding from subjective arbitrariness. What such rules would look like is never explained, and that they exist is merely postulated. It is, furthermore, doubtful that Dilthey intended to view such a hermeneutics as a methodology of the human sciences. He certainly considered understanding as the foundational procedure of all the human sciences, but their methodological theory was always conceived, as the handwritten additions phrase it, to be an "epistemological, logical, and methodological analysis of understanding," and such analysis is not specifically linked to hermeneutics.[49] Instead, it is connected to the undeveloped plan for the second volume of the *Introduction*.

From the essay of 1900 we can surmise that Dilthey retained a classical, normative conception of hermeneutics to the very end. At best, he discerned that such an art has something to do with the epistemological methodology of the human sciences, but he did not fully trace out the implications of his program or define it with sufficient clarity. That he did not do so may be connected, as is often surmised, with the fact that over time he became increasingly aware of the narrowness of framing the question methodologically, as was his first impulse. For understanding is not just the special procedure of the human sciences; it is primordial to the way human beings negotiate their historical existence. Dilthey's final proposals occasionally proclaim a universal philosophy of historical life, which his students enthusiastically promised to carry out under the banner "hermeneutic philosophy."[50] Stimulated by his correspondence with Count Yorck von Wartenburg, Dilthey is sometimes thought to have finally begun relinquishing his methodological ambitions. As far as we can tell, however, Dilthey's last writings do not support the notion that he abandoned methodology. It seems more accurate to speak of a tension, never superseded, between Dilthey's scientist effort to find a fixed basis for the human sciences and his insight that the ineluctable historicity of our historical life cannot be developed in terms of a method-ological plan.[51] Twentieth-century hermeneutic philosophy initiated by Dilthey—both that of the Dilthey school in the strict sense and the wider-ranging work of Heidegger and Gadamer—was to dramatize this irreconcil-ability, proclaiming the universality of historicity and thereby jettisoning the narrow frame of the original methodological project.

The later Dilthey retained the classical conception of hermeneutics while envisioning a "significant new task" for it in the age of historicism, namely, to defend "the certainty of understanding against historical skepticism and subjective arbitrariness." Yet ultimately the following assertion offers noth-ing more than a promise: "The hermeneutics of our time must determine its relation to the universal epistemological task of demonstrating the possibil-ity of knowledge from the structure [Zusammenhang] of the historical world and finding ways to realize this possibility."[52] What for Dilthey was a program, however, soon became a problem for his successors. Virtually all of them con-curred that the important new task of hermeneutics could be performed only if one abandoned the search for a methodology based on a universally valid foundation. The fact that the human sciences lack an Archimedean point they no longer considered a mere deficiency. Rather, this absence shows the proximity of the human sciences to the new universality, that of historicity. Leading the way in this direction was Heidegger's ontology of factical life, which made hermeneutics the universal foundation of philosophy.

V

Heidegger: Hermeneutics as the Interpretation of Existence

What is experienced from within cannot be categorized in concepts that have been developed for the external world given to the senses.

Dilthey, GS 5:196

In the nineteenth century, hermeneutic reflection remained peripheral in certain respects (especially to philosophy). Though their founding intuitions were broadly based, the classic figures in hermeneutics who were representative of the century—Böckh, Schleiermacher, Droysen, and Dilthey—did not manage to develop a unified conception of hermeneutics or publish it in systematic form. Indicative of this state of affairs is that their hermeneutic inquiries had to be compiled from posthumous writings edited by their students and published mostly in the form of overviews and fragments. This situation slowly begins to change with Heidegger (1889–1976), who was demonstrably influenced early by Schleiermacher, Droysen, and Dilthey.[1] In his thought, hermeneutics is elevated to the center of philosophical concern. It is true, however, that Heidegger's hermeneutics long remained hidden, despite the appearance of *Being and Time.* He developed his hermeneutic initiatives during the early twenties in the course of lectures entitled "Hermeneutics of Facticity," without, however, publishing his inquiries in this area. The most important of them, as we can ascertain today, were incorporated in *Being and Time,* though clearly under the pressure of newer questions which were superimposed on the earlier problematic and which for a time obscured the hermeneutic horizon of his project. As noted above, the task of situating hermeneutics systematically takes up no more than a half page in the magnum opus of 1927, thus leaving more space for the ontological question about the originary meaning of being and its main articulations. At first glance, Heidegger's later work appears marked by its departure from the hermeneutic inquiry characteristic of the earlier. In his important 1927 lecture on the basic problems of phenomenology (in volume 24 of the collected works), which can be considered a continuation and slight correction of *Being and Time,*[2] the concept of hermeneutics had already disappeared entirely. Moreover, the references to hermeneutics (mostly retrospective) in the later work can almost be counted on the fingers of one hand. So there is a good deal of evidence suggesting that Heidegger's real hermeneutics is to be found in the early lectures. These provided substantial impetus for the subsequent development of hermeneutics, especially Gadamer's. The present moment is propitious for studying them in that several lectures and manuscripts from this period have recently been published.[3] These have occupied the center of recent Heidegger research because they throw so much light on what had previously been unknown or only surmised. Unfortunately, a detailed investigation of the hermeneutics developed in them cannot be undertaken within the restricted scope of the present introduction. Our objective must be limited to explaining how these lectures contribute philosophically to an improved understanding of the hermeneutics of *Being and Time* and the history of its influence.

1. The "Fore" of Fore-Understanding

Heidegger's insight into the so-called fore-structure of understanding is very well known. The theologian Rudolf Bultmann gave it definitive formulation: human understanding takes its direction from the fore-understanding deriving from its particular existential situation, and this fore-understanding stakes out the thematic framework and parameters of every interpretation. Rarely has anyone given much thought to the question of what this fore-structure is really "fore" to, and so (to put it rather awkwardly) the "wherefore" or "thereafter" of the fore-structure has remained for the most part in the dark. Heidegger assigns special emphasis to this "fore." What is its significance within the circumference of hermeneutic inquiry? If for purely heuristic purposes we take paragraphs 31 to 33 of *Being and Time* as the "exoteric" center of its hermeneutics, the title of the final paragraphs can be considered an initial answer: "Assertion as a Derivative Mode of Interpretation." This phrase suggests that what the fore-structure is "fore" to is assertion, if not language itself. Fore-structure means, then, that human Dasein is characterized by an interpretive tendency special to it that comes be-*fore* every statement—a disposition the fundamental character of which is care and which is always under threat of being concealed by the fact that propositional judgments tend to take center stage. This view may at first seem surprising, but I believe it can be shown that Heidegger's hermeneutics of facticity is intended to be a hermeneutics of everything that is at work behind statements. It is an interpretation of Dasein's care structure, which expresses itself before and behind every judgment and which has its most elemental manifestation in understanding.

In stark, fundamental opposition to the hermeneutic tradition, this understanding first of all divests itself of its purely "epistemic" character. Earlier, understanding had been understood as a theoretical *intelligere* that concerned itself with construing meaningful entities in an intelligible manner. In Droysen and Dilthey, understanding rose to the status of an autonomous process of knowledge that served to ground the historical sciences of man and explain their methodological uniqueness. Heidegger considers such epistemological understanding to be secondary and derivative from a still more universal hermeneutical understanding. He works out his new conception of understanding by exploring the implications of the phrase "be at home with something" [sich auf etwas verstehen], which refers to a kind of understanding that is more like readiness or facility than knowledge. "To understand something" in this sense means to be equal to or master of it. Thus we might say that an athlete "understands" or knows how to play soccer. By this we do not mean some knowledge, of course, but a largely unexpressed capacity, a mastery, indeed an "art." Such capacities do not just include special accomplishments. They are interwoven through our whole lives: we understand how to get along with people, to care for things, to kill time, and so forth, without having any special knowledge at our disposal. This "practical" understanding Heidegger calls "existential" because it is a way of existing, a fundamental mode of being, by the power of which we deal with and try to find our way around in our world. Understanding means less a "kind of knowledge" than a "knowing one's way around" (Sichauskennen) that is undergirded by care (Sorge).[4] The fact that the scientist's epistemological understanding can be viewed as a subspecies of such mastery shows that this unheard-of understanding is universal. To understand a subject in a theoretic or scientific manner in fact means to be up to it, be able to cope with it, so that one can proceed from there.

This everyday understanding, Heidegger observes, almost always remains implicit. As a "mode of being" it is not consciously thematized. We live too much within it for it to need to be made explicit. Nevertheless, all the "things" and events that we deal with in our life-world are preinterpreted by this anticipatory understanding "as" things destined for this or that use. (Heidegger notes that the Greek word for thing, *pragma,* derives from the context of praxis, that is, from the care-ful having to do with things.) This instrumentalizing, interpretive "as" that is constitutive of things for human understanding is correlative to Dasein's inexplicit manner of dealing with its world. Heidegger designates this inexplicitness by drawing a distinction between the "hermeneutic" and the "apophantic" (or propositional) "as."[5] More fundamental than the apophantic "as" (that is, the explicitness of phenomena that have been explicated in propositions), a hermeneutic "as" is at work: a primally interpretive fore-understanding of the world operates on the level of Dasein. This thesis may well seem strange from the point of view of present-day philosophy of language. It can be well substantiated phenomenologically, however. When we enter a room through a door, for example, we have an understanding of what a door is for; we understand it "as" a means of entry or exit, without wasting words about the matter: "This as-structure, therefore, is not necessarily dependent on predication. In having to do with something I make no thematically predicative statement."[6] The as-structure, then, is essentially prelinguistic; it belongs simply to our "behavior," Heidegger writes.[7] The fore-structure of understanding is the philosophical description of the pre-predicative level of existence. It is extraordinarily significant that Heidegger applies precisely the concept of "hermeneutics" to pre-predicative understanding. This is consonant with the fundamental effort of hermeneutics to reach what is be-fore (or better, in and behind) statements—in brief, the mind and soul that expresses itself in the word. There can be no doubt that Heidegger appropriates the notion of hermeneutic understanding in order to radicalize it by demonstrating its universal embeddedness in the care structure of Dasein.

It is no accident that we understand the world "hermeneutically" in orienting ourselves to its use. Behind this concern for using objects in the world stands the fundamental care of Dasein, namely, its concern for itself. Dasein is distinguished by the fact that it is the being that is concerned with its own being, its ability to be, in the world. Heidegger does not state it on every page, but it is apparent that understanding's circumspective or caring mode of being is existentially rooted in Dasein's concern for itself. Care is thus the more or less unconscious hook that gives understanding its purchase on things.

From care stems the specific character of our understanding as project. In order to deal with the potentially threatening world, as it were, our understanding orients itself toward certain inexplicit projects which embody, in Heidegger's words, our own possibilities, our being able to be. Understanding means being able: to realize this or that project of understanding, instead of some other. According to Heidegger, however, it is not the case that first there are naked things "out there" which are subsequently given a certain coloring by our "subjective" and circumspective understanding. On the contrary, what is primarily there is precisely our involvement in the world, which takes the form of interpretive projects. The purely theoretic gaze upon the world, the possibility of which Heidegger never denies, comes from suspending these projects of concern. But the fundamental thing, more primary than theoretical knowledge, is the hermeneutic "as," which is basic to everything that confronts and engages us.

Our projections are not in the first place a matter of choice. Rather, we are "thrown" into them. The ineluctable thrownness and historicity of Dasein are the distinctive characteristics of its "facticity." Correlative to the factical and therefore fundamentally projective fore-structure of understanding is that it always finds itself within pregiven perspectives that guide its expectations of meaning: "These mostly inexplicit views, which are more often to be met with as customs than developed expressly, map out the lines of action for the movements of care."[8] Yet we are not blindly at the mercy of this fore-structure of pregiven interpretation nor inescapably imprisoned in our prejudices, as the common reading of the hermeneutic circle would have it. Heidegger's hermeneutics shows just the opposite. Its goal is the explicit elucidation of the fore-structure pregiven by history. For him, this elucidation is called interpretation.

2. Its Transparency in Interpretation

> *From the fact that words are absent, it cannot be concluded that interpretation is absent.*
>
> *Heidegger,* Being and Time

For traditional hermeneutics, interpretation (interpretatio) functioned self-evidently as a means to the end of understanding (intelligere). If people did not comprehend a particular passage of a text, they had to resort to interpretation, for the natural telos of interpreting was to enable understanding.[9] Viewed in Chladenius's way, the mediating function of interpretation is to provide the necessary means of understanding. First, then, comes interpretation, and understanding results from it thereafter. In bold new contrast to this tradition, Heidegger's existential hermeneutics flatly reverses this teleological sequence. Now, the primary thing is understanding, and interpretation consists in merely cultivating [Ausbildung] or extending this understanding.

Such a conception of interpretation is fundamentally critical. As we have seen, understanding lives in or from a certain situation-specific interpretive disposition. As an aspect of Dasein's care for its own being, understanding makes it possible for Dasein to cultivate itself as such, indeed understand itself. It is just this self-elucidation that is to be accomplished by interpretation or explication—literally, the unfolding of what was already implicated in understanding. Such unfolding follows "after" the first understanding, and yet so as to broaden and perfect the perspectives that interpretation characteristically opens up. As the self-appropriation of understanding, it represents understanding carried to completion or brought to an understanding of itself: "In it the understanding appropriates understandingly that which is understood by it. In interpretation, understanding does not become something different. It becomes itself."[10]

Interpretation thus tries to help the *fore-understanding* achieve transparency. In the first place, it assists in appropriating one's own situation of understanding and the presuppositions that determine caring cognition and action.[11] Its critical impulse lies in the effort to avoid self-misunderstanding as far as possible. *Because* our understanding can mistake itself, every effort of understanding needs to be "appropriated, strengthened, and secured."[12] Thus in every correct interpretation the very first task must be to become reflectively conscious of one's own fore-structure of understanding.

Heidegger ought not be misconstrued as saying that textual interpretation, for example, consists merely in explicating the interpreter's subjective fore-understanding, as it were, without paying any attention to the text one is trying to understand. An interpretation that disregarded the other would be perverted into a strange monologue of the interpreter with his own fore-understanding. Clearly Heidegger means something much more basic: in order to interpret a text, for example, it is necessary to make our *own* situation transparent *so that* we can appreciate precisely the otherness and alterity of the text—that is, without allowing our unelucidated prejudices to dominate the text unwittingly and so conceal what is proper to it. Interpreters who affirm their own sovereignty and deny their hermeneutic situation run the risk of embracing it all the more uncritically. Thus Heidegger remarks with respect to the conflict between philosophy and its history: "All interpretations in the field of history of philosophy, and others as well, that refrain from reading things into texts and offering historically problematic 'constructions,' find to their surprise that they read things in nevertheless, only without direction and with conceptual means of the most disparate and unregulable origins."[13] In contrast, by reflectively returning to one's own fore-structure, one can at least partially regulate one's implicit interpretive dispositions and so allow the otherness of the things to be disclosed and appear against that background. On the basis of this critical effort at self-understanding it becomes clear why Heidegger employs the hermeneutic circle: namely, for the purpose of transcending historicism. There is admittedly a circular relation between interpretation and understanding—that is, between every interpretation and the fore-conceptions that nourish it; but this circularity properly belongs to the ontological or ineluctable care-structure, and thus to the fore-structure of Dasein. It is pointless to shut one's eyes in the face of this "vicious" circle and wish it away in order to usher in some Dasein-free objectivity. "What is decisive," Heidegger pointedly writes, "is not to get out of the circle but to come into it in the right way."[14] To get into it in the right way means, concretely, that the first priority and the continual task of a conscientious interpretation are always to work through one's own fore-conceptions for oneself and bring them to interpretation. What Heidegger has in mind here is not a reflection that would remove such fore-conceptions from the field of play but instead a reflective foregrounding of one's own fore-structure to the end of opening up a genuine *dialogue* between the two particular positions, that is, with the subject matter and the other's unfamiliar thought. Without this process of foregrounding, understanding is in danger of letting the direction of its gaze be dictated "by fancies and popular conceptions."[15] There can be no question of eliminating the interpretive dispositions that prestructure and direct interpretive inquiry in the first place; the point is to make them conscious— insofar as possible, of course. Once the interpretively developed fore-structure has been thus foregrounded, then, it needs to be positively engaged in the process of interpreting.[16]

3. The Idea of a Philosophical Hermeneutics of Facticity

As a philosophical program, Heidegger's hermeneutics conceives of itself as the radicalization of the interpretive dispositions immanent in understanding. Hermeneutics, Heidegger remarks, is to be taken in "the primordial signification of the word, where it designates the business of interpreting."[17] This understanding of the term rejects the view, dominant since Schleiermacher and Dilthey, that hermeneutics is an art or technique of understanding, the purpose of which is to construct a methodological foundation for the human sciences. Not theory of interpretation but interpretation itself is the subject matter of a hermeneutics that is to achieve the status of philosophy; its end is to heighten the self-transparency of Dasein, a process in which philosophical clarification merely furthers the interpretive activity that Dasein, as an understanding being, is always performing. In this way philosophical hermeneutics has as its goal the self-interpretation of facticity—as it were, the interpretation of interpretation—so that Dasein can become transparent to itself. Through the interpretive process the "basic structures of Being which Dasein itself possesses, are *made known*" to Dasein. Stemming from Dasein's concern for itself, philosophy—understood as "the genuine explicitation of the interpretive tendencies in the basic movements of life"—functions to clarify Dasein's own self-interpretation.[18]

This philosophical vision becomes fully clear in Heidegger's lecture "The Hermeneutics of Facticity" (summer 1923). There hermeneutics refers to "the unified way of engaging, beginning, accessing, and explicating facticity," which presents "intimations of possible modes of being aware."[19] Conceived with a view to Dasein's possible *self*-transparency, hermeneutics does not itself carve out a trail to this awareness or propose models for doing so. It must remain the task of each individual Dasein to open up its own path to self-transparency. Philosophical hermeneutics contents itself with the task of recalling Dasein to this path already indicated in the underlying structure of interpretation. More precisely, "Hermeneutics has the task of informing; of making each Dasein, in its being, accessible to this Dasein itself; of going back to the self-alienation with which Dasein is oppressed. In hermeneutics the possibility is of Dasein's becoming and being for itself *understandingly.*"[20]

The early lectures resound with a battle cry against "self-alienation" that makes them almost reminiscent of the young Hegelians or even ideology critique.[21] What hermeneutics is protesting against is the self-misunderstanding, the self-mistaking of Dasein that *Being and Time* calls "fallenness" and the early texts call "ruin." Dasein has a natural propensity to overlook itself, to deny that its possibilities for transparency are of its own making. This is especially evident in that human beings dissolve unawares into their world and so are lost to themselves. Instead of undertaking their own interpretations of themselves, they take up interpretations that are already available and so relieve themselves of the burden of self-elucidation. A critical hermeneutics of facticity that calls Dasein back to itself and its possible freedom thus has the purpose of dismantling or deconstructing these traditional explications of Dasein which have become self-evident and resistant to criticism. "Hermeneutics fulfills its task only on the way to destruction."[22] Destruction here means the dismantling of tradition to the extent, and only to the extent, that it conceals existence from itself and spares it from the necessity of self-appropriation. Viewed in a positive light, destruction tries to reawaken the primordial experiences of Dasein, experiences that lurk behind the categories of the ontological tradition and that have since become inimical to reappropriation.

In order to make these basic experiences once again accessible, philosophical hermeneutics must of course work out a new set of concepts for itself. Heidegger is very careful about this point. To avoid the danger of a new scholasticism as much as possible, he introduces his concepts as "formally indicative." The concept of a formal indication basic to the early Heidegger suggests that statements about Dasein require a specific act of appropriation on the part of understanding. They are not theoretical propositions describing a subject matter that is present at hand; instead, they are to be viewed as invitations to self-appropriation that are issued to every individual Dasein. The "primary sense" of formal indications, then, is not "reference to what is present at hand" but rather "Dasein's letting itself be understood" that calls for an act of Dasein-specific interpretation.[23] Philosophical assertions have the character of indications which are understood only to the extent they are realized and concretized in an act of personal appropriation—that is, each

in its own way and on its own responsibility. Such indications are wholly misunderstood if taken as expressions of present-at-hand matters of fact: "They
are only indicators of Dasein, though as express assertions their immediate
meaning is presence-at-hand. . . . They indicate *possible* ways of understanding and possible ways of conceiving the Dasein structure made accessible in
such understanding. (As assertions indicating a hermeneuein, they have the
character of *hermeneutic* indications.)"[24]

The allusion to hermeneuein is significant here. It points in an enlighten-
ing way to the inescapable appropriation that is performed by each Dasein
in the act of understanding. Dasein must hermeneutically engage itself in the
process of understanding. Since philosophy always concerns itself with
Dasein's care for itself, formal indications uniquely display a methodologically fundamental meaning for all philosophical concepts.[25] Thus Heidegger
calls precisely for *"hermeneutic* concepts"—that is, expressions that are not
merely capable of reflecting a neutral, present-at-hand fact; rather, they are
"accessible only in repeated new interpretations."[26] Consequently a sentence
is hermeneutical when it calls the interpreter to an act of self-reflection or
interpretation, and so to self-application. Thus it is necessary to pierce
through the facade of universal concepts in order to return to the specific
experiences that reveal themselves through them.

4. The Derivative Status of Statements?

We first discussed this hermeneutic return to what is behind the statement
in the context of distinguishing between the hermeneutic and the apophantic "as." Heidegger never tires of accentuating the pre-predicative element in
hermeneutics. We would be misunderstanding Heidegger's intention, however, if we believed that Dasein's self-interpretation had to take place outside
language. Here, too, we cannot take Heidegger literally but must read
between the lines, as Schleiermacher suggests. Heidegger's interpretation of
interpretation cannot be conceived as overlooking or repressing language.
He merely means that in every spoken word Dasein's care also makes itself
heard. He is simply protesting against the tendency of statements to monop-
olize our view of language, and so produce a "modification" of the fundamental hermeneutic relation to the world. This is the place to recall Heidegger's famous example of the heavy hammer. The use of the tool, at first
wordless, gradually becomes noticeably difficult for the worker. In this way
the hammer comes to be understood "as" heavy (for Dasein). This "as" thus

leads to a process of interpretation, though initially it need not be expressed: "Interpretation is carried out primordially not in a theoretical statement but in an action of circumspective concern—laying aside the unsuitable tool, or exchanging it, 'without wasting words.'"[27] In the act of laying it aside, the hermeneutic "as" is already at work in interpreting the world. This interpretation can be put in words, of course: "the hammer is heavy," but the hermeneutic "as" thereby undergoes a certain change. Out of the primordial "as" a predicative statement is formed about an object present at hand (the hammer) and a quality (its heaviness) is ascribed to it. As Heidegger puts it, "By making a statement in the form of predication . . . the primordially interpretive 'as' is at the same time leveled out in the pure and simple determination of the thing."[28] The assertion, so to speak, reifies or thing-izes the original—that is, the hermeneutical—relation, so that "the whereby of the having to do with becomes the whereof of a signification."[29]

It could certainly be objected that this is a minor alteration insofar as each sentence is comprehended as the utterance of the Dasein doing the hammering, and not as the description of some present-at-hand thing. Heidegger does not maintain that *every* statement implies the reversal of the original, inexplicit "as." Language is not that impotent, after all. If we understand Heidegger rightly, we see that he is merely warning us against taking statements as simple assertions about determinate, present-at-hand objects, because to do so is to overlook the fact that language is rooted in the care structure of Dasein. His reference to the pre-predicative, hermeneutic "as" serves to remind us that in principle every statement bears witness to this rootedness and, moreover, is dependent on an act of interpretive completion. Whoever wants to understand something verbal in a hermeneutical manner must constantly attend to what is tacitly meant, though not openly expressed.[30]

The hermeneutic glance, then, is not directed away from language. Its objective is not in suspense "be-fore" language in any trivial mental or esoteric sense. The interpreter merely wants to understand what the verbal utterance is trying to say, and avoid the potentially objectivizing view of language that confines it to the purely logical content of what is stated. Even though Heidegger speaks of the "derivative character" of assertions and mentions with a certain smugness that language is not thematized until fairly late in *Being and Time*,[31] still the 1927 work does take into account the linguistic nature of our understanding and interpreting in that it stresses the *originary* character of "discourse" [Rede]. Discourse—or, better, discoursing—is the self-interpretation of Dasein as it manifests itself in its usual unselfconscious use of language. This familiar discourse, in which Dasein's care still immediately expresses itself, is "equiprimordial"[32] with understanding conceived as the verbal articulation of the understanding within which every event of meaning occurs. Common discourse shows something further about the circumspective care-structure of Dasein: namely, that colloquial language must be distinguished from statements considered as logical constructs. Only a truncated view of logic would reduce language to mere predication or logicality—that is, to the process of assigning attributes to a present-at-hand object while ignoring the Dasein that is expressing itself thereby as well. To try to exclude Dasein's involvement as constructive care would be almost like looking for the rainbow when there isn't any sun, or trying to capture the logos without the real thing that manifests itself through the explicitness of the legein.

5. Hermeneutics after the Turn

The hermeneutic view of language presented in *Being and Time* only seems to undergo fundamental revision in Heidegger's later work. To be sure, language is there affirmed more emphatically as the "house of being," as if it were thereafter to take over Dasein's role as the originary and untranscendable revelation of Being. Yet Heidegger's suspicion of statements has not diminished. Even though he himself had written a good deal already, Heidegger warns against mistaking propositions for the full expression of philosophical truth. His recently published *Beiträge zur Philosophie* (1936–1938), which presents perhaps the most extensive evidence of the new accents in his thought, repeats the warning in its opening pages: "In philosophy propositions never constitute proof . . . because here 'propositions' are not at all the true."[33] This warning remains in effect up to the lecture titled "Time and Being," which can reasonably be considered the end point of Heidegger's thought. Its final lines are as follows: "It is inescapably necessary to overcome the obstacles which make such a saying [of experience] obviously inadequate. Even the saying that occurs in the form of lecture remains an obstacle of this kind. Its saying has been only in propositions."[34] It is easy to expose the aporia of a speaking that no longer trusts propositions and that occasionally takes flight into a sigetic, a philosophy of silence which it nevertheless proclaims for all to hear.[35] Yet the aporia dissolves as soon as we learn that the only essential thing is to preserve the hermeneutic character of language that is manifest in the struggle to find the right words. A philosophy that begins with refusal as a fundamental form of being can no longer blindly assume that the suffering of finite creatures can be adequately expressed in propositions. This explains Heidegger's Sisyphus-like resistance to universal cybernetics and the global technology that reduces language to a means of communication capable of expressing and calculating everything. These elements of Heidegger's later work obviously exceed the framework of the present study.[36]

If the hermeneutic understanding of language has not disappeared from his thought after the turn,[37] the same holds true of hermeneutics' critical task, namely, to elucidate the interpreter's own situation. Often disparaged as an unintelligible deviation from the Enlightenment, Heidegger's entry into the history of being, quite the contrary, simply furthers the destruction of tradition—called for in *Being and Time*—in the sense of the reflexive appropriation of our understanding's historical situation. The interpretive dispositions underlying the fore-structure of our understanding are thus to be raised to transparency—that is, to interpretation—through the elucidation of the history of Being. The later Heidegger is still so conscious of human understanding as "thrown" that his thought is almost completely preoccupied with interpretation and the confrontation with the ontological tradition that determines us. Who would want to deny that in the later Heidegger the confrontation with the history of Being occurs, though unexpressed, with regard to an awareness or serenity that is to be achieved by and for Dasein. This self-transparency should not be conceived as self-patency, of course; rather, like the Delphic "Know thyself," it should be understood as insight into one's own limits and insuperable thrownness—indeed, as the consciousness of one's finitude and situatedness in the history of Being.

Heidegger's philosophy after the turn ultimately results from thinking through Dasein's thrownness as worked out in the hermeneutics of facticity. Dasein is no longer considered the potential agent of its interpretive projects, as appeared to be the case in 1927; rather, it receives them beforehand from the mostly subliminal history of being, the elucidation of which must become the very first task of hermeneutic interpretation. Viewed from the perspective of his practice in the later work, then, Heidegger's thought remains permeated by hermeneutics; indeed, it is thus concretized. The word *hermeneutics,* like almost all the key words of *Being and Time,* was not retained in the later work, however; and to all appearances its absence is connected to the dethroning of human subjectivity that is the consequence of radicalizing thrownness and, therefore, finitude. It may be that Heidegger labored under a certain self-misunderstanding, however, insofar as he believed hermeneutic thought had to be ascribed to the transcendental-subjective element of modernity.[38] For his own hermeneutic thought in *Being and Time* was indeed conceived as a counterbalance to a modernity obsessed with subjectivity, and it was for this reason that he called for the destruction of the ontological tradition.

The few references to hermeneutics in the later work almost all occur in *On the Way to Language* (1959), and particularly in the "Dialogue with a Japanese." Asked about the meaning of hermeneutics, Heidegger cites, practically without comment, the definition given in one of Schleiermacher's lectures (which Heidegger had just "at hand"). Hermeneutics, Schleiermacher says, is "the art of understanding rightly another man's language, particularly his written language."[39] Heidegger affirms Schleiermacher's definition of the task of hermeneutics, though he had distanced himself explicitly from it in the summer-semester lecture of 1923 and implicitly in *Being and Time*. He further explains—mysteriously and almost tautologically—that hermeneutics main task is more precisely to be understood as the attempt "to define the nature of interpretation first of all on hermeneutic grounds." What is intended by "hermeneutic" here? We ought not expect too much, Heidegger counters, "because the subject is enigmatic, and perhaps no subject matter is involved at all."[40] Once again the hermeneutic suspicion of what is thing-like and at our disposal is accompanied with a gesture toward the ineffable or enigmatic, the understanding of which calls for a hermeneutics.

Yet Heidegger abruptly returns, almost twenty pages later, to explain what the hermeneutical really is. It is most readily understood from the Greek verb *hermeneuein,* which means "the exposition which brings tidings because it can listen to a message."[41] Prior to every interpretation, the hermeneutical manifests itself as "the bearing of message and tidings."[42] These suggestions, like most others in the later work, are to be taken in pure simplicity. Most simply expressed, hermeneutics means the exposition of tidings that call for a hearing. Nowhere in his work is Heidegger closer to the hermeneutic tradition than here. This bringing of tidings is only possible through language; indeed, it occurs as the most elementary activity of language itself. It is language, Heidegger elaborates, that underlies "the hermeneutic relation." Consequently the question about hermeneutics fuses with that about language. What, then, is language but the communication of tidings to be understood by an interpretive hearing?

"Thus when I ask you about hermeneutics," the Japanese concludes in the dialogue, "and when you ask me what our word.is for what you call language, we ask each other the Same."[43] "Clearly," answers Heidegger in closing. For the later Heidegger, then, hermeneutics becomes another word for language, understood as the bringing of news for the sake of a co-respondent hearing and understanding. If so, we must admit that, not just in the later work but overall, the path of Heidegger's thought was not only consciously on the way to language but on the way to hermeneutics as well.

VI

Gadamer and
the Universe of
Hermeneutics

1. Back to the Human Sciences

In making language the essence of hermeneutics Gadamer clearly follows the later Heidegger's radicalization of historical thrownness. His aim, however, is to reconcile this radicalization with the young Heidegger's hermeneutical starting point, namely, understanding. Specifically, given that we are situated in a history articulated in linguistic tradition, what are the consequences for human understanding and self-knowledge? These consequences are elaborated in "The Ontological Shift of Hermeneutics Guided by Language," the title of the last third of Gadamer's magnum opus, *Truth and Method*. To understand what this ontological or universal shift in hermeneutics implies, we need to return to the underlying problem this work addresses: the question of the human sciences or of a hermeneutics commensurate with them. To be sure, the problem of methodology in the human sciences was not unknown to Heidegger. In large part, his familiarity with it came by way of Dilthey and his own neo-Kantian teachers. Yet beginning with his first project, grounded in facticity, he had firmly reduced understanding in the human sciences to a secondary or derivative status. Elevating understanding to the royal road of method ultimately struck him as merely an expression of the befuddlement in which historicism found itself. The attempt to methodologize understanding he considered fundamentally a desperate attempt to discover a "firm foothold," even though that seemed precluded by the historicity that had become pervasive in the nineteenth century. Basically, Heidegger problematized the idea of such a fixed Archimedean point by exposing its metaphysical presuppositions. The idea of a timeless, ultimate basis originated in humanity's flight from its own temporality.[1] The notion that there is an absolute truth thus grows out of the repression or forgetting of one's temporality. Instead of invoking yet again the phantom of an ultimate foundation, Heidegger proposed radically situating oneself within the level of finitude and working through the structure of prejudice as a positive ontological characteristic of understanding in order to perceive our genuine possibilities in our very situatedness. Thus Heidegger overcame historicism's epistemological way of putting the question. What is at issue in understanding is not the phantom of an absolute foundation—that child of positivism and ultimately of metaphysics—but Dasein's increased awareness of the possibilities at its disposal. The quest for universally valid truth undeniably threatens to conceal the reality of understanding and orient it toward a cognitive ideal that it can never in fact realize.

The process of working out his own, hermeneutically more radical position allowed Heidegger, as it were, to get beyond the problem of historicism and its corollary, the methodology of the human sciences, as well. When Gadamer reopens a dialogue with the human sciences, the point is not to develop its "methodology," as might seem to be the case, given the implications of the term hermeneutics in the wake of Dilthey. Rather, the example of the interpretive sciences is meant to demonstrate the untenability of the idea of universally valid knowledge, and thereby to sidestep the historicist way of putting the question. The conflict with historicism, of only marginal interest for Heidegger, becomes for Gadamer the main task.

Seven times between 1936 and 1959 Gadamer held lectures with the title "Introduction to the Human Sciences," where he elaborated a hermeneutics that could do justice to these sciences. He first presented his conclusions to the public during the fifties in important essays on the question of truth in the human sciences, in the Louvain lectures (1957) on the problem of historical consciousness, and then in his book *Truth and Method* (1960). His work was sparked by the question of how the human sciences should understand themselves vis-à-vis the natural sciences. Gadamer there argued against the idea, fostered by historicism and positivism, that the human sciences had to work out proper methods for themselves before they could attain to the status of science. The hope of doing so, however, had been the focal point for all the methodological efforts of Dilthey, Droysen, and neo-Kantianism. Gadamer places this focus fundamentally in doubt by asking whether the demand for method, considered to be the sole guarantee of validity, is really appropriate with regard to the human sciences. Gadamer takes his first orientation from Helmholtz's Heidelberg lecture of 1862 on the relationship of the natural and human sciences. According to this speech, still worth reading today, the natural sciences derive rules and laws from the collected materials of experience by means of logical induction. The human sciences proceed in a different manner. They arrive at knowledge by employing something like a psychological sense of tact. In this connection Helmholtz speaks of an "artistic induction" stemming from an instinctive sense or tact, for which there are no definable rules. Exaggerating only slightly, one could say that in the first part of *Truth and Method* Helmholtz is Gadamer's main interlocutor. If a book can be understood only by framing the question to which it is an answer, we can say it was Helmholtz's simple question about the way of knowing proper to the human sciences that provided the original impetus for *Truth and Method*. Thus at the beginning of *Truth and Method* Gadamer writes as follows:

> The human sciences have no method of their own. Yet one might well ask, with Helmholtz, to what extent method is significant in this case and whether the other logical presuppositions of the human sciences are perhaps not far more important than inductive logic. Helmholtz had indicated this correctly when, in order to do justice to the human sciences, he emphasized memory and authority, and spoke of the psychological tact that here replaced the conscious drawing of inferences. What is the basis of this tact? How is it acquired? Does not what is scientific about the human sciences lie rather here than in their methodology?[2]

Gadamer concurs with Helmholtz that at bottom the human sciences have far more to do with the practice of tact than with applying any kind of methods. Even though Helmholtz began with the model of the natural sciences—

in the second half of the nineteenth century nothing else was possible—nevertheless in 1862 he rightly grasped the uniqueness of the human sciences, in Gadamer's view. We ought not overlook how provocative is Gadamer's solidarity with Helmholtz: in going back to 1862, and indeed to a *natural scientist,* Gadamer skips over the entire discussion about the methodological uniqueness of the human sciences that had so preoccupied neo-Kantianism as well as such authors as Dilthey, Misch, Rothaker, and Weber at the end of the nineteenth and beginning of the twentieth century. The point is that this endlessly drawn-out debate was perhaps far too obsessed with the idea that the human sciences had to produce some kind of method that could be called their own in order to become sciences. To Gadamer it seemed much more appropriate—and here he follows Helmholtz—to trace the human sciences back to something like tact or an unmethodizable "je ne sais quoi." Helmholtz, not Dilthey,[3] thus becomes the silent partner of hermeneutics because he does more justice to the human sciences' specific way of knowing. In this sense *Truth and Method* can be aptly described as a fundamental critique of the obsession with method that typified those concerned with the scientificity of the human sciences.

It is therefore Gadamer's initial thesis that the scientific character of the human sciences "can be understood more easily from the tradition of the concept of Bildung than from the modern idea of scientific method."[4] This explains why Gadamer recurs to the humanistic tradition at the beginning of *Truth and Method.* It was over the course of this tradition that the concepts were formed which make possible a just assessment of the cognitive claims proper to the human sciences. According to Gadamer, this tradition was still very much alive before Kant, though afterward it was repressed and dominated by a conception of method alien to it. Thus Gadamer must address the question "how this tradition became so impoverished and how the human sciences' claim to knowledge came to be measured by a standard foreign to it—namely the methodical thinking of modern science."[5] How did it happen, then, that the humanistic tradition so declined as to be displaced by the increasingly dominant natural sciences and their idea of method? Gadamer answers: through the fateful aestheticization of humanism's basic concepts, especially judgment and taste, which had previously possessed a *cognitive* function. It was Kant's *Critique of Judgment* that in itself or through its successors (Gadamer vacillates somewhat on this question) subjectivized and aestheticized taste and (what amounts to the same thing) denied it any cognitive value. Whatever did not measure up to the standards of the objective and methodical natural sciences was thereafter considered merely "subjective" and "aesthetic"—that is, excommunicated from the realm of hard knowledge. "In discrediting any kind of theoretical knowledge except that of natural science, [Kant's subjectivization of taste] compelled the human sciences to rely on the methodology of the natural sciences in conceptualizing themselves."[6] It was in this way that the humanistic tradition in which the human sciences could recognize themselves was surrendered and the way paved for the aestheticization and subjectivization of judgment. As for the loss to the human sciences, "the importance of this cannot be easily overestimated, for what was here surrendered was the element in which philological and historical studies lived, and when they sought to ground themselves methodologically under the name of 'human sciences' side by side with the natural sciences, it was the only possible source of their full self-knowledge."[7]

For understanding the composition of *Truth and Method,* too, the importance of this historical process cannot be easily overestimated. For it is here, with Kant and his successors, that the artwork and aesthetics in general are subsumed into the observation of the work. That is to say, in the very description of how the humanistic tradition's fundamental grounds were subjectivized and aestheticized, the *basic issue* of the self-conception of the human sciences never entirely dropped out of sight. Gadamer keeps a firm grip on this issue when he submits the process that produced a completely new, specifically *aesthetical* consciousness to a devastating critique. The heart of the initial section of *Truth and Method* thus consists in a "Critique of the Abstraction Inherent in Aesthetic Consciousness."[8] For *Truth and Method,* the path through aesthetics amounts to a *detour,* as it were. For all the positive insights into art that *Truth and Method* offers, its opening chapters offer less an aesthetic than an anti-aesthetic. The creation of an autonomous aesthetics is therefore nothing but an abstraction which—to use the early Heidegger's terms—needs to be destroyed or relativized in order for us to better understand the kind of knowing that occurs in the human sciences.

2. The Overcoming of Historicist Hermeneutics

The second part of *Truth and Method* deals with recuperating the hermeneutic specificity of the human sciences, and it is here that Gadamer's "hermeneutics of the human sciences," as he systematically terms it,[9] is to be found. The first section considers the history of hermeneutics during the nineteenth century in order to review the aporias of historicism. The most basic among them consists in the fact that historicism, while recognizing the universal historicity of all human knowledge, nevertheless aims at something like absolute knowledge. Dilthey, in particular, found it impossible to reconcile his discovery of the historicity of all life with his epistemological efforts to ground the human sciences methodologically. Not until after Husserl revaluated the life-world and Heidegger developed the more fundamental hermeneutics of facticity did it become possible to overcome historicism's obsession with epistemological foundations. Starting with the ground they had prepared, Gadamer elaborates the "Elements of a Theory of Hermeneutic Experience" in the systematic second part of his magnum opus.

He begins with Heidegger's discovery of the ontological structure of the hermeneutic circle. Ontological here means, as so often with Gadamer, universal. The circle is universal because every act of understanding is conditioned by its motivation or prejudices. Prejudices or fore-understandings, Gadamer writes, should be considered almost like transcendental "conditions of understanding." Our historicity is not a restriction but the very principle of understanding. We understand and strive for truth because we are led on by expectations of meaning. Thus Gadamer provocatively titles the first section of *Truth and Method*'s systematic second part "The Elevation of the Historicity of Understanding to the Status of a Hermeneutic Principle." According to Gadamer, historicism's delusion consisted in trying to displace our prejudices with methods in order to make something like certainty and objectivity possible in the human sciences. Deriving from the Enlightenment, this struggle was itself motivated by a nineteenth-century prejudice, the belief that objectivity could be achieved only by precluding the operation of situated subjectivity in understanding. Historicism was overcome by applying it to itself, as it were, since historicism itself had taught that every doctrine can be understood only against the backdrop of its time. This insight could be applied reflexively to historicism itself. As soon as the scientific ideal of knowledge was revealed, with Heidegger's help, to be dependent on metaphysics, a more appropriate understanding became possible—one that takes into account the ontological fore-structure of understanding in defining the objectivity proper to the human sciences.

There can be no question of merely setting aside one's prejudices; the object is, rather, to recognize and work them out interpretively. Thus Gadamer allies his position with Heidegger's idea that the very first task of interpretation consists in self-critique: working out one's own fore-projections so that the subject matter to be understood can affirm its own validity in regard to them. Since the understanding can often be misled by erroneous fore-conceptions, and since this danger can never be wholly avoided, interpreters must endeavor to develop appropriate interpretive initiatives from within their own situation: "Working out appropriate projections, anticipatory in nature, to be confirmed 'by the things' themselves, is the constant task of understanding."[10] This quotation does not fit the typical picture of Gadamer. His hermeneutic position is usually taken to be something for which there seems to be plentiful evidence: namely, that given the prejudice structure of understanding, there can never be any "confirmation by the things themselves." But it is easy to show that his hermeneutics is quite misunderstood when taken thus. Even if Gadamer's utterances are not always perfectly consistent, his "rehabilitation" of prejudices still warns us to be critically "aware of one's own bias, so that the text can present itself in all its otherness and thus assert its own truth against one's own fore-meanings."[11] On the other hand, Gadamer does not fall into the positivist extreme of calling for a negation of the prejudice structure of understanding in order to let the thing speak for itself without being obfuscated by subjectivity. A reflexively critical understanding of the kind contended for will be concerned "not merely to form anticipatory ideas, but to make them conscious, so as to monitor them and thus acquire right understanding from the things themselves."[12] This is what Gadamer finds in Heidegger: the mean between the positivist dissolution of the self and Nietzsche's universal perspectivism. The question is only how one is to come by the "appropriate" fore-projections that permit the "thing itself" to speak.

Thus everything comes down to the "question of genuine critique in hermeneutics."[13] How, insofar as we can become conscious of them, can we distinguish the right prejudices from the wrong ones, the fore-conceptions that lead to misunderstanding? Is there a criterion for doing so? According to Gadamer, this yearning for a criterion that would certify objectivity once and for all is at best a vestige of historicism. Even if there is no such criterion at hand, however, there are indicators. In this regard, *Truth and Method* emphasizes the productivity of temporal distance. In investigating the past, we are often able to recognize interpretive approaches that have proved themselves. The inability to discern them, for instance, is what makes for problems in evaluating contemporary art. It is almost impossible for critics to distinguish the really valuable artistic efforts of their own time. Thanks to historical distance such judgments become somewhat more certain, and this is what accounts for what might be called the fruitfulness of historical distance. In 1960 Gadamer identified this productivity as the solution to the "critical" task of hermeneutics: "It is only temporal distance that can solve the question of critique in hermeneutics, namely how to distinguish the *true* prejudices, by which we *understand,* from the *false* ones, by which we *misunderstand.*"[14]

However, this solution was somewhat one-sided, for the question arises whether temporal distance always proves to be so productive. A Heideggerian like Gadamer knows full well that history very often has a concealing effect, and interpretive approaches often block access to the very things they mean to reveal. At times it is precisely getting over and beyond historically influential interpretations that proves to be hermeneutically fruitful.[15] Moreover, temporal distance offers virtually no help when it comes to overcoming the provincial temporality of the present. In any case, Gadamer has himself recently discerned the one-sidedness of his views in this respect. When *Truth and Method* appeared in the fifth, Gesammelte Werke edition of 1986, he revised the above passage and replaced "it is only" with "often." The text now reads: "Often temporal distance can solve the question of genuine critique in hermeneutics." Even if the problem persists unresolved, Gadamer's revision nicely illustrates a distinctive characteristic of hermeneutics, namely, that it remains continually ready to alter its opinion when better insight comes along.

3. Effective History as Principle

Gadamer's far-reaching demand for a new kind of understanding in the human sciences, one that concerns itself with subject matter, is elucidated in his elaboration of historically effected consciousness. Since the nineteenth century, history of effect or influence has referred to the study of a given work's interpretations—that is, the history of its reception. Such study has shown that works call forth different interpretations at different times, and must do so. We can say, then, that developing a consciousness of historical effect parallels becoming aware of one's own hermeneutic situation and the productivity of temporal distance. By historically effected consciousness, however, Gadamer means something much more basic. For him it has the status of a "principle"[16] from which virtually his whole hermeneutics can be deduced.

Beyond its relevance to conceptualizing the discipline of literary criticism, the principle of effective history expresses the mandate that one's own situatedness be raised to consciousness in order to "monitor" the way it deals with texts or traditions. This is the interpretation of one's own fore-understanding that Heidegger calls for. Perhaps even more emphatically than Heidegger, however, Gadamer recognizes that this task can never be completed or fulfilled.[17] Effective history is never entirely under our power or at our disposal. We are more subject to history than it can be subjected to consciousness. Whenever we understand, history effects the horizon, never susceptible of ultimate clarification, of everything that can appear meaningful and worth inquiring into. Thus effective history acquires the function of authorizing and affecting each individual act of understanding—even, of course, where its effects are denied. Subsequent to *Truth and Method* Gadamer formulated the principle in this memorable aphorism: "wirkungsgeschichtliches Bewußtsein ist mehr Sein als Bewußtsein"—historically effected consciousness is more being than consciousness.[18] History interpenetrates our "substance" in such a way that we cannot ultimately clarify it or distance ourselves from it.

This insight into the fact that we are conditioned by effective history finds immediate application in Gadamer's dispute with historicism and modern methodological consciousness. Historicism hoped to escape historical conditionedness by distancing itself from the determining effects of history. According to historicism, the historian needs to develop a sense of history emancipated from its conditionedness, thereby making objective historiography possible. Gadamer shows, by contrast, that the power of effective history is not diminished by the recognition of it.[19] Historical consciousness as it emerged in the nineteenth century was not such a radical innovation that it precluded history's subterranean effect on all understanding. History is at work even where we imagine ourselves superior to it (so much so that even historicism was oblivious to its own positivist roots). It is history that determines the background of our values, cognitions, and even our critical judgments. "That is why," says Gadamer, "the prejudices of the individual, far more than his judgments, constitute the historical reality of his being."[20]

Thus the concept of historically effected consciousness proves to be subtly ambiguous. On one hand, it means that present-day consciousness is itself shaped—indeed, constituted—by history. Our consciousness is thus "effected" by history.[21] On the other hand, the concept suggests that becoming conscious of being so effected is a task always still to be undertaken. Further, the consciousness of being effected itself has two meanings: first, it is a call for the elucidation of our historicity in the sense of working out our hermeneutic situation, but also and more fundamentally it involves the awareness of the limits placed on any such enlightenment. In the latter form, historically effected consciousness is the most unequivocal philosophical expression of the consciousness of one's own finitude. The recognition of human limits, however, does not paralyze reflection. On the contrary, what was actually restrictive was historicism's attempt to align understanding with a metaphysically conditioned ideal of knowledge. Historically effected consciousness promises, rather, a heightening of reflection. Gadamer's hermeneutics of finitude is designed to provide this reflection—that is, to demonstrate the universal and specifically *hermeneutical* character of our experience of the world.

4. Understanding as Questioning and Therefore Application

After establishing the principle of effective history, *Truth and Method* takes on the task of recovering the "basic phenomenon of hermeneutics" that had gotten lost in the nineteenth-century detour into method. The main impetus of this recovery comes from the problem of application.[22] Pre-Heideggerian hermeneutics had viewed application as something subsequent to hermeneutic understanding. The proper goal of understanding was thought to be purely epistemic, even noetic. The object was to understand an unfamiliar meaning as such. The application of what was so understood occurred at best ex post facto in such disciplines as jurisprudence, where a law is applied to an individual case, or theology, for example in the homiletic elucidation of a particular passage of Scripture. According to Gadamer, however, application is anything but after-the-fact. He follows Heidegger's intuition that understanding always includes self-understanding—indeed, self-encounter. Understanding, then, involves something like applying a meaning to our situation, to the questions we want answered. It is not the case that there is first a pure, objective understanding of meaning, to which special significance accrues when it is subsequently applied to our questions. We always take ourselves along whenever we understand, so much so that for Gadamer understanding and application are indivisibly fused. This can best be seen by means of a negative example, non-understanding. Whenever we cannot understand a text, the reason is that it says nothing to *us* or has nothing to say. So there is nothing to be surprised or complain about if understanding occurs differently from one period to another, or even from one individual to another.

Motivated by the particular questions of the moment, understanding is not just reproductive but, because it involves application, always also a productive activity.[23] So much is understanding co-determined by the individual effective-historical situation that it seems inappropriate to speak of progress in interpretation or (with Schleiermacher) of understanding better over the course of history. If we acknowledge the productive element of application in every successful interpretation, it is enough to say, in Gadamer's well-known dictum, that we "understand differently" if we understand at all.[24]

Application does not need to be undertaken consciously in order to occur. It, too, is impelled by effective history. Understanding or, what is the same, application is less an action of autonomous subjectivity than "participating in an event of tradition, a process of transmission in which past and present are constantly mediated."[25] To understand a text from the past means to translate it into our situation, to hear in it an answer to the questions of our time. Historicism's error was to have made objectivity dependent on eliminating the interpreting subject and its situatedness, for truth—here understood as the disclosure of meaning (aletheia)—occurs only in the process of effective-historical application.

Gadamer's depiction of understanding as participating in an occurrence of tradition means that subjectivity is not completely in control of what in particular strikes it as being sense or nonsense. As the young Heidegger observed, we discern the interpretive dispositions of our time more as custom and habit than as something we perform intentionally. Effective history is "mehr Sein als Bewußtsein," more being than consciousness—or, in Hegelian terms, more substance than subjectivity. Thus we belong to history more than it belongs to us. This historicity of application precludes talk of a zero point when understanding has not yet begun. Understanding is the continuation of a dialogue that precedes us and has always already begun.[26] Thrown into certain interpretive dispositions, we carry on the conversation. Thus in each new encounter with meaning we take over and modify the views of what makes sense that have been passed down from tradition and are present in us.

In this way the hermeneutics of application belongs, as Gadamer indicates, to the dialectic of question and answer. To understand something means to have related it to ourselves in such a way that we discover in it an answer to our own questions—but "our own" in a way that these questions, too, are assimilated into a tradition and metamorphosed by it. Every act of understanding, even self-understanding, is motivated, stimulated by questions that determine in advance the sight lines of understanding. A text is given voice only by reason of the questions that are put to it today. There is no interpretation, no understanding, that does not answer specific questions that prescribe a specific orientation. Unmotivated questions of the kind that positivism desiderates would pertain to no one and consequently be of no cognitive interest. The point is not to exclude the anticipations of meaning implicit in our questions but to foreground them so that the texts that we are trying to understand can answer them all the more clearly. Thus successful understanding can be described as the effective-historical concretion of the dialectic of question and answer. It is precisely here that we can see the philosophical import of historically effected consciousness. Gadamer himself calls attention to it at the end of the second part of *Truth and Method,* before he goes on to extend the significance of hermeneutics beyond the boundaries of the human sciences: "The dialectic of question and answer . . . now permits us to state more exactly what kind of consciousness historically effected consciousness is. For the dialectic of question and answer that we demonstrated makes understanding appear to be a reciprocal relationship of the same kind as conversation." Understanding is here defined as a relationship and, more exactly, as dialogue. In terms of its form, understanding is less like grasping a content, a noetic meaning, than like engaging in a dialogue—the "dialogue that we are," Gadamer adds, in an allusion to Hölderlin.[27]

Significantly, it is historically effected consciousness that occurs in the form of dialogue. Consciousness loses the autonomy and self-possession accorded it by the tradition of idealism and reflective philosophy from which Gadamer here distances himself. The task of the final section of *Truth and Method* is to demonstrate that our verbal experience of the world universally takes the form not of isolated consciousness but of hermeneutic dialogue as realized in the dialectic of question and answer.

5. Language as Dialogue

> *We are endeavoring to approach the*
> *mystery of language by beginning with*
> *the conversation that we are.*
> Gadamer, Truth and Method

Gadamer's hermeneutics of language is the most misunderstood aspect of his philosophy. The aphorism "Being that can be understood is language" has seemed to justify accusing his philosophy of—or, according to another school of thought, celebrating it for—reducing all being to language. Readers have also objected to the occasional moments of vague diction in the final section of *Truth and Method,* which is sometimes lacking in precise conceptual distinctions. Thus we detect a certain resignation when distinguished students of Gadamer such as Walter Schulz believe they have discovered that for Gadamer everything collapses into an all-embracing synonymy: "History, language, dialogue, and game—all of these, and this is the decisive thing, are interchangeable quantities."[28] The question, then, is *why* language and dialogue can become so. Against whom is Gadamer's foregrounding of the dialogical nature of language directed? Clearly it is directed against the propositional logic that dominates Western philosophy. The point is to call into question philosophy's traditional fixation on the theoretical logos apophantikos—that is, the demonstrative proposition, which is "theoretical in that it abstracts from everything that is not explicitly expressed."[29] To restrict language to what is thus theoretically explicit narrows it artificially. Like Heidegger, Gadamer considers the "construction of logic on the basis of the proposition" to be one of the "most fateful decisions of Western culture."[30] To reverse this decision is the primary intent of Gadamer's hermeneutics of dialogue. Its simplest insight can be expressed thus: "Language is most itself not in propositions but in dialogue."[31] Against propositional logic, in which the sentence consists in a self-sufficient unity of meaning, hermeneutics reminds us that a proposition can never be prescinded from the context of motivation—that is, the dialogue—in which it is embedded and which is the only place it has any meaning. Ultimately a proposition is just an abstraction that is never really encountered in a living language. Thus Gadamer asks, "Are there such things as pure propositions? When and where?"[32]

The privileging of method is clearly connected to the privileging of propositions in Western and especially modern consciousness, for the idea of method draws its power from the fact that certain objects and processes can be experimentally isolated and thereby controlled.[33] Such isolation does violence to language, however. Specifically, understanding what is said cannot be reduced to a cognizing subject's intellectual comprehension of an objectivizable, isolable content; understanding results just as much from belonging to an ongoing, changing tradition—that is, to a dialogue in the context of which everything that is said becomes meaningful and logical for us. In his observations on language, Gadamer brings to a climax the objections against modernity's privileging of method which he had first problematized in the context of the human sciences. This privilege is perfectly obvious because method promises the domination of things that it has isolated, made repeatable and reusable, and thus put at our disposal. It is an open question, however, whether such isolation ever succeeds in the case of language or of one's own understanding. Do we understand if and to the extent that we control? Isn't this a case of finitude explaining itself away? The hermeneut answers that we understand, rather, because something speaks to us from a tradition to which we—more or less loosely—belong.

Against the primacy of propositional logic, which conceives—or, rather, misconceives—understanding as something at our disposal, Gadamer elaborates a logic of question and answer that understands understanding as participation—participation in meaning, a tradition, and ultimately a dialogue. In this dialogue there are no statements, only questions and answers that call forth new questions in turn. "There are no propositions which can be understood exclusively with respect to the content that they present, if one wants to understand them in their truth. . . . Every proposition has presuppositions that it does not express. Only those who think with these presuppositions can really assess the truth of a proposition. I maintain, then, that the ultimate logical form of the presuppositions that motivate every proposition is the *question*."[34] Here we come to the heart of hermeneutic philosophy—namely, as Gadamer expresses it, "the hermeneutic ur-phenomenon, that there is no possible statement that cannot be understood as the answer to a question, and can only be understood thus."[35]

To formulate this phenomenon we have frequently referred to the ancient and perhaps antiquated doctrine of the verbum interius: the "inner word" that is never spoken but nevertheless resounds in everything that is said. In the third part of *Truth and Method,* Gadamer takes this Stoic and Augustinian doctrine as the single piece of evidence that Western forgetfulness of language never quite became total.[36] His seldom noticed rehabilitation of this doctrine cannot be constructed as a regression into naive mentalism; instead, it is a hermeneutic critique of propositional logic and its corollary, the dominion of method. To be sure, this doctrine suggests, bluntly put, that the words we use cannot themselves exhaust what we have "in mind"—that is, the dialogue that we are. The inner word "behind" what is said refers to none other than this dialogue, this rootedness of language in our questioning and to us questionable existence, a dialogue which no propositions can wholly capture: "What is stated is not everything. The unsaid is what first makes what is stated into a word that can reach us."[37]

It must be emphasized once again, however, that this is intended to be a hermeneutic theory of *language,* not some mysticism of ineffability. Precisely in order to view language rightly, rather than overlook it or peer behind it, we need to acknowledge what never is but always remains to be said, the inner dialogue. To affirm this means that the hermeneutics of language takes the end point of language (or, better, of propositions) as its starting point: "Of course, the idea that understanding is in principle linguistic cannot be taken to mean that all our experience of the world occurs only as language and in language."[38] This statement should warn us once and for all against hasty interpretations that saddle Gadamer with the basic thesis of language ontology: everything that is must be expressible in propositional form.

If, however, Gadamer can maintain that understanding is *in principle* linguistic, it is because language embodies the sole means for carrying out the conversation that we are and that we hope to convey to each other. It is for this reason that hermeneutics permits itself an aphorism such as "Being that can be understood is language." The emphasis should be on the "can." Understanding, itself always linguistically formed and dealing with things verbal, must be capable of engaging the whole content of language in order to arrive at the being that language helps bring to expression. The essential linguisticality of understanding expresses itself less in our statements than in our search for the language to say what we have on our minds and hearts. For hermeneutics, it is less constitutive that understanding is expressed in language—which is true but trivial—than that it lives in the unending process of "summoning the word" and the search for a sharable language. Indeed, understanding is to be conceived *as* this process, for this process—the corresponding realization of the inner word—is what grounds the universality of hermeneutics.[39]

6. The Universality of the Hermeneutic Universe

The claim characteristic of hermeneutics, that understanding is universal, has occasioned a good deal of discussion and debate. Is it to be understood as a claim for the universal validity of Gadamer's philosophy? If so, how can it be reconciled with the fundamental thesis of hermeneutics: the historicity of all understanding?

We should notice first in this regard that in Gadamer's usage the word *universality* is especially polysemic. If we confine ourselves literally to *Truth and Method,* we find a number of highly various candidates for universality. The title of the book's last section refers to a "universal aspect of hermeneutics," leaving it open whether hermeneutics here refers to philosophical hermeneutics (say, that of Gadamer), or understanding, or else language viewed hermeneutically. All three possibilities are genuinely possible and defensible. Gadamer speaks de facto of the "universality" of the "linguisticality of understanding,"[49] of a "universal hermeneutic" concerned with the general relationship of man to the world,[41] as well as of broadening hermeneutics into a "universal inquiry."[42] Often we meet with general titles like that of his 1966 essay, "The Universality of the Hermeneutic Problem," or the "hermeneutic dimension."[43] It would be hard to contend that the wide-ranging controversies about universality have shed much light on the question. Gadamer notoriously does not put much stock in clarifying his concepts precisely, thus refusing to pay tribute to the trend toward propositional logic that parcels out language in fixed units of meaning.

A few guideposts are necessary to trace out the universality of the dimension that Gadamer has in mind. At the outset we need to remark that what is at issue is more the universality of a "dimension" than of a philosophy— namely, Gadamer's—as Habermas's talk of the "universal claim of hermeneutics" seems to suggest. Never has Gadamer himself claimed universal validity for his position: " 'hermeneutic' philosophy . . . does not understand itself to be an 'absolute' position."[44] In fact, precisely in the name of insuperable historicity, Gadamer characterizes transcendental philosophy's claim to be absolute, for example, as philosophy's misunderstanding of itself.[45] It is not for nothing that the final paragraphs of *Truth and Method* allude to the maxim of Plato's *Symposium:* None of the gods philosophizes. We philosophize not because we possess the absolute truth but because we do not. Itself a function of finitude, philosophy has to be mindful of its own finitude. It is just when we think we have acquired definitive knowledge that we most need to keep our universal finitude in mind.[46]

Within the framework of *Truth and Method,* the "universal aspect" of hermeneutics has at least one meaning that is easily explained. It indicates that traditional hermeneutics—that of the *human sciences*—has been superseded in the direction of a philosophical hermeneutics that accords the "hermeneutic phenomenon" its full breadth. For philosophy, this universality means that hermeneutic inquiry cannot be limited to the ancillary problem of devising a methodology for the human sciences. The quest for understanding and language is not merely a methodological problem but a fundamental characteristic of human facticity. Emphasizing the "universal aspect" of hermeneutics, then, opposes confining hermeneutics to the human sciences: "Hermeneutics is in this way a universal aspect of philosophy and *not just* the methodological basis of the so-called human sciences."[47] The whole of Gadamer's philosophical, emphatically *speculative* efforts are directed toward broadening the horizon of hermeneutics so far beyond the human sciences narrowly conceived that it becomes a central occupation of philosophy. It is precisely this that is meant by *broadening* hermeneutics to become the universal inquiry of philosophy and by the "Ontological Turn of Hermeneutics," as the title of the third section of *Truth and Method* phrases it. In this final part, Gadamer turns hermeneutic inquiry away from and beyond the hermeneutics of the human sciences, the subject of the first two parts, and toward the greater universality, that of the ontological or philosophical dimension.

How can we speak of the universality of a hermeneutic dimension or experience without investing this philosophy with a claim to absoluteness? It is easy to be misled by the word universality. Consequently it is important to follow the suggestions in various of Gadamer's texts that the real basis for the talk about universality in *Truth and Method* should be sought in the semantic field of the word "universe." Accordingly, we can take the claim that language and understanding are universal to mean that they constitute our universe—that is, the element or the totality in which we live as finite beings. Thus Gadamer alludes, apparently just in passing, to the biologist von Uexküll's contrast between a "universe of life" and the "world of physics."[48] Gadamer also appeals to Leibniz's notion that the monad is a universe in the sense that it can reflect the entire world within itself. In the context of *Truth and Method* the conception of the *universe* or the universality of language and understanding is directed against the thesis that any given language is limited because there are many different languages. In fact it may seem that reason itself is limited insofar as it is circumscribed within a specific language. But that is not the case, Gadamer counters, because it is a distinctive characteristic of language that it can give expression to *everything*. It is in this sphere that we can best understand the "universality of language," that is, the fact that language can keep pace with the boundlessness of reason.[49]

This dimension of language is universal and forms the universe in that all understanding and human existence occur within it. This does not mean, of course, that an expression for everything already exists in language. The universality of language consists not in creating what is to be said but rather in that language can always be sought. The universal dimension of hermeneutics is therefore that of the inner word, the dialogue from which every expression receives its life. To be sure, we do find completely precise, communicative words. Yet these words are, as it were, nothing but the visible terminus signaling the interminable desire for further understanding and language. What is hermeneutically significant about language in this respect is the dimension of inner dialogue, the fact that what we say always means more than is actually expressed: "A meaning, an intention always goes above and beyond what is actually captured in language, in words that reach others. An insatiable yearning for the right word—that is what constitutes the genuine life and nature of language."[50]

In this yearning our finitude reveals itself. No ultimate self-possession is guaranteed to us, in word or concept. We live in and from a dialogue that can never end because no words can grasp what we are or state how we should understand ourselves. Through this finitude is expressed our human consciousness of death, which—speechlessly seeking speech—strives against its own end. Thus Gadamer shows that there is a close connection between the interminability of our search for the right word and "the fact that our own existence is situated in time and before death."[51]

In the inner word, in the drive to understanding and language that constitutes the universe of our finitude, is rooted the universality of hermeneutic philosophizing. Can there be anything more universal for philosophy than finitude? The contemporary philosophy that concerns itself with the universality of the finitude revealed in our ceaseless endeavor to understand and say what we understand erects its claim to universality on this very basis. This claim does not express itself in definitively grounded propositions, however. For a philosophy of finitude, that would be a contradiction. Instead, hermeneutic philosophy advocates the self-interpretation of facticity and, in the sure knowledge that none of the gods philosophizes, tries to give full cognizance to finitude as the universal horizon within which everything makes sense for us.

VII

Hermeneutics

in Dialogue

The possibility that the other person
may be right is the soul of hermeneutics.
Gadamer, July 9, 1989, Heidelberg
Colloquium

If anything is universal in philosophical hermeneutics, it is probably the recognition of one's own finitude, the consciousness that actual speech does not suffice to exhaust the inner conversation that impels us toward understanding. Gadamer ties the universality of the hermeneutic process to the fact that understanding depends on this ongoing conversation: "That a conversation occurs, no matter when or where or with whom, wherever something comes to language, whether this is another person, a thing, a word, a flame (Gottfried Benn)—this is what constitutes the universality of hermeneutic experience."[1] Only in conversation, only in confrontation with another's thought that could also come to dwell within us, can we hope to get beyond the limits of our present horizon. For this reason philosophical hermeneutics recognizes no principle higher than dialogue.

Gadamer's philosophy presents what is probably the most recent original and comprehensive conception of hermeneutics. It is generally considered one of the most epoch-making contributions to philosophy since Heidegger's *Being and Time*. Though Heidegger's influence was never small, after the thirties he withdrew somewhat from the circle of philosophical discussion. Gadamer reintroduced hermeneutics into the discussion, and after the Second World War it received increasing international attention. Since its publication in 1960 *Truth and Method* has had an enormous effect on the development of philosophy, for example, in the marked turn toward language, whereby the Continent converged with the linguistic turn of Anglo-American philosophy; then in the rehabilitation of practical philosophy, first in the form of a return to a new Aristotelianism that supplemented Kant's ethics of duty with an attention to the historical contingency of life-forms; but also in theory of science, where Kuhnian contextualism could welcome the assistance of hermeneutics in its critique of positivism; and finally in sharpening hermeneutic consciousness for the purpose of providing a critical social theory—not to mention applications of hermeneutics in such fields as literary theory (that of H. R. Jauß and W. Iser, who concretized the dialectic of question and answer in the form of reception aesthetics), in history (R. Koselleck), in law, and in theology. Even a skeletal analysis of the developments occasioned, formed, and furthered by hermeneutics would exceed the framework of the present study and would still be merely a general overview. Thus we will discuss what is, I hope, a representative selection of the debates that were directly ignited by hermeneutics and thus stimulated the philosophical conversation of the present generation.

What aroused opposition at the beginning of the sixties was the departure of hermeneutics from methodologism and apparently from a claim to objectivity; in the seventies it was the overdependence of hermeneutics on traditions and its lack of a critical element; in the eighties it was the fact that hermeneutics clung to the idea of a will to understand, to consensus, and to truth, and this was considered a regress into metaphysics. The most important representatives of these debates were Betti, Habermas, and Derrida. Against Gadamer, Betti defended a methodologism designed to guarantee objectivity; Habermas, ideology critique; and Derrida, deconstruction.

1. Betti's Epistemological Return to the Inner Spirit

It is certainly a historical injustice to bring Emilio Betti's hermeneutics into discussion after Gadamer's, for the older jurist (1890–1968) preceded

Gadamer in presenting a detailed hermeneutics in 1955 under the title *General Theory of Interpretation*. Perhaps the thousand pages of the work limited its readership, but the book soon appeared—probably at Gadamer's suggestion—in an abbreviated German edition in 1967. Earlier Betti had apprised his German readers of his hermeneutic position in two short polemical "manifestos," appearing in 1954 and 1962.[2] The curtain was thus ready to open on the discussion between Gadamer and Betti right at the beginning of the sixties.

Betti's whole hermeneutics can justly be characterized as polemical, even "reactionary."[3] This term is intended not in the banal ideological sense but rather in the sense that his whole energy is devoted to reacting against the "subjectivistic" and "relativistic" tendencies he detected in the existential hermeneutics of Heidegger and Bultmann. In contrast to them, he aimed to rehabilitate the idea of a hermeneutics obeying strict scientific standards that could guarantee the objectivity of interpretation in the human sciences. His hermeneutics is no less universal in scope than Gadamer's. He himself speaks of a *universal* theory of interpretation. In his usage, however "universal" has a purely epistemological significance. It means that *all* forms of scholarly interpretation—as they are practiced in philology, history, theology, and law—have at bottom a common gnoseological structure; and to hermeneutics as the methodological basis of all the human sciences falls the job of working out the criteria of their objectivity. Understanding is the epistemological task common to all these sciences. So conceived, understanding is the mental process concerned with comprehending the mind of another insofar as it has expressed itself in interpretable, meaning-bearing forms. With hermeneutics as its theory, interpretation proposes itself as the solution for the epistemological problem of understanding.[4] We come into contact with another mind not immediately but only by taking a detour through the objectivizations or meaning-bearing forms whereby it makes itself cognizable. "Sinnhaltige Formen" (meaning-bearing forms) here is the German translation of the Italian "forma rappresentativa."[5] The objectivizations to be interpreted (language, but also gestures, monuments, traces, tones of voice, and so on) represent or stand for the inner spirit or mind that one is trying to understand. Naturally Betti can find support for this view in the entire hermeneutic tradition, and particularly in the romantic notion that understanding consists in reversing the creative act from within to without. Betti frankly avails himself of the idealist and romantic way of expressing the matter, and in respect to the doctrine of the inner spirit we have not here disputed the justice of doing so: our understanding really does attempt to experience what words mean—the meaning that is, as it were, behind the words and is intended to be expressed through them. Whether that involves postulating a reified inner spirit is not very important from our point of view.

For Betti, however, the whole question revolves around the cognitive understanding of a mens auctoris, the meaning intended by the author. The interpreter must therefore exclude personal interests and projections, and respect the autonomy of the author's intended meaning. In Betti's view it is a dangerous error for relativist hermeneutics to describe prejudices as "conditions of understanding." This objection is specifically directed at Gadamer's theory of application. Understanding has nothing at all to do with application, Betti argues, once we become aware that the interpretive process can be controlled and therefore rendered objective. Application pertains only to particular spheres of interpretation, for example, theology and jurisprudence, and even they need to be erected on the foundation of epistemological understanding. Before a passage of Scripture or a law can be applied to a concrete situation, its purely noetic meaning must first be ascertained. Of course, the interpreter can actualize a meaning and assimilate it to present-day expectations, but a meaning thus modernized must be distinguished from the text's original meaning. In this way, Betti formulates an important hermeneutic distinction between the *meaning* of a text and the *significance* which one and the same meaning acquires over the course of its various interpretations.[6] These two should not be confused, as Gadamer's theory of application seems to imply. Betti's distinction is highly practicable in hermeneutics. We cannot in practice avoid recognizing interpretations that are overmodernized and deviate too far from the text's original meaning. Otherwise, interpreting would be a purely arbitrary act. And yet, however clearly significance can be known as such, it still remains a question whether the original meaning, on the other hand, can ever be definitively nailed down. For example, we can say that Plato's Ideas cannot be reduced to Kant's interpretation of them as ideas of pure reason or to the methods of neo-Kantianism, but this does not amount to getting a grasp on its original meaning. That meaning remains at best the asymptote of understanding, the telos that the interpreter is trying to reach behind the words. Whether anyone ever succeeds can never, because of our finitude, be determined. Moreover, we can understand the meaning, as distinguished from its significance, only with respect to what it means to us and what its signs evoke for us. That is what Gadamer means when he talks about an interpenetration of meaning and significance.

To the end of precluding subjective preference from affecting the process of reconstruction, Betti's hermeneutics attempts to lay down the principles or canons that make interpretation verifiably objective. He proposes four: (1) the canon of hermeneutic autonomy, or the immanence of the hermeneutic criterion (that is, the meaning to be interpreted is the text's original, immanent meaning and not the interpreter's projection); (2) the canon of wholeness (totality) and of the inner semantic integration, which requires that hermeneutic inquiry take the text as bearing a self-consistent and coherent meaning; (3) the more subjective-sounding canon of the relevance of understanding reminiscent of Gadamer's notion of application, but for Betti it merely means that the interpreter is constrained "to retrace the creative process in his own thoughts, and to reconstruct from within, to translate back an unfamiliar thought, a piece of the past, a recollected experience, from within the actuality of his own life";[7] (4) finally, the canon of hermeneutic correspondence of meaning or hermeneutic congeniality. This means that the "interpreter should attempt to bring his own living actuality into the closest accord and harmony with the stimulus that he receives coming from the object, so that the two vibrate in consonance, that is, in tune with each other."[8]

No philosophical hermeneutics, insofar as it concedes limited justification to the project of a purely methodological hermeneutics of the human sciences, will be able to fault the motives of such canons. In principle every interpretation begins with the fact that the autonomy and coherence of its object must be respected. What seems dubious is only whether such canons do in fact serve to ground the objectivity of interpretation in the human sciences or positively distinguish correct from incorrect interpretations. The fact is that every interpretation will aim at consistency and correspondence to its object. The question, then, is not whether an interpretation ought to be appropriate to its object; rather, the question is when this happens and whether its occurrence can be verified. But for this verification there are no canons, no rule for the application of the rule itself. This might give one the impression that Betti contented himself with purely verbal solutions.[9]

In his answer to Gadamer, Betti later admitted that his rules had a merely negative function: "Besides, the hermeneutic canons play not so much a positive as the negative, critical role of preventing those prejudices and prepossessions that can lead one down the wrong path."[10] However, such concessions raise doubts about the viability of a positive hermeneutics conceived as a theory of the methods guaranteeing objectivity in the human sciences. Certainly an interpretation can be criticized when it does not do justice to the object and its coherence, but where and when an interpretation is objectively valid—and not merely rhetorically convincing—is not a problem any methodology can solve.

Betti's hermeneutics proves to be a late birth of historicism. In order to keep clear of the danger of historical relativization, Betti's hermeneutics tries to construct a definitively grounded methodology of the human sciences governed by strict rules and procedures. Ultimately, however, it does not perform what it promises: a hermeneutics that will positively guarantee objectivity. Historicity does not cease merely because someone scientistically wishes it away. That is merely the way to fundamentally misunderstand its function as the condition of understanding. The limited justification for Betti's hermeneutic efforts consists in its reminding us, however, that some interpretations are more and some less frivolous than others because they conform to general, though negative standards. Meaning does not dissolve into modernized significance. This meaning and the inner spirit behind meaning-bearing forms can flourish only on the productive ground of our open-ended inquiries and expectations, and this is brought out much more clearly by Gadamer's hermeneutics of application.

2. Habermas's Critique of Hermeneutics in the Name of Agreement

> *One is tempted to enlist Gadamer against Gadamer.*
> Habermas, Zur Logik der Sozialwissenschaften

The title of this section may well seem paradoxical, but it is meant merely to indicate a possible evolution in Habermas's relation to hermeneutics. From 1967 to 1970 Habermas tried to legitimize an emancipatory critique of ideology conceived on the model of objectivizing sciences such as psychoanalysis and designed to counter the universalization of the hermeneutic concept of understanding. In the 1980s he then proposed a theory of communicative action and a correlative ethics of discourse that drew its legitimacy from the universal idea of agreement presupposed in language. This later development, or shift of emphasis, evidences a tacit and certainly seldom noticed indebtedness to hermeneutic philosophy's claim to universality.

Habermas's first productive encounter with hermeneutics occurred in the framework of *On the Logic of the Social Sciences,* a survey of the literature that appeared in *Philosophische Rundschau,* a journal edited by Gadamer and Helmut Kuhn.[11] There Habermas was already concerned with grounding the social sciences in a theory of language, as a step toward devising a theory of communicative action that could offer successful resistance to objectivist positivism.[12] By contrast to positivism and its apparently value-free sociology—where social action was conceived on the model of atomistic centers of power causally affecting each other, and therefore in abstraction from the agents' linguistically mediated life-world—Habermas went in search of a normative and linguistically based foundation for the social sciences. For help in developing this foundation he first turned to Wittgenstein's theory of language games that embody a form of life. Yet he found a vestige of positivism in Wittgenstein's thesis that these linguistically constituted life-forms were closed, as if each agent were monadically trapped in its language-world. It was precisely to overcome this limitation that Habermas brought hermeneutics into play. From Gadamer he learned that language can transcend itself and thereby exhibits the potential for rationality.[13] Hermeneutics, Habermas writes, shows that linguistic spheres are never monadically shut but are, rather, permeable, from without as well as within.[14] From without, because a language is open, being in principle able to express everything that can be said and understood. Its horizon is continually in the process of expanding. But also from within, since linguistic agents can distance themselves from their own expressions in order to interpret them, to reflect on them, etc. Hermeneutics' claim to universality is well substantiated in these respects, and Habermas can enthusiastically appropriate "Gadamer's masterly critique of the objectivist self-understanding of the human sciences"[15] in constructing an interpretive and emancipatory sociology based on theory of language.

Given this fundamental solidarity, the controversy between hermeneutics and ideology critique, however vociferous, concerns only secondary matters. The first misunderstanding, since cleared up, revolved around the concept of tradition. Following previous opponents, Habermas pointed indignantly to the discrediting of the Enlightenment which Gadamer's rehabilitation of tradition seemed to imply. Admittedly, many of Gadamer's formulations were provocative enough. The fact that "authority [was] accorded superiority over knowledge"[16] seemed a slap in the face of Enlightenment. The debate that followed, as well as a rereading of *Truth and Method,* showed, however, that Gadamer always began with the idea that authority could be considered legitimate only if it was based on an act of recognition and thus of reason. He never gave authority and tradition precedence over reason, but only recalled that they depend on a situated reason that plays itself out in communication. Indeed, it is ironic to note that, in this section of *Truth and Method,* Gadamer cites Karl Jaspers's and Gerhard Krüger's accounts of tradition and faults them for giving authority precedence over reason.[17] Habermas's critique of Gadamer in this regard merely repeats Gadamer's own critique of some of his predecessors.

Moreover, Habermas believed that hermeneutics had to be charged with "linguistic idealism,"[18] because it overlooked the factical limits of language. If the present introduction has made anything clear, it is, I hope, that the hermeneutic conception of language is based, from the ground up, on the experience of just these limits. The ceaseless striving for words and understanding indeed presupposes the experience of the inadequacy of linguistic understanding. The universality of language is not that of any particular language-state, as though everything could be said and understood effortlessly; it is the search for words. It is an apparent paradox that, hermeneutically, we are in search of understanding and language, because they fail us in principle. Habermas is combatting a merely imaginary opponent when he argues against the hermeneutic claim to universality that there are in fact "specifically unintelligible utterances of life."[19] We don't need psychoanalysis or ideology critique to tell us that!

The deployment of ideology critique and psychoanalysis serves to ignite a further conflict between Gadamer and Habermas. With their support Habermas wants to relativize the apparently sharp opposition between truth (in the human sciences or life-world) and (scientific) methods. This, in order to show that there can be a kind of understanding that is methodical and explanatory, that can get behind a false consciousness (that of an individual in the case of psychoanalysis, and a society in that of ideology critique), and that can practice critique in the name of undistorted communication. Psychoanalysis and ideology critique, Habermas claims, offer striking examples of the fact that methodical and objective knowledge is to be had in the social realm. In this respect the Gadamer-Habermas quarrel was especially conditioned by its time, because it was in fact fought out during the period when Marxist psychoanalysis and ideology critique were booming. It also resonated with political undertones (conservatism vs. social emancipation) by which we are perhaps less affected today. Moreover, it cannot be said that the scientific status of psychoanalysis and ideology critique has become any more certain of late.

We must restrict ourselves here to charges that pertain directly to the self-understanding of hermeneutics.

Gadamer first retorted that he never intended any sharp opposition between truth and method. Certainly truth can be achieved by way of method. What he considered dubious was merely the claim on the part of modern methodical consciousness to a monopoly, its dogmatic assertion that there can be no truth outside of method. Gadamer never questions the explanatory achievements of psychoanalysis, though he might well have pointed out the hermeneutic basis of its constructs and called it to task for its scientistic understanding of itself (as had Paul Ricoeur a few years earlier).[20] Above all, however, what Gadamer problematized was the simple extrapolation of the psychoanalytical model to society. In a therapeutic conversation there is actually a patient seeking help and a doctor who is competent and responsible for giving it. In society, by contrast, there can be no question of informing a group that doesn't feel especially sick that it is afflicted with false consciousness—all this in the name of a certain conception of freedom and a competence purporting to be the sole province of emancipatory social science. The "anticipation of the good life," as Habermas calls it, is indeed common to all. It is not the privilege of ideology critique, battened on psychoanalytical metaphors.

Gadamer and Habermas have both learned something from their confrontation. Stimulated by Habermas, Gadamer was able to work out the critical potential of his hermeneutics more incisively than before. His hermeneutics does not exhaust itself in resignation to finitude; it strives for a "critically reflexive knowledge,"[21] the effectiveness of which is most manifest where correcting objectivistic self-misunderstandings increases the individual's freedom. Gadamer is thinking in particular of the dichotomy Habermas creates between tradition, which grows and lives on, and the reflexive appropriation of it. Undoubtedly people can reflect themselves out of a given tradition; but the tradition that one thus gets a view of becomes understandable only thanks to critical questions and expectations of meaning which in their totality can never be rendered transparent by reflection. For hermeneutics, critically reflexive knowledge is also called for, Gadamer insists, whenever the narrowness of "logic's false claims" needs to be made manifest.[22] Thus hermeneutics defends "speaking intelligibly" against the propositional logic that measures language by the criterion of a propositional calculus. Here hermeneutics serves to remind us that each human language is grounded in dialogue. Propositions are not everything. As critically reflexive knowledge,

hermeneutics "makes us critically conscious what the *scopus* of a given proposition is and what hermeneutic efforts its truth claim calls for."[23] Many propositions can be disproved using the criteria of self-regulatory logic, to be sure,
but there still remains the question whether we thereby reach, in Plato's
words, "the soul of speech."[24] In reminding us of the inner conversation that
is always going on behind propositions, hermeneutics proves its value as critically reflexive knowledge.

For Habermas, too, the debate has proved fruitful. Perhaps there are other
reasons for it, but since 1970 psychoanalysis has to all intents and purposes
gradually ceased to occupy a central place in his thought and no longer serves
as his model for a critical social science. As if Gadamer's charges had hit
home, Habermas thereafter virtually never transposed psychoanalysis to sociology. Furthermore, he began to root his critical theory of society all the more
deeply in the ground of language theory as he forged his way toward universal pragmatics and a theory of communicative action. His basic intuition was
that the normative bases of a social theory and its discourse ethics as well are
to be found in the pragmatic implications or validity claims implicit in language used to communicate and understand. The task of a critical philosophy must be to offer a rational reconstruction of the intuitive presuppositions
involved in language use. Habermas's leading supposition is that in principle
language use must be conceptualized as a process of coming to agreement.
"I concur with Wittgenstein that 'language' and 'agreement' [Verständigung]
are equiprimordial, reciprocally explanatory concepts."[25] Gadamer would fit
here just as well as Wittgenstein. Perhaps even better, because Habermas's
Logic of the Social Sciences had earlier corrected Wittgenstein's conception of
monadically closed language games by appealing to the hermeneutic insight
that language is fundamentally open and reflexive. From Gadamer he learned
that universal understanding was in principle achievable in conversation. That
the later Habermas appeals to Wittgenstein against his earlier and better
judgment may be connected with the fact that in his later works he increasingly trivializes hermeneutics by associating it with the preservation of "cultural tradition" and loses sight of the way it universalizes language. However
that may be, the basic hermeneutic category of understanding or agreement
receives a renewed universalization from Habermas. It now becomes the
silent telos and common denominator of all language use. Even where the
language of coming to agreement is perverted for strategic purposes, such
tactics are merely "parasitical" on the idea of coming to an agreement, as
shown by the fact that even purposes inimical to this idea are nevertheless

absolutely dependent on its validity. From this all-embracing anticipation of agreement, Habermas derives the ethical implications that will be rationally reconstructed by his discourse ethics.

What is without doubt significant in Habermas's renewal of hermeneutics' claim to universality is that identifying the idea of coming to an understanding with the telos of language implies certain ethical consequences. Gadamer was hardly unaware of these implications. Since his first encounter with Heidegger, the main orientation of his study of Greek philosophy had been to work out the ethical dimensions of the hermeneutics of facticity.[26] In an appeal to the situational ethics of Aristotle, he showed that the exercise of practical wisdom, phronesis, always occurs against the background of a community that develops over time and articulates itself linguistically. Habermas emphasizes more of the Kantian element behind the hermeneutic *universalization* of agreement [Verständigung]. Anyone who enters into conversation has already accepted universal contrafactual principles of understanding. In 1973, K.-O. Apel did not hesitate to call the project of constructing such an ethics a "transcendental hermeneutics."[27]

The notion of mutual understanding and agreement can therefore be expanded into an ethics of discourse coherent with hermeneutics. It remains an open question, however, on what level this discourse should be situated and what is supposed to be gained by such an ethics: merely clarifying the "moral point of view"[28] that has already manifested itself in custom or, beyond that, developing a "planetary macroethics" (Apel), which itself claims immediate and urgent moral relevance? The usual answer is that the pertinent norms are to be negotiated by the participants, and that philosophy must merely clarify the procedure whereby the individuals involved can judge what kind of norms are universal or acceptable in their particular situation.

From a hermeneutic point of view, this procedure, extrapolated from the idea of understanding, still has something abstract about it. Despite the talk of a "postconventional morality," are norms really something that can be the object of negotiation? Moreover, there remains the question about what concrete form a procedure for grounding norms might take, when human conflicts are dominated by interests that are not all susceptible to being communicated. Finally, whether or not a rational reconstruction of the presuppositions of "communicative action" will ever succeed—and how one could know that it had—is also impossible to say. It would certainly be unhermeneutical to strive for anything like reified self-possession by reconstructing what is always intuitively presupposed and apparently not to be superseded by reflection. Such a claim might better be left to the divine noesis noeseos.

3. The Deconstructive Challenge to Hermeneutics

> *Now I really do not want to say that the solidarities that bind human beings to each other and make them partners in conversation suffice to make everything intelligible and bring people to complete consensus. For that, an unending dialogue between two people would be necessary; and for the inner dialogue of the soul with itself, the same holds true.*
>
> Gadamer, Text und Interpretation

Even though Gadamer employs the model of Platonic dialogue in which we only participate, and Habermas starts with the example of scientific, argumentative communication, their profound solidarity on the issue of dialogical understanding manifests itself once more in the common front with which both meet the challenge of deconstruction and neohistorical postmodernism. In the hermeneutic idea of coming to an understanding, deconstruction discerns a perpetuation of the metaphysical will to power, which it claims is the real force behind the dialogical model of rationality and which totally represses all anomalous individuality, difference, and dissidence. Habermas countered that Derrida cannot in principle maintain his protest against communicative reason without self-contradiction because he himself is seeking understanding and consensus. Moreover, the meaning of communicative reason is not to level out individuality; quite the contrary, it is to bring the individual's communicative possibilities to the point where they can unfold themselves freely and articulate their justifiable claims to validity. It is only in the context of a dialogical community that the pluralism and difference of lifeforms favored by deconstruction are possible.[29]

The encounter between Gadamer and Derrida occurred in the context of a meeting arranged by the Goethe Institute of Paris in April 1981 for the purpose of opening a conversation between the two streams of thought defining Continental philosophy—French deconstruction and German hermeneutics—itself a genuinely hermeneutical initiative. Based on the actual contributions, however, it seems to have been more a case of talking past each other, as demonstrated by the proceedings since published in the several languages concerned.[30] Directly engaging Derrida's textual deconstruction, Gadamer held an opening lecture entitled "Text and Interpretation," to which Derrida answered on the next day with three brief questions. Derrida then gave a lecture on Heidegger and Nietzsche, without directly concerning himself with Gadamer or hermeneutics. In the years that followed, Gadamer wrote significant essays on the deconstructive challenge, in which he clarified the theoretical contribution of his hermeneutics. To understand this challenge, we will need to limit ourselves here to Derrida's three questions, since his encounter with Gadamer has subsequently issued in no further texts. These questions all converge on a central point: the status of (good) will in understanding as presupposed by hermeneutics. Is not a metaphysical premise involved here? Not in the trivial sense, of course, as if hermeneutics postulated a second world; rather, in the sense of "metaphysics" elaborated by Heidegger, that the will to understanding is complicitous with the drive for the total domination of beings. The will that Gadamer makes a claim for could ultimately be taken as the last successor of the metaphysics of will. This Derridean charge is plausible or intelligible to the extent that in the process of understanding occurs an appropriation of the other that could be construed as an absolute assimilation of otherness.

Already in *Truth and Method* Gadamer had dealt with the possibility of such a misunderstanding of his intentions. In discussing applicatio, where the danger of appropriation seems especially great, he distinguishes hermeneutics from all knowledge aiming at domination [Herrschaftswissen].[31] Against the metaphysical and specifically Hegelian will to conceive, Gadamer explicitly appeals to the model of Platonic dialogue (which is also easily misunderstood, for Plato is generally considered the father of metaphysics, particularly in the wake of Heidegger and Nietzsche). The truth that can be achieved and experienced in dialogue has nothing to do with taking possession. Describing it as participatory truth seems nearer the mark, for in dialogue with others and oneself as we are thinking, we arrive at truths that enlighten us without knowing what is happening to us or how. We can hardly be said to dominate these truths. Rather, we are possessed by them, as it were. Understanding is experienced as a passion when an interpretation "occurs" to us. In this connection Gadamer recalls the maxim of Heraclitus, "The lightning guides everything," which was scratched over the doorway of Heidegger's hut. Lightning here means "the suddenness of lightning-like illumination that makes everything visible with one stroke, and yet is immediately swallowed up in darkness again."[32] To that extent the truth of understanding means more something like participation than ceaseless, irremediable appropriation.

The confrontation between Gadamer and Derrida has raised another far-reaching question as well: whether we can speak at all of the understanding of "truth." Is it not the case, rather, that interpretation drifts from sign to sign, without ever coming up against meaning in the form of bodily presence, as it were? Especially in his studies on Husserl, the early Derrida pointed out the problem of the "vouloir dire"—wanting or meaning to say.[33] A sign, according to the traditional conception, "wants" to say something, but what it means can never be definitively fixed. The meaning whose presence it claims to represent is so constantly "deferred/differed" that Derrida considers all signs to be animated by irreducible différance. The whole illusion of metaphysics (with which Heidegger, too, is supposed to have been afflicted, in that he was looking for something like the meaning of being) culminates in just this: searching for meaning and striving after understanding. This broad suspicion of metaphysics forms the backdrop of deconstruction's attack on hermeneutics.

We might well greet this charge by shaking our heads and affirming the undeniable fact that it does not in principle affect the capacity for understanding; even Derrida wants to understand and be understood when he engages in conversation. It has been primarily Habermas's devastating critique that has called attention to Derrida's self-contradiction. In this respect, however, hermeneutics can show more sympathy for Derrida's position, because the hermeneutic conception of participatory truth and its constant dependency on conversation demonstrate precisely that the notion of a reified meaning of the sort suggested by the metaphysics of presence and classical philosophy of language is untenable. Here, too, the hermeneutic conception of the inner word must be brought into play. It is indeed the conviction of hermeneutic philosophy that no word quite captures the soul's inner strivings. A word or a sign can never be ultimately taken as the absolute presence of meaning. It is precisely indication, différance, if you will, or reference to something else that can be meant but not said. Language lives in this unsatisfied yearning, the irreducible différance between word and meaning.[34]

It would be fatal to maintain that there is no such yearning and to content oneself like Derrida with the notion that signs refer only to other signs and they to still others, without meaning anything, without any vouloir dire, as it were. Returning to a kind of semiotic positivism is what it ultimately amounts to when one denies the inner word or the inner conversation that nourishes language and is nourished by it. Insisting on the sign, as if it did not refer to something else, something unreachable, is the purest positivism—it is indeed, if the label still means anything, bad metaphysics. To take language as pure sound that means nothing but itself is to pursue the metaphysics of the absolutely present-at-hand.

A similar semiotic physicalism is to be found in Lyotard's apparent truism that philosophy has to do only with sentences: sentences are the only things that are always and everywhere presupposed.[35] It is indeed true that sentences are to be found everywhere, but these sentences are the result, optimally the proof, of a conversation that precedes them, and they depend on the interpretation that follows in order to be heard or understood. To take voices or sentences in their pure present-at-handness as ultimate givens signifies a regression into the propositional logic of metaphysics that dominated the entire West, excepting only the doctrine of the logos endiathetos. For propositional logic, statements reflect content in an instrumental manner, as if every word corresponded to an idea. The theory of the verbum interius is much more adequate in that it discloses the genuine life and complexity of language, and it reflects our experience of the fact that our speaking remains bound to prior meanings when we express a meaning that cannot be reduced to the signs we use.

It would nevertheless be inadequate to posit an outer limit of language, as if thought were somehow irremediably imprisoned within metaphysical language. Anyone who considers language such a "Babylonian slavery of the spirit" overlooks the fact that language is conversation.[36] Language is permeable, as Habermas says: although our desire for expression always exceeds our capacity, yet to a certain degree—the degree to which thought is possible—it can reflect on its own limits and expand them. To limit language once and for all to an écriture with nothing behind it is positively to truncate the reach of the logos—"as if," Gadamer responds to Derrida, "all discourse consisted in propositional judgments."[37] The logos of metaphysics cannot—à la Derrida and, in part, Heidegger—be reduced to a metaphysics of the will that is in principle blind to otherness. If one understands logos to mean talking with one another and thus mutual interdependence, then the hermeneutical logos has its real place in conversation and, above all, in the conversation of the soul with itself, as Plato liked to describe thought.[38] Because there is no ultimate or definitive closure from a post-metaphysical standpoint, it is upon this conversation that the universality of hermeneutics is based.

Afterword

The argument between Derrida and Gadamer has made at least one thing clear: the charge brought against the universal search for truth and understanding is universal perspectivism, as Nietzsche inscribed it in philosophical consciousness. What is the point of striving for understanding, when everything is perspectival and historically conditioned? Often Gadamer has himself been viewed as the spokesman for historical relativism, since he had written that we do not understand better, but only differently. What would it mean to talk about the universality of understanding differently? Ultimately, does it not destroy the whole notion of truth?

All appearances to the contrary notwithstanding, to equate understanding differently with nihilistic relativism would be a historicist mistake, since understandings are different only from an exterior perspective. If one were to view all the interpretations of a given text in diachronic, historical sequence, it might well seem that always and everywhere the only understanding is understanding differently. This would be true only to a limited extent, however, if viewed from the interior perspective that we are all involved in here and now. Of course, we can work up the admission that what we consider true today may look much different tomorrow, so that even our own understanding might seem provincial, one among many possibilities. This view, however, does not correspond to the situation of people who are actually in the process of striving for and achieving understanding. Everyone who is trying to understand is trying to find something true. This can be shown first from the negative fact that everyone knows what lies and falsehood are. To make a mistake is to overlook the truth; to lie is to twist it. Positively defining and characterizing truth is admittedly a very difficult task. Yet when we say we understand, we are laying claim to truth, and by truth we mean simply a meaningful account that corresponds to things. How can such a truth claim be consonant with understanding differently?

We understand differently every time because we bring a truth anew to language by applying it (an apt affirmation, a criticism, a plausible view, and so on) to our situation. Every individual, every time, does so in his or her own way and therefore "differently." And yet what each attempt to understand is striving for remains a truth, something that can be discussed in a given case. We would commit a historicist fallacy if we tried to describe truth as relative when it is thus taken in different ways. Insofar as hermeneutics speaks of relativism, it is merely as a ghost—as a fiction that is supposed to frighten people but that does not exist.[1] For relativism—generally understood as the view that every opinion about a given thing, or even every thing per se, is just as good as any other—is not in fact a view that was ever seriously held by anyone.[2] Certainly not by hermeneutics. To be sure, hermeneutics does maintain that the experiences we have with truth are embedded in our situation— and that means in the inner conversation that we are continually having with ourselves and others. But this is just what renders relativism untenable in the sense that "anything goes." No one is of a mind to accept everything as equally justified and equally valuable. The soul's inner conversation, which cannot be conceived as otherwise than situated, precludes all arbitrariness of interpretation.

This is precisely why for hermeneutics relativism has never existed anywhere. Rather, there are opponents of hermeneutics who suspect it of entertaining a relativistic understanding of truth because the hermeneutic view of truth does not answer their foundationalist expectations. Thus in present-day philosophy relativism functions like a scarecrow or bogey in the service of foundationalist positions that would like to do away with the inner dialogue of the soul that constitutes understanding.

Those who talk about relativism presuppose that there could be a truth without the horizon of this conversation—that is, an absolute truth separate from our questions. The notion of merely relative truth exists only against the backdrop of a truth considered absolute. Yet how can we know when we have arrived at a truth that is absolute and no longer discussable? It could never be satisfactorily demonstrated. At best ex negativo: This truth would be non-finite, nontemporal, unconditional, and irreplaceable. Common to the defining qualities of absolute truth is the insistent negation of finitude, and in this negation one detects the basic moves of metaphysics. By metaphysics is meant—etymologically, historically, and thematically—the overcoming of temporality. What could make such transcendence possible? Do we have some access to an absolute truth? Nothing would be more welcome. According to Heidegger, however, such transcendence is based on the repression of our temporality; the claim to infinite truth results from the negation of finitude. But it belongs to finitude (if the tautology is not meaningless) that it remains finite, even and especially when the claim to infinitude is made.

A nonrelative truth has to be absolute. From the absence of absolute truth it does not follow, however, that we have no truth. As shown by the indubitable experiences of lies and falsehood, we make lasting claims to truth—that is, to things that make sense, that are in harmony with the things we experience and for which arguments, evidence, witnesses, and conclusions can be marshaled. To deny this would be mere sophistry. The truths we share and which we have good reason to affirm are neither arbitrary nor absolutely certain. The impulse to equate truth with methodologically certified knowledge is a modern Cartesianism. Even the methods that have proved so fertile over the course of scientific development were not absolute—that is, detached from human interests. As exemplified in Descartes's very meditation on the cogito, they were dependent on the inner conversation of the soul with itself—in this case, on the human striving for a higher degree of verifiability in a few branches of knowledge, especially the science of external nature. Rooted in its Cartesian origin, this highly successful model subsequently became the criterion of all knowledge whatsoever. From this perspective, everything else did indeed seem irremediably relativistic.

The philosophical age based on this dogma was that of historicism. The danger of relativism that it had in view and the untenability of its implications led hermeneutics to relativize this very criterion, and so to turn historicism against itself. In this process it appeared that historicism, though aware that knowledge is historically conditioned, had been measuring its own knowledge by a metaphysical or absolute criterion. The historicist fallacy, rich in consequences, consisted in considering the historical conversation—that every soul conducts within itself and is carried forward in every cognition of the world—to be an obstacle to truth. Hermeneutics was the first to discover that historicity is the motive force behind every effort to understand. "Historicity no longer defines the limit of reason and its claim to comprehend truth, but instead represents a positive condition for our knowledge of the truth. Thus the argument of historical relativism really loses all basis. A criterion of absolute truth reveals itself to be an abstract metaphysical idol and loses all methodological significance. Historicity stops summoning the ghost of historical relativism."[3]

Only a new historicism could infer from this that everything is therefore merely relative. It is necessary to free oneself from such a view in order to get closer to the truths we actually experience, share, and defend. One of the most important accomplishments of hermeneutics has been to show how philosophical thought, stuck since Hegel in the problem of historicism, can get beyond this cockeyed way of going about the question. This is what is suggested by the hermeneutic distinction between truth and method. Truth is to be found outside or beyond the narrow circle of knowledge that can be methodized. Of course, there is a good deal of nonsense outside method as well. Do we therefore need a "criterion" to separate the true from the false? What is meant by a criterion? Something like a formal, undeceptive means that we can automatically apply to all situations? This search for a criterion does not overcome historicism, since it still tries to replace the soul's questioning with method. What we forget is that the conversation which we never cease to be cannot accept everything and at the same moment experiences a capacity for truth within itself.

This faculty of critique and reason has its locus in the verbum interius, in the conversation with oneself that every person is. It deserves mentioning that the Stoic doctrine of the logos endiathetos originated in the context of an argument about the human race's distinguishing characteristic.[4] What separates humans from animals is not language or the external logos, for animals, too, can make audible sounds. The only thing that distinguishes us is that an inner deliberation is going on behind the voice. It allows us to play off the views that occur to us against each other and place them at a critical distance. Human beings are not hopelessly consigned to their instincts or the sounds that circulate in the air. What liberates us for the possibility of being human is the realm of free and measured reflection constituted by the inner logos, the most basic theme of hermeneutics, which has long since promised, and been called, reason.

Notes

Preface

1. Compare W. Schulz, "Die Aufhebung der Metaphysik in Heideggers Denken," in *Heideggers These vom Ende der Philosophie: Verhandlungen des Leidener Heidegger-Symposiums April 1984*, ed. M. F. Fresco, p. 33.

Introduction

1. Letter from M. Heidegger to O. Pöggeler, May 1, 1973, cited in O. Pöggeler, *Heidegger und die hermeneutische Philosophie*, p. 395.
2. Compare C. von Bormann, "Hermeneutik," in *Theologische Realencyklopädie* 15:130: "In Gadamer's work hermeneutics may well have received its last great formulation. Since then no new initiatives have been developed. Ricoeur's attempt at a 'philosophical hermeneutics' leads back to older forms of understanding meaning."

3. Compare H.-G. Gadamer, *Gesammelte Werke* 2:219. Hereafter cited as *GW.*

4. Compare C. F. Gethmann, "Philosophie als Vollzug und als Begriff: Heideggers Identitätsphilosophie des Lebens in der Vorlesung vom Wintersemester 1921/22 und ihr Verhältnis zu *Sein und Zeit,*" *Dilthey-Jahrbuch* 4 (1986–1987):29ff.

5. See P. Szondi, *Introduction to Literary Hermeneutics,* trans. M. Woodmansee, with a foreword by J. Weinsheimer; and J. Hörisch, *Die Wut des Verstehens,* as well as E. Behler, "Friedrich Schlegels Theorie des Verstehens: Hermeneutik oder Destruktion?" in *Die Aktualität der Frühromantik,* ed. E. Behler and J. Hörisch, pp. 141–160.

6. See E. Behler, "Schlegels Theorie," p. 145.

7. Compare W. Dilthey, "Das hermeneutische System Schleiermachers in der Auseinandersetzung mit der älteren protestantischen Hermeneutik" (1860), in *Gesammelte Schriften* (Göttingen, 1966), 14:243–262. Hereafter cited as *GS.*

8. Compare H.-E. Hasso Jaeger, "Studien zur Frühgeschichte der Hermeneutik," *Archiv für Begriffsgeschichte* 18 (1974):35–84; as well as L. Geldsetzer's illuminating introductions to his editions of J. M. Chladenius, *Einleitung zur richtigen Auslegung vernünftiger Reden und Schriften* (1742; Düsseldorf, 1969); and G. F. Meier, *Versuch einer allgemeinen Auslegungskunst* (1757; Düsseldorf, 1965).

9. Compare, e.g., F. Blass, "Hermeneutik und Kritik," in *Handbuch der klassischen Altertums-Wissenschaft in systematischer Darstellung,* pp. 148ff.

10. Reprint of the second edition of 1886: Darmstadt, 1966.

11. Compare F. Rodi, "Diltheys Kritik der historischen Vernunft—Programm oder System?" *Dilthey-Jahrbuch* 3 (1985):140–165.

12. O. F. Bollnow, *Dilthey: Eine Einführung in seine Philosophie* (1936), 4th ed.

13. In "Why the First Draft of *Being and Time* Was Never Published," *Journal of the British Society for Phenomenology* 20 (1989):3–22, T. Kisiel refers to the possibly purely contingent conditions that delayed the publication of Heidegger's magnum opus. It was originally destined for the *Vierteljahresschrift für Literaturwissenschaft und Geistesgeschichte* but was declined because of his highly mannered diction.

14. M. Heidegger, *Being and Time,* trans. John Macquarrie and Edward Robinson, pp. 61–62. Hereafter cited as *BT.*

15. H.-G. Gadamer, "Erinnerungen an Heideggers Anfänge," *Dilthey-Jahrbuch* 4 (1986–1987):16.

16. See C. F. Gethmann, "Philosophie als Vollzug," pp. 28ff.

17. See H.-G. Gadamer, *Truth and Method,* trans. Joel Weinsheimer and Donald G. Marshall, p. 255, hereafter cited as *TM,* and C. F. Gethmann, "Philosophie als Vollzug."

18. Thus Gadamer (*GW* 3:423) speaks of the "turn before the turn."

19. Compare Gadamer, *TM,* p. xxv; *Kleine Schriften* 4:259; *Das Erbe Hegels,* p. 45 (= *GW* 4:467); "Introduction," to *Seminar: Philosophische Hermeneutik,* ed. H.-

G. Gadamer and G. Boehm, pp. 39–40. See also my monograph *Hermeneutische Wahrheit? Zum Wahrheitsbegriff Hans-Georg Gadamers*, pp. 83ff.

20. K.-O. Apel, Introduction to *C. S. Peirce, Schriften zur Entstehung des Pragmatismus* 1:13. This tripartite division is still followed by R. Bubner, *Modern German Philosophy*. In *Nachmetaphysisches Denken*, J. Habermas adds structuralism as the fourth twentieth-century form of mind, in addition to the other three strands named above.

21. See H. Schnädelbach, "Was ist Neoaristotelianismus?" in *Moralität und Sittlichkeit*, ed. W. Kuhlmann (Frankfurt, 1986), pp. 38–63.

22. See, e.g., M. Riedel, ed., *Rehabilitierung der praktischen Philosophie*.

23. In *Hermeneutics as Politics*, S. Rosen includes under the rubric "hermeneutics" the present-day French philosophy of Derrida, Foucault, Deleuze, and Lyotard—a term they would hardly apply to themselves, although it is true that in his essay devoted to Nietzsche, Freud, and Marx, Foucault described these three authors as preparing the way for "modern hermeneutics."

24. Compare R. Rorty, *Philosophy and the Mirror of Nature;* J. Grondin, "Hermeneutical Truth and Its Historical Presuppositions: A Possible Bridge between Analysis and Hermeneutics," in *Anti-Foundationalism and Practical Reasoning,* ed. E. Simpson, pp. 45–58; R. Bubner, "Wohin tendiert die analytische Philosophie?" *Philosophische Rundschau* 34 (1987):257–281.

25. *BT,* p. 272.

26. *TM,* p. 344.

27. See H.-G. Gadamer, *Das Erbe Europas*, p. 123: "Misuse of power is the most fundamental problem of human social life, and complete prevention of this misuse is possible only in utopia."

28. On the universal perspectivism of Nietzsche, see W. Müller-Lauter, *Nietzsche: Seine Philosophie der Gegensätze und die Gegensätze seiner Philosophie,* and also his "Nietzsches Lehre vom Willen zur Macht," *Nietzsche-Studien* 3 (1974):1–60; J. Figl, *Interpretation als philosophisches Prinzip;* and V. Gerhardt, "Die Perspektive des Perspektivismus," *Nietzsche-Studien* 18 (1989): 260–281; A. Schrift, *Nietzsche and the Question of Interpretation: Between Hermeneutics and Deconstruction.*

29. J. Habermas, *Theorie des Kommunikativen Handelns* 1:72.

30. Ibid., 1:82.

31. Compare J. Habermas, *Nachmetaphysisches Denken* (1988), p. 55. It is no wonder, then, that despite his long-projected discourse theory of truth Habermas considers working out a theory of truth as a desideratum of his work (see his "Entgegnung," in *Kommunikatives Handeln,* ed. A. Honneth and H. Joas [Frankfurt, 1986], p. 327). The correspondence theory he has always considered untenable (*Nachmetaphysisches Denken*, p. 149).

32. Moreover, the position (argued by K.-O. Apel, e.g.) that hermeneutic universalism should be surpassed by transcendental reflection on the indubitable condi-

tions of argumentation must keep in mind that, for its part, it only represents an interpretation of the kind of argumentation taken as fundamental.

33. See V. Gerhardt, "Die Perspektive des Perspektivismus," p. 271.

34. P. Ricoeur, *Freud and Philosophy*, trans. Denis Savage. See also M. Foucault's positive recuperation of the hermeneutics of suspicion in "Nietzsche, Freud, Marx."

Chapter 1: On the Prehistory of Hermeneutics

1. John Findlay's book, *Kant and the Transcendental Object* (Oxford, 1981), for example, carries the subtitle *A Hermeneutic Study*, though the word *hermeneutic* occurs nowhere in it. He just means that the book consists in an interpretation of Kant.

2. G. Ebeling, "Art: Hermeneutik," in *Religion in Geschichte und Gegenwart*, 3d ed., 3:243.

3. J. Pépin, "Hermeneutik," in *Reallexikon für Antike und Christentum* 14:724. This includes considerable documentation from the entirety of Greek writing.

4. According to Aristotle's commentator, Ammonios (*Comm. in Arist. GR.* 4, 5, 5, 17/23). Cf. J. Pépin, "Hermeneutik," p. 723.

5. See J. Pépin, "Hermeneutik," p. 728. Here Pépin traces the thread of Aristotelian philosophy of language through the Stoa up to the exegeses of Philo. In fact, the distinction between an inner and an uttered logos is initiated in the first lines of Aristotle's *Peri hermeneias*, where the sound is described as the phonetic index of experiences residing in the soul. See also M. Pohlenz, "Die Begründung der abendländischen Sprachlehre durch die Stoa," *Nachrichten von der Gesellschaft der Wissenschaften zu Göttingen*, Philologische-Historische Klasse, n.s., 3 (1938–1939):151–198 (esp. 191ff.).

6. See L. Taran, "Academica: Plato, Philip of Opus, and the Pseudo-Platonic *Epinomis*," *Memoirs of the American Philosophical Society* 107 (1975):223–24.

7. See M. C. van der Kolf, "Prophetes," in *Pauly's Realencyclopädie der klassischen Altertumswissenschaft* 23, 1:797–816.

8. See P. Chantraine, *Dictionnaire étymologique de la langue grecque*, 4 vols. In "Der Gott Hermes und die Hermeneutik," *Tijdschrift voor Filosofie* 30 (1968):525–635, F. K. Mayr argues for retaining the connection between Hermes and hermeneutics.

9. Compare Aristotle's equation of hermeneia and dialektos (manner of speaking, language, dialect) in *De Anima*, 2.2.420b.18–20.

10. See J. Pépin, "Hermeneutik," p. 726 (with considerable documentation).

11. This book belongs to the Peripatetic heritage (see the collected edition: Aristotle, *The Poetics;* Longinus, *On the Sublime;* and Demetrius, *On Style* [Cambridge, 1927]), but its date is uncertain. See also F. K. Kerényi, "Origine e

senso dell'ermeneutica," in *Ermeneutica e tradizione,* ed. E. Castelli (Padua, 1963), p. 134.

12. Boethius, *Commentarium in librum Aristotelis "Peri hermeneias," liber primus,* ed. C. Meiser (Leipzig, 1877), p. 32 (rpt. in *Commentaries on Aristotle's "De interpretatione"* [New York, 1987]).

13. De migratione Abrahami, 1:12 *(Les oeuvres de Philon d'Alexandrie* [Paris, 1965], 14:100 [hermeneia = prophora logou]).

14. Clement of Alexandria, *Stromateis,* 8.20.5. Cf. J. Pépin, "Hermeneutik," p. 732. Moreover, H.-E. Hasso Jaeger, "Studien," pp. 64–65, makes it very clear that hermeneia basically means bringing thought to expression—i.e., the transference of the thought to utterance. However, Hasso Jaeger is completely mistaken to imply, contrary to the thesis of present-day hermeneutics, that hermeneia so understood has nothing to do with interpretation.

15. Compare J. Pépin, "Hermeneutik," p. 744.

16. See H.-J. Klauck's careful investigation of the word in *Allegorie und Allegorese in synoptischen Gleichnistexten,* p. 39.

17. Compare *Stoa und Stoiker,* trans. M. Pohlenz, 2d ed., p. 29.

18. Cicero, *De natura deorum,* 2.25. See J. Pépin, *Mythe et allégorie: Les origines grecques et les contestations judéo-chrétiennes,* 2d ed., pp. 125–127.

19. Pseudo-Herakleitos, *Questiones Homericae,* ed. F. Oelmann (Leipzig, 1910), p. 2. See also H.-J. Klauck, *Allegorie,* pp. 45–53; and J. Pépin, *Mythe,* pp. 159–167.

20. In *Allegorie,* p. 39, H.-J. Klauck refers to Stoic philosophy of language in this connection.

21. See H.-J. Klauck, *Allegorie,* p. 52.

22. See H. de Lubac, *Histoire et esprit: L'intelligence de l'Ecriture d'après Origène,* p. 160.

23. See H.-J. Klauck, *Allegorie,* p. 39: "The one rational logos, which holds the entire whole together, realizes itself in language, myth, and poetry as well."

24. Fragment 11 (Diels): "Homer and Hesiod have ascribed to the gods everything that is considered disgraceful and contemptible among men: theft, adultery, and reciprocal betrayal."

25. See J. Pépin, *Mythe,* pp. 112–121.

26. See the recent collection of J. Pépin's essays, *La tradition de l'allégorie: De Philon d'Alexandrie à Dante.*

27. See I. Christiansen, *Die Technik der allegorischen Auslegungswissenschaft bei Philo von Alexandrien,* p. 134.

28. See J. Pépin, "Les indices de l'allégorie," *La tradition,* pp. 34ff.

29. See J. Pépin, *La tradition,* pp. 36ff.; and I. Christiansen, *Die Technik,* p. 152.

30. This is clearly the point at which Philo's above-mentioned readoption of the doctrine of outer and inner logos comes into play. See K. Otte, *Das Sprachver-*

ständnis bei Philo von Alexandrien: Sprache als Mittel der Hermeneutik, pp. 131–142.

31. *Philo of Alexandria: The Contemplative Life, the Giants, and Selections,* trans. and ed. David Winston (New York, 1981), p. 55.

32. On Philo's esoteric background, see J. Pépin, *La tradition,* p. 13. This background remained profoundly significant for the Church Fathers. A few passages in the New Testament (esp. in the fourth Gospel: "The word came into the world, but the world knew him not") seem to suggest a mystical mode of reading. See John 1:5, 3:12.

33. See H.-J. Klauck, *Allegorie,* p. 43.

34. Here the heritage of Plato's *Phaedrus* (274–278) is apparent. On the universality of this problematic in Plato, see the essay by T. Szlezák, "Dialogform und Esoterik: Zur Deutung des platonischen Dialogs 'Phaidros,'" *Museum Helveticum* 35 (1978):18–32, and his book *Platon und die Schriftlichkeit der Philosophie.*

35. H.-J. Klauck, *Allegorie,* p. 98.

36. That is, until the epoch-making essay by H. de Lubac, "Typologie et allégorisme," *Recherches de science religieuse* 34 (1947):180–266.

37. Augustine still speaks of "allegorica praefiguratio" in the Old Testament (*De civitate Dei,* 17.5.n2). See H. de Lubac, "Typologie," p. 189.

38. Thus G. Ebeling, "Hermeneutik," p. 247. See also J. Pépin's judgment in his lexicon article on hermeneutics, p. 753: "the most significant text by far on the theme" of hermeneutics.

39. See J. Daniélou, *Origène* (1948), pp. 179–190, as opposed to H. de Lubac, *Histoire et esprit* (1950), pp. 159–161, who minimizes Origen's dependence on Philo in order to emphasize the Pauline strand.

40. Origen follows an older reading; today the text reads "thirty."

41. Origen, *Über die Prinzipien,* 4.2.4.

42. On Origen's terminological and in part substantive oscillations on this question, see H. de Lubac, *Histoire et esprit* (1950), pp. 141ff.

43. *Über die Prinzipien,* 4.2.6.

44. Ibid., 4.4.10, which refers to 4.1.16.

45. See J. Daniélou, *Origène,* p. 180. Cf. H. de Lubac, *Histoire et esprit,* p. 107: "If there were not a secret intention of the Holy Ghost beneath the letter, an intention that would point beyond the literal, then this letter itself would often seem incredible, either because of its occasionally shocking nature, its apparent contradictions, its illogicalities, or finally by virtue of its sheer banality. . . . The spiritual meaning that discloses the true value of the text also justifies the literal in its literality. It serves to save the literal."

46. See J. Daniélou, *Origène,* p. 147; and H. de Lubac, *Histoire et esprit,* p. 170.

47. See J. Daniélou, *Origène,* p. 163.

48. Ibid., p. 172.

49. *Über die Prinzipien,* 4.3.5. See J. Daniélou, *Origène,* p. 182; and esp. H. de Lubac, *Histoire et esprit,* pp. 92–93.

50. See H. de Lubac's four-volume exposition, *Exégèse médiévale: Les quatre sens de l'Ecriture.*

51. *Summa theologica,* 1.10, conclusio.

52. See the most important book on the subject by Christoph Schäublin, *Untersuchungen zur Methode und Herkunft der antiochenischen Exegese.* On Theodoret of Cyrrhus, see A. Viciano, "'Homeron ex Homero saphenizein': Principios hermenéuticos de Teodoreto de Ciro en su Comentario a las Epístolas paulinas," *Scripta Theologica* 21 (1989):13–61.

53. It will appear in volume 59/60 of the *Gesamtausgabe.* In the meantime, see the report of J. Barash, "Les sciences de l'histoire et le problème de la théologie: Autour du cours inédit de Heidegger sur saint Augustin," in *Saint Augustin,* ed. P. Ranson (Lausanne, 1988), pp. 421–433; as well as O. Pöggeler's statements in *Der Denkweg Martin Heideggers,* 2d ed. (Pfullingen, 1983), pp. 38ff.

54. H.-G. Gadamer, "Erinnerungen an Heideggers Anfänge," p. 21.

55. *TM,* p. 418.

56. G. Ebeling, "Hermeneutik," p. 249.

57. M. Heidegger, *Ontologie (Hermeneutik der Faktizität),* ed. K. Bröcker-Oltmans, p. 12. Heidegger cites Augustine in Latin. English translation from *On Christian Doctrine,* trans. D. W. Robertson, Jr. (Indianapolis, 1958), p. 78.

58. Heidegger, *Ontologie,* p. 12.

59. See *De trinitate,* 1.2: "Sancta Scriptura parvulis congruens."

60. *On Christian Doctrine,* 1.35.

61. Ibid., 2.7.

62. Ibid., 2.12.

63. Ibid., 3.18.

64. Ibid., 3.1: "ut per nos instrui valeat, sciat ambiguatatem Scripturae aut in verbis propriis esse, aut in translatis."

65. Ibid., 3.29.

66. Ibid., 3.37.

67. *De trinitate,* 15.10.19: "verbum est quod in corde dicimus: quod nec graecum est, nec latinum, nec linguae alicujus alterius."

68. Ibid., 15.11.20.

69. Ibid. On the construal of hermeneia as the mediation of thought, see also Augustine, *De civitate Dei,* 8.14: "ideo Hermes Graece, quod sermo vel interpretatio, quae ad sermonem utique pertinet; hermeneia dicitur . . . , per sermonem omnia cogitata enuntiantur."

70. See I Cor. 1:24. Cf. *De trinitate,* 4.20.27; 4.1.1; 7.3.4–6; 15.12.222, and passim.

71. *De trinitate,* 15.15.24: "numquid verbum nostrum de sola scientia nostra nascitur?"

72. Ibid., 15.15.25.
73. See *TM,* p. 421.
74. Ibid.
75. Ibid., p. 422.
76. Ibid., p. 427.
77. See ibid., pp. 427–428: "The unity of the word that explicates itself in the multiplicity of words manifests something that is not covered by the structure of logic and that brings out the *character of language as event.*"
78. Ibid., p. 11 (my italics).
79. H.-G. Gadamer, "Von der Wahrheit des Wortes," *Jahresgabe der Martin-Heidegger-Gesellschaft* (1988), p. 17.
80. *GW* 2:52; see also on the same page: "It is not judgments but questions that have primacy in logic, as the Platonic dialogues and the dialectical origins of Greek logic show as well."
81. Compare H.-G. Gadamer's essay, "Grenzen der Sprache," *Evolution und Sprache: Über Entstehung und Wesen der Sprache, Herrenalber Texte* 66 (1985):89–99.
82. *GW* 2:185.
83. "Grenzen der Sprache," pp. 97–98.
84. G. Ebeling, "Hermeneutik," p. 249.
85. G. Gusdorf's book suffers from this simplification: *Les origines de l'herméneutique,* esp. pp. 68–70, 77 ("leurs oeuvres doivent être rangées au musée des erreurs et des horreurs de l'histoire").
86. H. de Lubac, *Exégèse médiévale;* H. Brinkmann, *Mittelalterliche Hermeneutik* (Tübingen, 1980).
87. See esp. Gadamer's essay that arose from the immediate context of *TM,* and was described in the second volume of his *GW* as the first "further development" of *TM:* "Zur Problematik des Selbstverständnisses: Ein hermeneutischer Beitrag zur Frage der Entmythologisierung" (*GW* 2:121–132), as well as the numerous religiously oriented works and his relation to Marburg theology in *Heideggers Wege* (Tübingen, 1983; *GW* 2:92–120). Generally speaking, Gadamer's presentations of the history of hermeneutics are heavily influenced by the Protestant tradition: including those in *TM* itself, in the hermeneutics article in *Historisches Wörterbuch der Philosophie,* and the introduction to the volume he edited with G. Boehm, *Seminar: Philosophische Hermeneutik.*
88. According to the first sentence of Dilthey's essay "Das hermeneutische System Schleiermachers in der Auseinandersetzung mit der älteren Hermeneutik" (*GS* 14, 1:597). On this subject, see also C. von Bormann, "Hermeneutik," p. 112.
89. See G. Ebeling, "Die Anfänge von Luthers Hermeneutik," *Zeitschrift für Theologie und Kirche* 48 (1951):174n.
90. Thus G. Ebeling, ibid., proceeds accordingly.

91. See ibid., p. 176.

92. On the eventful life of Flacius, see the details in L. Geldsetzer's introduction to the reprint of the second part of the *Clavis: De ratione cognoscendi sacras literas,* in *Über den Erkenntnisgrund der heiligen Schrift.*

93. "Introduction," *Clavis,* n.p.: "horrendum in modum blasphemant, vociferantes Scripturam esse obscuram, ambiguam, non etiam sufficientem ad plenam institutionem hominis Christiani ad salutem." See also W. Dilthey, *GS* 14, 1:600ff.

94. Thus L. Geldsetzer (in the introduction to *De ratione*) rightly sees the significance of the *Clavis* in the "step that Flacius took toward grounding theological dogma exclusively in the text of the Bible, thereby giving biblical exegesis pride of place within scientific theology."

95. Flacius, *De ratione,* p. 7.

96. Ibid., p. 25.

97. See L. Geldsetzer, introduction to *De ratione.*

98. Flacius, *De ratione,* p. 27.

99. W. Dilthey, *GS* 14, 1:602.

100. R. Simon, *Histoire critique du Vieux Testament* (Rotterdam, 1685), p. 430: "Pour ce qui est des règles qu'il prescrit, comme d'expliquer un passage obscur par un autre qui est clair et d'avoir de bonnes versions de la Bible, on les peut trouver dans les Livres des Pères."

101. See J. Wach, *Das Verstehen* 1:14.

102. Paying attention to the scope of the text, which Melanchthon also advocated (see H.-G. Gadamer, *GW* 2:282), had also been an ancient exegetical rule. Ultimately it also goes back to Plato's warning in the *Phaedrus* that in writing down speeches the whole context of meaning needs to be taken into account.

103. Flacius, *De ratione,* p. 23.

104. Ibid., p. 69.

Chapter 2: Hermeneutics between Grammar and Critique

1. See the overview by C. von Bormann, "Kritik," in *Historisches Wörterbuch der Philosophie,* ed. J. Ritter, 4:1249–1262.

2. This omission was remedied by two pieces published in the seventies. See *GW* 2:276–291 and 292–300.

3. H.-E. Hasso Jaeger, "Studien," pp. 35–84.

4. Titles then were awfully long: *Idea boni interpretis et malitiosi calumniatoris quae obscuritate dispulsa, verum sensum a falso discernere in omnibus auctorum scriptis ac orationibus docet, & plene respondet ad quaestionem Unde scis hunc esse sensum, non alium? Omnium facultatum studiosis perquam utilis.* The book stayed in print up to a fifth edition in Augsburg in 1670.

5. *Idea boni interpretis,* Art. 1, §3: "Omne scibile habet aliquam respondentem scientiam philosophicam. Modus interpretandi est aliquod scibile. Ergo: Modus interpretandi habet aliquam respondentem scientiam philosophicam." See L. Geldsetzer, "Che cos'è l'ermeneutica?" *Rivista di filosofia neoscolastica* 73 (1983):594–622.

6. *Idea boni interpretis,* Art. 1, §6: "Una generalis est hermeneutica, quamvis in obiectis particularibus sit diversitas."

7. See H.-E. Hasso Jaeger, "Studien," p. 50.

8. See ibid. and H.-G. Gadamer, *GW* 2:279, 296.

9. Johannes Clauberg, *Logica vetus et nova* (1654), cited from M. Beetz's useful discussion: "Nachgeholte Hermeneutik: Zum Verhältnis von Interpretations- und Logiklehren in Barock und Aufklärung," *Deutsche Vierteljahresschrift für Literaturwissenschaft und Geistesgeschichte* 55 (1981):591.

10. See H.-E. Hasso Jaeger, "Studien," p. 52.

11. Ibid.

12. Ibid., p. 56; see also M. Beetz, "Nachgeholte Hermeneutik," p. 598.

13. *Idea boni interpretis,* p. 4: "Hermeneuticam . . . organi Aristotelici adjectione novae civitatis aucturi." See H.-E. Hasso Jaeger, "Studien," p. 51; and H.-G. Gadamer, *GW* 2:287.

14. *Idea boni interpretis,* p. 29: "interpres enim est analyticus orationum omnium quatenus sunt obscurae, sed exponibiles, ad discernendum verum sensum a falso."

15. For the details, see H.-E. Hasso Jaeger, "Studien," p. 46; and on the scopus, see M. Beetz, "Nachgeholte Hermeneutik," p. 612 (*Idea boni interpretis,* p. 231: "scopus est certissima interpretationis clavis").

16. For the titles, see the above-cited articles of Hasso Jaeger, Geldsetzer, and Beetz.

17. F. Schleiermacher, *Hermeneutik und Kritik,* ed. M. Frank (Frankfurt, 1977), p. 75.

18. See H.-G. Gadamer, *GW* 2:288.

19. J. M. Chladenius, *Einleitung zur richtigen Auslegung vernünftiger Reden und Schriften.* On the overcoming of hermeneutics by logic in the eighteenth century, see M. Beetz, "Nachgeholte Hermeneutik," p. 608. For an evaluation of Chladenius's contribution to philology and literary criticism, see P. Szondi, *Introduction to Literary Hermeneutics.*

20. On the four kinds of obscurity, see J. M. Chladenius, *Einleitung,* preface, n.p.

21. F. Schleiermacher, *Hermeneutik und Kritik,* p. 71.

22. F. A. Wolf, *Museum der Altertumswissenschaften.*

23. See A. Böckh, *Enzyklopädie und Methodenlehre der philologischen Wissenschaften,* ed. E. Bratuschek, pt. 1: *Formale Theorie der philologischen Wissenschaft,* 2d ed. Thus Böckh had thereby removed grammar from among the philological sci-

ences (on this move, see G. Pflug, "Hermeneutik und Kritik: August Böckh in der Tradition des Begriffspaars," *Archiv für Begriffsgeschichte* 18 (1975):138–196). I should also mention the compendium—probably the last compiled in this spirit—published by F. Blass in 1892 under the title "Hermeneutik und Kritik."

24. F. Schlegel is one. In his view, there is a genuine antinomy concerning the relative primacy of critique or hermeneutics (F. Schlegel, *Zur Philologie,* in the *Kritische Friedrich-Schlegel-Ausgabe,* ed. E. Behler, 16:55). Schlegel expresses it as follows: "If one goes by the historical impression, the restoration of the text is most important. The *higher* criticism belongs to this task as well. — Likewise in respect to art, virtuosity, etc., as well, hermeneutics requires the aid of critique. No! They have in every respect, at least in the scholarly, the same rank. Of what use is the text to me if I don't understand it?"

25. J. M. Chladenius, *Einleitung,* preface.

26. See J. M. Chladenius, *Einleitung,* §176, p. 96: "Thus there is no doubt that interpreting according to the rules corresponds to a science that we call hermeneutics. In our language it is rightly called the art of interpretation."

27. See L. Geldsetzer's introduction to Chladenius's *Einleitung,* p. xx.

28. J. M. Chladenius, *Einleitung,* §309.

29. Ibid.

30. Reprinted with an introduction by L. Geldsetzer (Düsseldorf, 1965).

31. Ibid., §1.

32. Ibid., §3.

33. Ibid., §9.

34. See G. W. F. Leibniz, *Betrachtungen über die Erkenntnis, die Wahrheit und die Idee,* Gerhardt edition, 4:422ff. Also to be found in the collection *Fünf Schriften zur Logik und Metaphysik* (Stuttgart, 1966).

35. G. F. Meier, *Versuch,* §9.

36. Ibid., §35.

37. Ibid., §118: "That meaning of discourse is hermeneutically true (sensus hermeneutice verus) which is a genuine signification of the discourse. . . . Now, since a finite author can deceive and be deceived, one cannot, from the hermeneutic truth of a meaning, deduce its logical, metaphysical, or moral truth."

38. Ibid., §123. On the enormous significance of authorial intention for Enlightenment hermeneutics, see M. Beetz, "Nachgeholte Hermeneutik," p. 611.

39. G. F. Meier, *Versuch,* §138.

40. Ibid., §136.

41. Ibid., §39.

42. Ibid., §134.

43. Ibid., §249.

44. Ibid., §251.

45. Even in the rationalist A. G. Baumgarten, the mantic enjoys a privileged place. It is divided into almost thirty subdivisions, among them onirocritique or the interpretation of dreams, rhabdomantic (interpreting using little sticks), libanomantic (using sacred smoke), alectriomantic (using chickens), and so forth. See A. G. Baumgarten, *Texte zur Grundlegung der Ästhetik* (Hamburg, 1983), appendix.

46. It appears as early as his youthful work, *Methodus Nova Discendai Docendaeque Jurisprudentiae,* pt. 2, §67. On this, see H.-E. Hasso Jaeger, "Studien," p. 74n.

47. See L. Geldsetzer, introduction to Chladenius's *Einleitung,* p. xviii: "With Georg Friedrich Meier's *Versuch einer allgemeinen Auslegungskunst* . . . all these tendencies toward the constitution of a universal hermeneutics came to a provisional end. The special hermeneutics of the two great dogmatic disciplines, theology and jurisprudence, completely stifled it, and Enlightenment philosophy also shied away from cultivating the knowledge gained by the labor [of interpretation] because it believed itself capable of developing such knowledge much more easily by means of its own thought."

48. J. M. Chladenius, *Einleitung,* §187.

49. Dilthey tried to view it as a prefiguration of psychological interpretation. Heidegger's overview of the history of hermeneutics (*Gesamtausgabe* 63:13) mentions only Rambach's *Institutiones hermeneuticae sacrae* of 1723, who is the only one between Flacius and Schleiermacher he quotes extensively. Gadamer is indebted to pietism for his theory of the fundamental function of the "subtilitas applicandi." Moreover, at one point in his debate with Derrida, Gadamer mentions the pietistic undertones of his own conception of self-understanding, which refers less to self-presence than to the impossibility of it ("Dekonstruktion und Hermeneutik," in *Philosophie und Poesie: Otto Pöggeler zum 60. Geburtstag,* ed. A. Gethmann-Siefert, 1:8).

50. On pietism's influence on romanticism, see H.-G. Gadamer, *GW* 2:97; and G. Gusdorf, *Les origines,* p. 118.

51. A. H. Francke, *Praelectiones hermeneuticae ad viam dextre indagandi et exponendi sensum Sacrae Scripturae,* p. 196: "Omni, quem homines proferunt sermoni, ex ipsa animi destinatione unde is procedit, affectus inest." See W. Dilthey, *GS* 14, 1:619. A theory of affects had already been projected in the appendix to Francke's *Manductio ad lectionem Scripturae Sacrae* (1693).

52. See W. Dilthey, *GS* 14, 1:619.

53. Cited from the excerpt in *Seminar: Philosophische Hermeneutik,* ed. H.-G. Gadamer and G. Boehm, p. 62.

54. Ibid., p. 65.

55. From this double task, Meier (*Versuch,* §1) derives his definition of hermeneutics as the science of the rules to be observed "in order (1) to know the sense of something said and (2) convey it to others." See also J. A. Ernesti, *Institutio inter-*

pretis Novi Testamenti, §4, p. 4: "Interpretatio igitur omnis duabus rebus continetur, sententiarum (idearum) verbis subiectarum intellectu, earumque idonea explicatione. Unde in bone interprete esse debet subtilitas intelligendi, et subtilitas explicandi."

56. See M. Beetz, "Nachgeholte Hermeneutik," p. 602.

57. *GW* 2:80.

Chapter 3: Romantic Hermeneutics and Schleiermacher

1. F. Schleiermacher, *Hermeneutik und Kritik* (1977), p. 75.

2. P. Szondi, *Einführung in die literarische Hermeneutik,* p. 136. [*Introduction to Literary Hermeneutics,* trans. M. Woodmansee (London, 1994).]

3. For a less rabid assessment of the Kantian revolution, see my *Kant et le problème de la philosophie: L'a priori* and *Emmanuel Kant: Avant/Après.*

4. See P. Szondi, *Einführung,* pp. 135–136.

5. G. A. F. Ast, *Grundlinien der Grammatik, Hermeneutik und Kritik,* §71 (cf. the excerpt in H.-G. Gadamer and G. Boehm, eds. *Seminar: Philosophische Hermeneutik,* p. 112).

6. Ibid., §71 (Gadamer and Boehm, pp. 113–114).

7. Ibid., §75 (Gadamer and Boehm, p. 116).

8. Ibid. On the prefigurative function of this theory of the circle, see W. Dilthey, *GS* 14, 1:657–659.

9. Friedrich Schlegel's "Philosophie der Philologie," with an introduction by Josef Körner, *Logos* 17 (1928):1–72. Now titled *Zur Philologie* in the *Kritische Friedrich-Schlegel-Ausgabe* 16:33–81, hereafter cited as *KA.* On Schleiermacher's acquaintance with these notebooks, see H. Patsch, "Friedrich Schlegels 'Philosophie der Philologie' und Schleiermachers frühe Entwürfe zur Hermeneutik: Zur Frühgeschichte der romantischen Hermeneutik," *Zeitschrift für Theologie und Kirche* 63 (1966):432–472. See also Dilthey's learned discussion of Schlegel in *GS* 14, 1:670–677.

10. F. Schlegel, 16:38 (3:49).

11. See the programmatic but also symptomatically uncertain assertion in *KA* 16:69 (4:93): "Even a philosophy of hermeneutics could probably make great strides. It, too, is perhaps a real science, just like grammar. Isn't it rather an art?—If it's art, it's science too."

12. *KA* 16:37 (3:25).

13. See E. Behler, "Friedrich Schlegels Theorie des Verstehens," pp. 141–160. See also Schlegel's essay "On Unintelligibility" (1800).

14. For what follows, see W. Virmond, "Neue Textgrundlagen zu Schleiermachers früher Hermeneutik," *Schleiermacher-Archiv* 1 (1985):575–590.

15. A copy of this hitherto unknown lecture has recently been published: "Friedrich Schleiermachers 'Allgemeine Hermeneutik von 1809–10,'" ed. W. Virmond, *Schleiermacher-Archiv* 1 (1985):1269–1310. Following the well-known editions by Lücke, Kimmerle, and M. Frank, it offers a refreshing overview of Schleiermacher's hermeneutic project.

16. See W. Virmond, "Neue Textgrundlagen," p. 576.

17. According to M. Frank, introduction to *Hermeneutik und Kritik,* p. 57.

18. W. Hübener writes with good reason that "a relatively complete historical ignorance of the hermeneutic tradition made it easier for Schleiermacher scholars to emphasize Schleiermacher's originality." In "Schleiermacher und die hermeneutische Tradition," *Schleiermacher-Archiv* 1 (1985):565.

19. *Hermeneutik und Kritik,* ed. M. Frank, p. 76.

20. Ibid., p. 78.

21. F. Schleiermacher, "Allgemeine Hermeneutik von 1809–10," p. 1276.

22. Ibid.: "The task is to understand the meaning of an utterance on the basis of language."

23. *Hermeneutik,* ed. H. Kimmerle (1959), p. 38.

24. "Allgemeine Hermeneutik von 1809–10," p. 1276.

25. Ibid.

26. Though Schleiermacher's views changed little, his terminology changed a good deal, and this has caused no little confusion among his interpreters. See H. Birus, "Schleiermachers Begriff der 'Technischen Interpretation,'" *Schleiermacher-Archiv* 1 (1985):591–600.

27. *Hermeneutik und Kritik,* ed. M. Frank, p. 92; *Hermeneutik,* ed. H. Kimmerle, pp. 29–30.

28. See W. H. Pleger, *Schleiermachers Philosophie,* pp. 173–174; and M. Potepa, "Hermeneutik und Dialektik bei Schleiermacher," *Schleiermacher-Archiv* 1 (1985):492.

29. See W. Virmond, "Neue Textgrundlage," p. 582.

30. "Allgemeine Hermeneutik von 1809–10," p. 1272.

31. F. Schleiermacher, "Über den Begriff der Hermeneutik," *Hermeneutik und Kritik,* ed. M. Frank, p. 328.

32. *Hermeneutik und Kritik,* ed. M. Frank, pp. 94, 104; "Über den Begriff der Hermeneutik," p. 325; "Allgemeine Hermeneutik von 1809–10," p. 1308. On the history of this maxim before Schleiermacher, see O. F. Bollnow, "Was heißt einen Schriftsteller besser verstehen, als er sich selber verstanden hat?" (1940), in Bollnow's *Studien zur Hermeneutik* 1:48–72.

33. See W. Hinrichs, "Standpunktfrage und Gesprächsmodell: Das vergessene Elementarproblem der hermeneutisch-dialektischen Wissenschaftstheorie seit Schleiermacher," *Schleiermacher-Archiv* 1 (1985):529.

34. See *Hermeneutik und Kritik,* ed. M. Frank, pp. 81, 360; see also Frank's "Par-

tialität oder Universalität der 'Divination,'" *Deutsche Vierteljahresschrift für Literaturwissenschaft und Geistesgeschichte* 58 (1984):249, and W. H. Pleger, *Schleiermachers Philosophie,* p. 186.

35. See M. Frank, *Das individuelle Allgemeine: Textstrukturierung und -interpretation nach Schleiermacher,* pp. 313ff.

36. This is H. Kimmerle's main thesis in "Die Hermeneutik Schleiermachers im Zusammenhang seines spekulativen Denkens" (Ph.D. diss., University of Heidelberg, 1957). As far as we can tell, the basic outlines of this pattern of development have not yet met definitive refutation. This is confirmed by M. Potepa ("Hermeneutik und Dialektik") and H. Birus ("Schleiermachers Begriff"). The only thing still under dispute is what "psychological" means. We think it can be rescued from the charge of trivial "psychologism."

37. M. Potepa ("Hermeneutik und Dialektik," p. 495) rightly views this as the underlying motivation of Schleiermacher's later hermeneutics.

38. H.-G. Gadamer, *TM,* p. 196.

39. W. Dilthey, *GS* 14, 1:689.

40. "Über den Begriff der Hermeneutik," p. 321.

41. F. Schleiermacher, *Dialektik,* ed. R. Odebrecht, §1.5. See the excerpt in *Hermeneutik und Kritik,* ed. M. Frank, p. 419.

42. *Hermeneutik und Kritik,* ed. M. Frank, p. 71.

43. "Über den Begriff der Hermeneutik," pp. 315–316.

44. See W. H. Pleger, *Schleiermachers Philosophie,* p. 10. On the relation between dialectic and hermeneutics, see also the work by Potepa and Hinrichs cited above, as well as "Hermeneutik," by C. von Bormann, p. 118.

45. "Über den Begriff der Hermeneutik," p. 316.

46. Ibid., p. 335.

47. Ibid.

Chapter 4: The Problems of Historicism

1. A. Böckh, *Enzyklopädie,* p. 75.

2. Ibid., p. 10.

3. Ibid., p. 80.

4. Ibid., p. 11. See F. Rodi, *Erkenntnis des Erkannten* (Frankfurt, 1990), pp. 70ff., for the interpretation of this formula as indicative of the fact that interpretation is in principle interminable.

5. Böckh, *Enzyklopädie,* p. 76.

6. Ibid., p. 46.

7. J. G. Droysen, *Historik,* p. 324.

8. J. G. Droysen, "Erhebung der Geschichte zum Rang einer Wissenschaft," ibid., p. 386.

9. J. G. Droysen, "Kunst und Methode," ibid., p. 417. See also Droysen's *Texte zur Geschichtstheorie*, ed. G. Birtsch and J. Rüsen, p. 56: "It would be silly not to celebrate the masterly progress of the mathematical-physical disciplines; the fact that their presuppositions, their methods, their results have come to be considered the sole scientific norms of validity is no charge against them but at most a reproach to the spheres of scientific life that are defenseless against them."

10. "Kunst und Methode," p. 424.

11. Ibid., p. 378.

12. See *Texte zur Geschichtstheorie*, p. 56.

13. *Historik*, pp. 22, 328.

14. Ibid., p. 22.

15. See ibid., p. 20.

16. Ibid., p. 133.

17. Ibid., p. 23.

18. Ibid., p. 316.

19. Ibid., pp. 25, 329.

20. Ibid., p. 27.

21. Ibid., pp. 28, 322, 394, 422; and *Texte zur Geschichtstheorie*, p. 61.

22. *Historik*, pp. 28ff.

23. Ibid., p. 14.

24. Ibid., p. 203.

25. See *TM*, p. 216.

26. *Historik*, p. 357.

27. Ibid. On the idea of historical research as knowledge of God, see *Texte zur Geschichtstheorie*, pp. 17, 20f., and 38.

28. *Historik*, p. 358.

29. Ibid., p. 316.

30. This phrase occurs as early as a diary entry of 1860 (see *Der junge Dilthey: Ein Lebensbild in Briefen und Tagebüchern, 1852–1870*, ed. C. [Dilthey] Misch).

31. W. Dilthey, *GS* 1:xvii.

32. Ibid.

33. Ibid., 19:60. See also 5:148: "Without these relations to the psychic structure in which their relations are grounded, the human sciences are an aggregate, a collection of things, but no system."

34. See Dilthey's letter of March 9, 1895, to P. Natorp in H.-U. Lessing, "Briefe an Dilthey anläßlich der Veröffentlichung seiner 'Ideen über eine beschreibende und zergliedernde Psychologie,'" *Dilthey-Jahrbuch* 3 (1985):200.

35. The projections and elaborations for this second volume have been collected in *GS* 19, published in 1982. Despite this volume's excellent contributions to the study of these matters, it still cannot be said that the precise meaning of epistemology, logic, and methodology emerges here with satisfactory clarity. An

insightful reconstruction is to be found in H.-U. Lessing's monograph, *Die Idee einer Kritik der historischen Vernunft.*

36. H. Ebbinghaus, *Über erklärende und beschreibende Psychologie* (1896), rpt. in *Materialien zur Philosophie Wilhelm Diltheys,* ed. F. Rodi and H.-U. Lessing, pp. 45–87.

37. *GS* 5:144.

38. Ibid., p. 173.

39. Ibid., p. 193.

40. Hermeneutics is only occasionally mentioned here, usually in a general list along with "critique." See *GS* 19:265, 293, 336. It has virtually no place, and need have none, in Lessing's faithful attempt (see n. 36) to reconstruct the projected Critique of Historical Reason.

41. *GS* 7:80.

42. Ibid., p. 230.

43. Ibid., p. 82. On the central significance of deliberating with oneself in Dilthey, see M. Riedel, "Das erkenntnistheoretische Motiv in Diltheys Theorie der Geisteswissenschaften," in *Hermeneutik und Dialektik,* ed. R. Bubner, K. Cramer, and R. Wiehl, rpt. in Riedel's *Verstehen oder Erklären? Zur Theorie und Geschichte der hermeneutischen Wissenschaften* (Stuttgart, 1978).

44. *GS* 7:85.

45. Ibid.

46. O. F. Bollnow, *Dilthey: Eine Einführung in seine Philosophie* (1936), 4th ed. In *Du texte à l'action: Essais d'herméneutique* 2:81ff., Paul Ricoeur remains indebted to this reading.

47. See F. Rodi, "Diltheys Kritik der historischen Vernunft—Programm oder System?" *Dilthey-Jahrbuch* 3(1985):140–165 (where he points out Dilthey's tendency to give various degrees of emphasis at various times to the several elements of a unitary starting point); see also M. Ermarth, *Wilhelm Dilthey: The Critique of Historical Reason,* p. 235.

48. *GS* 5:318.

49. Ibid., p. 333.

50. See, e.g., G. Misch, *Lebensphilosophie und Phänomenologie: Eine Auseinandersetzung der Diltheyschen Richtung mit Heidegger und Husserl,* 2d ed. (1931); and O. F. Bollnow, *Studien zur Hermeneutik.*

51. See H.-G. Gadamer, *TM,* pp. 231ff.

52. *GS* 7:217–218.

Chapter 5: Heidegger: Hermeneutics as the Interpretation of Existence

1. Heidegger himself refers to his early attention to Schleiermacher and Dilthey (in *On the Way to Language*) as well as to the fact that his first introduction to

hermeneutics occurred within a theological context. As a theology student, Heidegger actually attended a lecture on hermeneutics in the summer semester of 1910; see T. Sheehan, "Heidegger's Lehrjahre," in *The Collegium Phaenomenologicum: The First Ten Years* (Dordrecht, 1988), p. 92. On Heidegger's early attention to Dilthey, see F. Rodi's "Die Bedeutung Diltheys für die Konzeption von *Sein und Zeit,*" *Dilthey-Jahrbuch* 4 (1986–1987): 161–176. As for the connection to Droysen, it must suffice to mention that in the summer semester of 1926—that is, coincident with *Being and Time*—Heidegger held a seminar on Droysen's *Historik.* Admittedly, Heidegger's talk of a "new beginning" for hermeneutics is highly problematical, especially from a Diltheyan perspective (see F. Rodi, *Erkenntnis,* p. 89). For hermeneutics, as a matter of fact, there can never be a new beginning. But even a Dilthey scholar like Rodi (ibid., p. 81) recognizes that Dilthey's systematic and philosophical use of the term "hermeneutics" was still very muddy in 1910. Heidegger unquestionably set a new standard.

2. See T. Sheehan's interpretation, *"Time and Being,* 1925–27," in *Thinking about Being: Aspects of Heidegger's Thought,* ed. W. Shahan and J. N. Mohanty, pp. 177–219. See also my *Le tournant dans la pensée de Martin Heidegger.*

3. See especially vol. 20, 21, 24, 56/57, 61, 63 of the *Gesamtausgabe (GA),* as well as *Der Begriff der Zeit* and "Phänomenologische Interpretation zu Aristoteles (Anzeige der hermeneutischen Situation)," ed. H.-U. Lessing, *Dilthey-Jahrbuch* 6 (1989): 235–276, hereafter cited as "Anzeige." See also *The Early Heidegger,* ed. John Van Buren and T. Kisiel (Albany, 1995).

4. See *GA* 20:286.

5. See *BT,* p. 158, and *GA* 21:143–161 (the sections titled "Die Als-Struktur des primären Verstehens: Hermeneutisches 'als'" and "Die Modifikation der Als-Struktur beim Bestimmen: Apophantisches 'als'").

6. *GA* 21:144.

7. Ibid., p. 146.

8. "Anzeige," p. 241.

9. On this natural, teleological relation between interpreting and understanding, see E. Betti, "Zur Grundlegung einer allgemeinen Auslegungslehre," in *Festschrift für E. Rabel* 2:79–168.

10. *BT,* p. 148.

11. See *GA* 61:41, 160. On the early Heidegger's special emphasis on the term "Durchsichtigmachen" (making transparent), see H.-G. Gadamer, "Heideggers 'theologische' Jugendschrift," *Dilthey-Jahrbuch* 6 (1989):232.

12. *GA* 20:358.

13. "Anzeige," pp. 237–238.

14. *BT,* p. 153.

15. Ibid.

16. See Heidegger's "Anmerkungen zu Karl Jaspers' Psychologie der Weltanschauungen" (1919–1921), *Wegmarken,* 2d enl. ed., p. 9.

17. *BT,* p. 37.

18. Ibid. On hermeneutics as the self-interpretation of interpretation, see C. F. Gethmann, *Verstehen und Auslegung: Das Methodenproblem in der Philosophie Martin Heideggers,* p. 117; and R. Thurnher, "Hermeneutik und Verstehen in Heideggers *Sein und Zeit,*" *Salzburger Jahrbuch für Philosophie* 28–29 (1984–1985):107.

19. "Anzeige," p. 246.

20. *GA* 63:10.

21. See my "Die Hermeneutik der Faktizität als ontologische Destruktion und Ideologiekritik," in *Zur philosophischen Aktualität Heideggers,* ed. D. Pappenfuss and O. Pöggeler, 1:163–178.

22. "Anzeige," p. 249. See also *GA* 63:105.

23. See *GA* 21:410.

24. Ibid. (my italics). See also *GA* 63:80: "The formal indication is always misunderstood if it is . . . taken as a fixed, universal proposition."

25. See "Anmerkungen zu Karl Jaspers," pp. 10–11.

26. Ibid., p. 32.

27. *BT,* p. 157.

28. *GA* 21:153.

29. Ibid., p. 154. See *BT,* p. 158.

30. From this perspective, we can understand in what sense Gadamer can say that he is applying the expression "hermeneutically" in the "manner of speaking developed by the early Heidegger" (*GW* 2:219). What he means is the interpreter's cooperative completion of what a statement means, without being able to express it completely. In this context we need to keep in mind that Heidegger's thesis about the derivativeness of statements influenced the work of such important figures as Georg Misch (1878–1965) and Hans Lipps (1889–1941). Misch, Dilthey's student, developed the fruitful conception of "evocative" speaking that exceeded what is commensurate with statements, as well as the idea of a "hermeneutic logic" the business of which was to trace logical categories back to the context of practical life from which they had sprung. Unfortunately, Misch's lecture on hermeneutic logic remained unpublished. However, we have available a detailed report on this lecture in the useful work of O. F. Bollnow, *Studien zur Hermeneutik,* vol. 2: *Zur hermeneutischen Logik bei Georg Misch und Hans Lipps.* This project was carried further and given new emphases by Hans Lipps, the student of Husserl's and Heidegger's, in his very interesting though stylistically mannered *Untersuchungen zu einer hermeneutischen Logik.* Lipps pays special attention to the contextual or pragmatic nature of every judgment. At a programmatic moment, he writes, "instead of a morphology of judg-

ment, logic needs to develop a typic of discourse" (p. 134)—that is, a logic that would go behind the forms of objective discourse in order to understand the modes of behavior seeking expression in them. Lipps's proximity to pragmatism and to later hermeneutics has since been amply acknowledged. See, e.g., R. Bubner, *Modern German Philosophy,* pp. 43–46, as well as the more recent contributions on the occasion of Lipps's hundredth birthday in *Dilthey-Jahrbuch* 6 (1989). It is notable, however, that the term "hermeneutics" seldom appears in Lipps's work. It was only after the fact, after much hesitation, that he decided while his work was in press, to refer to hermeneutics in its title (see O. F. Bollnow, *Studien zur Hermeneutik,* pp. 27–28).

31. See *BT,* p. 160.
32. Ibid., p. 161.
33. *Beiträge zur Philosophie,* in *GA* 65:13.
34. *Zur Sache des Denkens* (Tübingen, 1969), p. 25.
35. See *Beiträge zur Philosophie,* pp. 78ff.
36. On the hermeneutic dimensions of the turn, see "Die hermeneutische Bedeutsamkeit der Kehre," which is chap. 3 of my *Hermeneutische Wahrheit?,* pp. 83–95.
37. On "the turn," see my *Le tournant dans la pensée de Martin Heidegger.*
38. On this point, see M. Riedel, "Gadamers dialektische Hermeneutik und der 'Schritt zurück' zum Ethos der Dialektik," *Allgemeine Zeitschrift für Philosophie* 15 (1990):43–49. On displacing "transcendental-hermeneutic" thought in favor of ontological-historical thought, see M. Heidegger, *Nietzsche* (Pfullingen, 1961), 2:415.
39. *On the Way to Language* (1959), trans. Peter D. Hertz (New York, 1971), p. 11.
40. Ibid.
41. Ibid., p. 29.
42. Ibid.
43. Ibid., p. 30.

Chapter 6: Gadamer and the Universe of Hermeneutics

1. See J. Grondin, "Le sens du titre *Etre et temps,*" and "Herméneutique et relativisme," in *L'horizon herméneutique de la pensée contemporaine.*
2. *TM,* pp. 7–8.
3. Ibid., p. 165: "Today's task could be to free ourselves from the dominant influence of Dilthey's approach to the question and from the prejudices of the discipline that he founded: namely 'Geistesgeschichte' [intellectual history]."
4. *TM,* p. 18.
5. Ibid., p. 24.

6. Ibid., p. 41.

7. Ibid.

8. This is the title of the section of *TM* beginning on p. 89. See also Gadamer's lecture "Zur Fragwürdigkeit des äesthetischen Bewußtsein" (Venice, 1958), rpt. in *Theorien der Kunst,* ed. D. Henrich and W. Iser, pp. 59–69.

9. *TM,* pp. 259, 282, 309, 311, 314, 324, 460.

10. Ibid., p. 267.

11. Ibid., p. 269.

12. Ibid.

13. Ibid., p. 298.

14. Ibid., pp. 298–299.

15. For an example, see Gadamer's own use of Helmholtz.

16. See the title of the section of *TM* beginning on p. 300 ("The Principle of History of Effect").

17. *TM,* p. 300.

18. *Kleine Schriften* (Tübingen, 1967), 1:127, 158; and *TM,* p. xxxiv.

19. See *TM,* p. 301: "But on the whole the power of effective history does not depend on its being recognized."

20. *TM,* pp. 276–277.

21. Ibid., p. xxiv.

22. See the subsection titles "The Recovery of the Fundamental Hermeneutical Problem, (A) The Hermeneutic Problem of Application" (*TM,* p. 307).

23. *TM,* p. 296.

24. Ibid., p. 297.

25. Ibid., p. 290.

26. Here Gadamer's analysis of historically effected consciousness overlaps with Ricoeur's narrative hermeneutics of historical consciousness (in the third volume of *Temps et récit,* pp. 300ff.). In this context see my "L'herméneutique positive de Paul Ricoeur: Du temps au récit," in *"Temps et récit" de Paul Ricoeur en débat,* ed. C. Bouchindhomme and R. Rochlitz, pp. 121–137.

27. *TM,* p. 377.

28. W. Schulz, "Anmerkungen zur Hermeneutik Gadamers," in *Hermeneutik und Dialektik,* ed. R. Bubner, K. Cramer, and R. Wiehl, 1:311.

29. *GW* 2:195.

30. Ibid.

31. H.-G. Gadamer, "Grenzen der Sprache," p. 98.

32. *GW* 2:195.

33. See ibid., pp. 49, 186–187.

34. Ibid., p. 52.

35. Ibid., p. 226.

36. See *TM,* p. 418, as well as the section above on Augustine.

37. *GW* 2:504. Thus when asked what in his life, or life generally, he considered worth telling, Gadamer had to reply, "I believe what is most worth telling is always what cannot be told" ("Die Kunst, unrecht haben zu können: Gespräch mit dem Philosophen Hans-Georg Gadamer," *Süddeutsche Zeitung,* no. 34 [February 10–11, 1990]:16).

38. *GW* 2:496.

39. See ibid., pp. 497–498.

40. *GW* 2:186. See also ibid., p. 73: "Universality of Language," and p. 233: "the universal phenomenon of human linguisticality."

41. *TM,* p. 476, inter alia.

42. Ibid., p. 483.

43. See *GW* 2:111.

44. Ibid., p. 505.

45. See ibid., p. 70. See also the interview in the *Süddeutsche Zeitung,* in n. 37 above.

46. See H.-G. Gadamer, "The Science of the Life-World," in *The Later Husserl and the Idea of Phenomenology,* ed. A.-T. Tymieniecka: "There is no claim of definite knowledge, with the exception of one: the acknowledgement of the finitude of human being in itself. Grasping the chances involved in it for the infinite self-correction, humanity goes further in the permanent dialogue of one with the other even about the life-world" (missing in the German version, "Die Wissenschaft von der Lebenswelt," in *GW* 3).

47. *TM,* p. 476 (my italics). See also *GW* 2:233: ". . . and to that extent there is no doubt possible about the universality of the hermeneutic problem. This is no secondary theme. Hermeneutics is no mere ancillary discipline to the human sciences of the Romantic period." On the transition from the human sciences to universal hermeneutics, see my essay "Zur Komposition von *Wahrheit und Methode,*" *Dilthey-Jahrbuch* 8 (1993):57–74.

48. *TM,* p. 451.

49. Ibid., p. 401.

50. "Grenzen der Sprache," p. 99.

51. Ibid.

Chapter 7: Hermeneutics in Dialogue

1. "Dekonstruktion und Hermeneutik" p. 5. See also *GW* 2:505, as well as H.-G. Gadamer and R. Koselleck, *Hermeneutik und Historik* (Heidelberg, 1987), p. 30: "The fundamental philosophical intention of my own hermeneutic project is not much more than the expression of my conviction that we can only reach things via conversation. Only when we suppose the possibility of opposed views do we have the chance of getting beyond the narrowness of our prepossessions."

2. E. Betti, *Teoria generale della interpretazione,* 2 vols. (Milan, 1955), German

trans.: *Allgemeine Auslegungslehre als Methodik der Geisteswissenschaften* (Tübingen, 1967); "Zur Grundlegung einer allgemeinen Auslegungslehre," pp. 79–168; *Die Hermeneutik als allgemeine Methodik der Geisteswissenschaften* (Tübingen, 1962).

3. See my essay "L'herméneutique comme science rigoureuse selon Emilio Betti (1890–1968)," *Archives de philosophie* 53 (1990):177–198.

4. E. Betti, *Die Hermeneutik,* esp. p. 11.

5. E. Betti, *Teoria* 1:62; *Allgemeine Auslegungslehre,* p. 44.

6. E. Betti, *Die Hermeneutik,* pp. 27–28. This theory was again employed in the influential work of E. D. Hirsch, especially *Validity in Interpretation.*

7. E. Betti, *Die Hermeneutik,* p. 19; see also *Teoria,* p. 314; *Allgemeine Auslegungslehre,* p. 226.

8. E. Betti, "Zur Grundlegung einer allgemeinen Auslegungslehre"; see also *Die Hermeneutik,* pp. 53–54.

9. See F. Bianco, "Oggettività dell'interpretazione e dimensioni del comprendere: Un'analisi critica dell'ermeneutica di Emilio Betti," in G. Crifò et al., eds., *Quaderni fiorentini per la storia del pensiero giuridico moderno,* p. 75.

10. E. Betti, *Allgemeine Auslegungslehre,* p. 217n.

11. On Gadamer's involvement in the promotion of the young Habermas, see R. Wiggershaus, *Die Frankfurter Schule,* p. 625; and R. Dahrendorf, "Zeitgenosse Habermas," *Merkur* 43 (1989):478–487.

12. See *Zur Logik der Sozialwissenschaften,* p. 7.

13. Ibid., p. 253.

14. Ibid., p. 258.

15. Ibid., p. 265.

16. H.-G. Gadamer, *GW* 2:244.

17. *TM,* p. 280 and n.

18. *Zur Logik der Sozialwissenschaften,* p. 289. See also P. Giurlanda, "Habermas' Critique of Gadamer: Does It Stand Up?" *International Philosophical Quarterly* 27 (1987):33–42.

19. J. Habermas, "Der Universalitätsanspruch der Hermeneutik," in K.-O. Apel et al., *Hermeneutik und Ideologiekritik,* p. 133.

20. P. Ricoeur, *De l'interprétation: Essai sur Freud.*

21. *GW* 2:254.

22. See "Replik zu Hermeneutik und Ideologiekritik," in *GW* 2:254.

23. Ibid.

24. Ibid., p. 255.

25. J. Habermas, *Vorstudien und Ergänzungen zur Theorie des kommunikativen Handelns,* esp. p. 497.

26. See esp. his Habilitation thesis, *Platos dialektische Ethik* (1928), now in *GW,* vol. 5, and the recently published study of 1930, *Praktisches Wissen* (ibid., pp. 230–248).

27. K.-O. Apel, *Transformation der Philosophie*, 2 vols.

28. Thus Habermas, *Moralbewußtsein und kommunikatives Handeln*, and strongly opposed by K.-O. Apel, "Normative Begründung der 'Kritischen Theorie' durch Rekurs auf lebensweltliche Sittlichkeit? Ein transzendentalpragmatisch orientierter Versuch, mit Habermas gegen Habermas zu denken," in *Zwischenbetrachtungen—Im Prozeß der Aufklärung* (Frankfurt, 1989). For his part, Gadamer declared his solidarity with the Kantian intention of clarifying conceptually what moral judgment always already presupposes and requires no philosophical legitimation in itself (see *GW* 3:357).

29. On this critique of Derrida, see J. Habermas, *Der philosophische Diskurs der Moderne*, as well as *Nachmetaphysisches Denken*, "Die Einheit der Vernunft in der Vielfalt ihrer Stimmen." Gadamer referred explicitly to Habermas's "first-rate critique of Derrida" (*GW* 2:23), a reference that appears to justify the postulation of a solidarity between hermeneutics and Habermas. This solidarity should not be overstated, of course.

30. In German, *Text und Interpretation* (Munich, 1984); in French, *Revue internationale de philosophie* 151 (1984); in English, *Dialogue and Deconstruction: The Gadamer-Derrida Encounter*, ed. D. Michelfelder and R. E. Palmer.

31. See *TM*, p. 311.

32. *GW* 6:232 and see also 241. On the immediacy of understanding, see the answer to Derrida in "Text und Interpretation," *GW* 2:357.

33. See especially *La voix et le phénomène*.

34. See H.-G. Gadamer, "Grenzen der Sprache," p. 99.

35. See J.-F. Lyotard, *Le différend*, p. 9: "*Objet.* Le seul qui soit indubitable, la phrase, parce qu'elle est immédiatement présupposée." On the critique of this unhermeneutical fetishism of the sentence, see M. Frank, *Die Grenzen der Verständigung.*

36. *GW* 2:364.

37. Ibid., p. 371.

38. *Theaetetus*, 184e; *Sophist*, 264a.

Afterword

1. See H.-G. Gadamer, *GW* 2:269, 299. This is described ironically in the interview with the *Süddeutsche Zeitung* of February 10–11, 1990: "Relativism is an invention of Habermas."

2. See R. Rorty, *Consequences of Pragmatism*, p. 166.

3. *GW* 2:103. See also *GW* 4:434.

4. See Pohlenz, *Stoa und Stoiker* (1950), pp. 25ff., as well as his "Die Begründung der abendländischen Sprachlehre durch die Stoa," pp. 193ff.

Bibliography

My deep thanks are due Mr. Denis Dumas for his tireless help in preparing this bibliography.

1. General Sources

A) BIBLIOGRAPHIES OF HERMENEUTICS

Bormann, C. von. "Art: Hermeneutik I: Philosophisch-theologisch." In *Theologische Realencyklopädie,* ed. G. Müller. Berlin, 1986. 15:108–137.

Bronk, A. *Rozumienie dzieje jezyk: Filozoficzna hermeneutiyka H.-G. Gadamera.* Lublin, 1988.

Ferraris, M. *Storia dell'Ermeneutica.* Milan, 1988.

Gadamer, H.-G., and G. Boehm, eds. *Seminar: Die Hermeneutik und die Wissenschaften.* Frankfurt, 1978. 473–485.

Gay, W. C., and P. Eckstein. "Bibliographic Guide to Hermeneutics and Critical Theory." *Cultural Hermeneutics* 2 (1974–1975):379–390.

Grondin, J. *Hermeneutische Wahrheit? Zum Wahrheitsbegriff Hans-Georg Gadamers.* Königstein, 1982. 198–210.

Heinrichs, N. *Bibliographie der Hermeneutik und ihrer Anwendungsbereiche seit Schleiermacher.* Düsseldorf, 1968.

Pépin, J. "Hermeneutik." In *Reallexikon für Antike und Christentum,* vol. 14. Stuttgart, 1988.

Petit, J.-C. *Répertoire bibliographique sur l'herméneutique.* Montreal, 1984. Includes a section devoted to Gadamer.

B) GENERAL INTRODUCTIONS TO HERMENEUTICS AND OVERVIEWS IN ENCYCLOPEDIAS

Apel, K.-O. "Das Verstehen (Eine Problemgeschichte als Begriffsgeschichte)." *Archiv für Begriffsgeschichte* 1 (1955):142–199.

Bea, A. "Art: Biblische Hermeneutik." In *Lexikon für Theologie und Kirche.* Freiburg, 1958. 2:435–439.

Bialoblocki, S. "Art: Hermeneutik." In *Encyclopedia Judaica: Das Judentum in Geschichte und Gegenwart.* Berlin, 1931.

Blass, F. "Hermeneutik und Kritik." In *Handbuch der klassischen Altertums-Wissenschaft in systematischer Darstellung,* ed. I. Von Müller. Munich, 1892. 1:147–295.

Bodammer, T., *Philosophie der Geisteswissenschaften.* Freiburg, 1987.

Bormann, C. von. "Art: Hermeneutik I: Philosophisch-theologisch." In *Theologische Realencyklopädie,* ed. G. Müller. Berlin, 1986. 15:108–137.

——. "Art: Kritik." In *Historisches Wörterbuch der Philosophie,* ed. J. Ritter. Basel, 1976. 4:1249–1262.

Bruns, G. *Hermeneutics Ancient and Modern.* New Haven, 1992.

Bubner, R. *Modern German Philosophy.* Cambridge, 1981.

Coreth, E. *Grundfragen der Hermeneutik: Ein philosophischer Beitrag.* Freiburg, 1969.

Diderot, D., and J. L. R. d'Alembert. "Art: Interprétation." In *Encyclopédie, ou Dictionnaire raisonné des Sciences, des Arts et des Métiers,* vol. 8. Paris, 1765.

Diemer, A. *Elementarkurs Philosophie: Hermeneutik.* Düsseldorf, 1977.

Dilthey, W. "Die Entstehung der Hermeneutik." In *Gesammelte Schriften* 5:317–338.

——. "Das hermeneutische System Schleiermachers in der Auseinandersetzung mit der älteren protestantischen Hermeneutik." In *Gesammelte Schriften* 14, 2:595–787.

Dupuy, B.-D. "Art: Herméneutique." In *Encyclopaedia Universalis.* 20 vols. Paris, 1968. 8:365–367.

Ebeling, G. "Art: Hermeneutik." In *Religion in Geschichte und Gegenwart,* 3d ed. Tübingen, 1959. 3:243–262.

Ferraris, M. *Storia dell'Ermeneutica.* Milan, 1988.

Gadamer, H.-G. "Art: Hermeneutik." In *Historisches Wörterbuch der Philosophie,* ed. J. Ritter. Basel, 1974. 3:1061–1073.

Gerber, W. E. "Art: Exegese III—Neues Testament und Alte Kirche." In *Reallexikon für Antike und Christentum,* ed. E. Dassmann. 6:1211–1229.

Granier, J. "Philosophie et interprétation." In *Encyclopédie philosophique universelle,* ed. A. Jacob. L'univers philosophique. Paris, 1989. 1:56–62.

Grondin, J. "Art: Herméneutique." In *Encyclopédie philosophique,* vol. 2, ed. A. Jacob. Paris, 1990.

———. *L'universalité de l'herméneutique.* Paris, 1993.

Gusdorf, G. *Les origines de l'herméneutique.* Paris, 1988.

Harvey, A. van. "Art: Hermeneutics." In *The Encyclopedia of Religion.* 16 vols., ed. M. Eliade. New York, 1987. 6:279–287.

Heinrici, G. "Art: Hermeneutik." In *Real-Encyklopädie für protestantische Theologie und Kirche,* 3d ed., ed. A. Hauck. Leipzig, 1899. 718–750.

Hermann, —. "Art: Herméneutique biblique." *Dictionnaire encyclopédique de la théologie catholique* 10 (1860):486–491.

Howard, R. J. *Three Faces of Hermeneutics: An Introduction to Current Theories of Understanding.* Berkeley, 1982.

Hoy, D. C. *The Critical Circle: Literature, History, and Philosophical Hermeneutics.* Berkeley, 1978.

Hufnagel, E. *Einführung in die Hermeneutik.* Stuttgart, 1976.

Ihde, D. "Interpreting Hermeneutics: Origins, Developments and Prospects." *Man and World* 13 (1980):325–343.

Ineichen, H. *Philosophische Hermeneutik.* Freiburg, 1991.

Kihn, Karl. "Art: Biblische Hermeneutik." In *Kirchenlexikon,* ed. Weßer and Welte. Freiburg, 1888. 1844–1875.

Klaus, G., and M. Buhr. "Art: Hermeneutik." In *Philosophisches Wörterbuch.* Leipzig, 1969. 473–477.

Kulenkampff, A. "Art: Hermeneutik." In *Handbuch wissenschaftstheoretischer Begriffe.* Göttingen, 1980. 2:270–281.

Landerer, M. A. "Art: Hermeneutik." In *Real-Encyklopädie für protestantische Theologie und Kirche.* Stuttgart, 1856.

Lehmann, K. "Art: Hermeneutics." In *Sacramentum Mundi: An Encyclopaedia of Theology.* 6 vols. New York, 1968–1970. 3:23–27.

Le Noir, Abbé. "Art: Herméneutique." In *Dictionnaire de théologie* 6 (1980):365–369.

Lücke, F. *Grundriß der neutestamentlichen Hermeneutik und ihrer Geschichte.* Göttingen, 1817.

Maas, A. J. "Art: Hermeneutics." In *The Catholic Encyclopedia* 7 (1910):271–276.

Mancini, I. "Art: Ermeneutica." In *Nuovo dizionario di teologia,* ed. G. Barbaglio and S. Dianich. Rome, 1976. 370–382.

Marle, Rene. *Introduction to Hermeneutics.* New York, 1967.

Mayer, G. "Art: Exegese II: Judentum." In *Reallexikon für Antike und Christentum*, ed. E. Dassmann. 6:1104–1211.

Molinaro, A., ed. *Il conflitto delle ermeneutische.* Rome, 1989.

Mussner, F. *Geschichte der Hermeneutik von Schleiermacher bis zur Gegenwart.* Freiburg, 1970.

Ormiston, G. L., and A. D. Schrift. *The Hermeneutic Tradition: From Ast to Ricoeur.* New York, 1989.

Ott, H. "Art: Hermeneutik." In *Theologie.* Stuttgart, 1967. 192–195.

Palmer, R. E. *Hermeneutics: Interpretation Theory in Schleiermacher, Dilthey, Heidegger and Gadamer.* Evanston, Ill., 1969.

Pattaro, G. "Art: Ermeneutica." In *Gli strumenti del sapere contemporaneo.* Turin, 1982. 2:264–270.

Pépin, J. "Art: Hermeneutik." In *Reallexikon für Antike und Christentum.* Stuttgart, 1988. 14:722–771.

Raddatz, W., G. Sauter, and H. G. Ulrich. "Art: Verstehen." In *Praktisch theologisches Handbuch,* ed. G. Otto. Hamburg, 1970. 483–513.

Ricoeur, P. "Narrativité, phénoménologie et herméneutique." In *Encyclopédie philosophique universelle*, ed. A. Jacob. L'univers philosophique. Paris, 1989. 1:63–71.

Riesenhuber, K. "Art: Hermeneutik." In *Philosophisches Wörterbuch,* 14th ed., ed. W. Brugger. Freiburg, 1976. 165–166.

Schaeffler, R. "Art: Verstehen." In *Handbuch philosophischer Grundbegriffe,* ed. H. Krings et al. Munich, 1974. 6:628–641.

Scharlemann, M. H. "Hermeneutic(s): A Survey Article." *Concordia Theological Monthly* 39:9 (1968):612–622.

Schenk, W. "Art: Hermeneutik III: Neues Testament." In *Theologische Realencyklopädie,* ed. G. Müller. Berlin, 1986. 15:144–150.

Schmidt, L. "Art: Hermeneutik II: Altes Testament." In *Theologische Realencyklopädie,* ed. G. Müller. Berlin, 1986. 15:137–143.

Schreckenberg, H. "Art: Exegese I: Heidnisch, Griechen und Römer." In *Reallexikon für Antike und Christentum,* ed. E. Dassmann. 6:1174–1194.

Schreiter, J. "Art: Hermeneutik." In *Enzyklopädie zur bürgerlichen Philosophie im 19. und 20. Jahrhundert.* Cologne, 1988. 411–438.

Schröer, H. "Art: Hermeneutik IV: Praktisch-theologisch." In *Theologische Realencyklopädie,* ed. G. Müller. Berlin, 1986. 15:150–156.

Stegmüller, W. *Hauptströmungen der Gegenwartsphilosophie: Eine Kritische Einführung.* Stuttgart, 1975. 2:103–147.

Sulzer, J. G. "Art: Theologische Hermeneutik." In *Kurzer Begriff aller Wissenschaften und anderer Theile der Gelehrsamkeit, worinnen jeder nach seinem Inhalt, Nutzen und Vollkommenheit kürzlich beschrieben wird.* Frankfurt, 1759. 214–223.

Szondi, P. *Einführung in die literarische Hermeneutik.* Frankfurt, 1975.

Thiel, M. *Interpretation: Philosophie, Jurisprudenz, Theologie.* Heidelberg, 1980.

Veraart, A., and R. Wimmer. "Art: Hermeneutik." In *Enzyklopädie für Philosophie und Wissenschaftstheorie.* 1984. 2:86–89.

Vogel, E. F. "Art: Interpres, Interpretation, Interpretieren." In *Allgemeine Encyklopädie der Wissenschaften und Künste,* ed. J. S. Ersch and J. G. Gruber. Leipzig, 1841. 2, 9:365–406.

Wach, J. *Das Verstehen: Grundzüge einer Geschichte der hermeneutischen Theorie im 19. Jahrhundert.* Tübingen, 1926; Hildesheim, 1966.

Walch, J. C. "Art: Auslegungskunst." In *Philosophisches Lexikon.* Leipzig, 1726. (Rpt. Hildesheim, 1968.)

Weber, O. "Art: Hermeneutik." In *Evangelisches Kirchenlexikon,* 2d ed., ed. H. Brunotte and O. Weber. Göttingen, 1962. 120–126.

Zedler, J. H. "Art: Hermeneutik." In *Großes vollständiges Universallexicon aller Künste und Wissenschaften.* Halle, 1735. 12:1729–1733.

C) READERS AND COLLECTIONS ON THE HISTORY OF HERMENEUTICS

Barbotin, E., ed. *Qu'est-ce qu'un texte? Eléments pour une herméneutique.* Paris, 1975.

Birus, H., ed. *Hermeneutische Positionen: Schleiermacher, Dilthey, Heidegger, Gadamer.* Göttingen, 1982. (Texts by H. Birus, H. Anz, G. Figal, and H. Turk.)

Bleicher, J. *Contemporary Hermeneutics: Hermeneutics as Method, Philosophy and Critique.* London, 1980.

Bubner, R., K. Cramer, and R. Wiehl, eds. *Hermeneutik und Dialektik.* 2 vols. Tübingen, 1970.

De Margerie, B. *Introduction à l'histoire de l'exégèse,* vol. 1: *Les Pères grecs et orientaux.* Paris, 1980; vol. 2: *Les premiers grands exégètes.* Paris, 1983; vol. 3: *Augustin.* Paris, 1983.

Diestel, L. *Geschichte des Alten Testamentes in der Christlichen Kirche.* Jena, 1869.

Doyle, E., and V. H. Floyd, eds. *Studies in Interpretation,* no. 2. Atlantic Highlands, N.J., 1977.

Flashar, H., K. Gründer, and A. Horstmann, eds. *Philologie und Hermeneutik im 19. Jahrhundert: Zur Geschichte und Methodologie der Geisteswissenschaften.* Göttingen, 1979.

Frei, H. W. *The Eclipse of Biblical Narrative: A Study of Eighteenth and Nineteenth Century Hermeneutics.* New Haven, 1974.

Gadamer, H.-G., and G. Boehm, eds. *Seminar: Die Hermeneutik und die Wissenschaften.* Frankfurt, 1978.

———. *Seminar: Philosophische Hermeneutik.* Frankfurt, 1976.

Hermeneutics in Ethics and Social Theory, a special issue of *Philosophical Forum* 22:1–2 (1989–1990). (Essays by J. Habermas, M. Walzer, A. Heller, S. Benhabib, R. Makkreel, T. McCarthy, A. Ophir, K. Baynes, G. Warnke, and A. Wellmer.)

Literary Hermeneutics, a special issue of *New Literary History* 10:1 (1978).

Manninen, J., and R. Tuomela, eds. *Essays of Explanation and Understanding: Studies in the Foundations of the Humanities and Social Sciences.* Dordrecht, 1976.

Müller-Vollmer, K., ed. *The Hermeneutics Reader: Texts of the German Tradition from the Enlightenment to the Present.* New York, 1985.

Nassen, U., ed. *Klassiker der Hermeneutik.* Paderborn, 1982.

Pöggeler, O., ed. *Hermeneutische Philosophie: Zehn Aufsätze.* Munich, 1972.

Ramm, B. L. *Hermeneutics.* Grand Rapids, Mich., 1971.

Riedel, M. *Erklären oder Verstehen? Zur Theorie und Geschichte der hermeneutischen Wissenschaften.* Stuttgart, 1978.

Robinson, J. M., and J. B. Cobb, Jr., eds. *The New Hermeneutic.* New York, 1964.

Shapiro, G., and A. Sica, eds. *Hermeneutics: Questions and Prospects.* Amherst, 1984. (Essays by E. Betti, H.-G. Gadamer, H. Dreyfus, R. E. Palmer, J. N. Mohanty, P. de Man, G. L. Bruns, J. O'Neill, G. L. Stonum, A. Giddens, F. R. Dalmayr, W. H. Dray, and R. Martin.)

Wachterhauser, B. R., ed. *Hermeneutics and Modern Philosophy.* Albany, 1986.

Warning, R., ed. *Rezeptionsästhetik: Theorie und Praxis.* Munich, 1975.

D. ON THE ETYMOLOGY OF HERMENEUEIN

Chantraine, P. "Art: 'hermeneus'." In *Dictionnaire étymologique de la langue grecque.* 4 vols., ed. P. Chantraine. Paris, 1968–1980.

Goclenius, R. "Art: Hermeneia." In his *Lexicon Philosophicum Graecum.* Marburg, 1615.

Hiltbrunner, O. *Latina Graeca: Samasiologische Studien über lateinische Wörter im Hinblick auf ihr Verhältnis zu griechischen Vorbildern.* Bern, 1958.

Kerényi, F. K. "Der Gott Hermes und die Hermeneutik." *Tijdschrift voor Filosofie* 30 (1968):525–635.

———. "Hermeneia und Hermeneutik: Ursprung und Sinn der Hermeneutik." In his *Griechische Grundbegriffe: Fragen und Antworten aus der heutigen Situation.* Zurich, 1964. 42–52.

———. "Origine e senso dell'ermeneutica." In *Ermeneutica e tradizione* (Archivio di filosofia). Padua, 1963. 129–137.

Mayer-Maly, T. "Art: Interpretatio." In *Der kleine Pauly.* Stuttgart, 1957. 2:1423–1424.

Vogel, E. F. "Art: Interpres, Interpretation, Interpretieren." In *Allgemeine Encyklopädie der Wissenschaften und Künste,* ed. J. S. Ersch and J. G. Grüber. Leipzig, 1841. 2, 9:365–406.

2. Stages of Hermeneutic History

A) ANTIQUITY AND THE MIDDLE AGES

Allegory

Aristotle. *Categories* and *De Interpretatione*. Trans. J. L. Ackrill. Oxford, 1963.

Bate, H. N. "Some Technical Terms of Greek Exegesis." *Journal for Theological Studies* 24 (1923):59–66.

Bouché-LeClerq, A. *Histoire de la divination dans l'antiquité*. Paris, 1879–1882.

Buffière, F. *Les mythes d'Homère et la pensée grecque*. Paris, 1956.

Burkert, W. *Greek Religion*. Oxford, 1985.

Canfora, L. *Storia della letteratura greca*. Rome, 1987. 477–482.

Cazeaux, J. *La trame et la chaîne: Ou les structures littéraires et l'exégèse dans cinq traités de Philon d'Alexandrie*. Leiden, 1983.

Christiansen, I. *Die Technik der allegorischen Auslegungswissenschaft bei Philo von Alexandrien*. Tübingen, 1969.

Daniélou, J. *Philon d'Alexandrie*. Paris, 1958.

Eco, U. "L'epistola XIII, l'allegorismo medievale, il simbolismo moderno." In his *Sugli specchi e altri saggi*. Milan, 1985.

Friedrich, W. H. "Allegorische Interpretation." In *Fischer Lexicon: Literatur*, ed. W. H. Friedrich and W. Kelly. Frankfurt, 1965.

Grondin, J. "The Task of Hermeneutics in Ancient Philosophy." *Boston Area Colloquium in Ancient Philosophy* 8 (1992): 211–230.

Halliday, W. R. *Greek Divination: A Study of Its Methods and Principles*. 1913; Chicago, 1967.

Havelock, W. R. *The Literate Revolution in Greece and Its Cultural Consequences*. Princeton, 1982.

———. *The Muse Learns to Write: Reflections on Orality and Literacy from Antiquity to the Present*. New Haven, 1986.

Heinemann, I. "Die Allegoristik der hellenistischen Juden außerhalb Philon." *Mnemosyne*, 4th ser., 5 (1952):130–138.

Hiemsch, P. *Der Einfluss Philos auf die älteste christliche Exegese*. Münster, 1908.

Kakridis, J. "The Ancient Greeks and Foreign Languages." *Hellenica* 22 (1966):22–34.

Klauck, H.-J. *Allegorie und Allegorese in synoptischen Gleichnistexten*. Münster, 1978.

Maass, F. "Von den Ursprüngen der rabbinischen Schriftauslegung." *Zeitschrift für Theologie und Kirche* (1952):129–161.

Méasson, A. *Du char ailé de Zeus à l'Arche d'Alliance: Images et mythes platoniciens chez Philon d'Alexandrie*. Paris, 1986.

Nikiprowetzly, V. *Le commentaire de l'écriture chez Philon d'Alexandrie: Son caractère et sa portée: Observations philologiques*. Leiden, 1977.

Oliver, J. H. *The Athenian Expounders of the Sacred and Ancestral Law*. Baltimore, 1950.

Otte, K. *Das Sprachverständnis bei Philo von Alexandrien: Sprache als Mittel der Hermeneutik*. Tübingen, 1967.

Pépin, J. *Mythe et allégorie: Les origines grecques et les contestations judéo-chrétiennes*. 2d ed. Paris, 1976.

————. *La tradition de l'allégorie: De Philon d'Alexandrie à Dante*. Paris, 1988.

Persson, A. W. "Die Exegeten und Delphi." In *Lunds Universitets Arsskrift*. Lund, 1918.

Pfeffer, F. *Studien zur Mantik in der Philosophie der Antike*. Meisenheim, 1976.

Philo of Alexandria. *Die Werke in deutscher Übersetzung*. Berlin, 1964.

Pohlenz, M. "Die Begründung der abendländischen Sprachlehre durch die Stoa." *Nachrichten von der Gesellschaft der Wissenschaften zu Göttingen*, n.s., 3 (1938–1939):151–198.

————, trans. *Stoa und Stoiker*. Zurich, 1950, 1964.

Runia, D. T. "Mosaic and Platonist Exegesis: Philo on 'Finding' and 'Refinding.'" *Vigiliae christianae* 40 (1986):209–217.

Sandys, J. E. *A History of Classical Scholarship*. London, 1903–1908. (Rpt. New York, 1958.)

Siegfried, C. *Philo von Alexandrien als Ausleger des Alten Testaments*. Aalen, 1875.

Sowers, S. G. *The Hermeneutics of Philo and Hebrews*. Zurich, 1965.

Szlezák, T. "Dialogform und Esoterik: Zur Deutung des platonischen Dialogs 'Phaidros.'" *Museum Helveticum* 35 (1978):18–32.

————. *Platon und die Schriftlichkeit der Philosophie: Interpretationen zu den frühen und mittleren Dialogen*. Berlin, 1985.

Tate, J. "On the History of Allegorism." *Classical Quarterly* 28 (1934):105–114.

————. "Plato and Allegorical Interpretation." *Classical Quarterly* 23 (1929):142–154.

Vermes, G. *Scripture and Tradition in Judaism*. Leiden, 1961.

Wehrli, F. *Zur Geschichte der allegorischen Deutung Homers im Altertum*. Zurich, 1928.

Wilson, N. G. "An Aristarchean Maxim." *Classical Review* 21 (1971):172.

New Testament Typology

Bonsirven, J. *Exégèse rabbinique et exégèse paulinienne*. Paris, 1939.

Bori, P. C. *L'interpretazione infinita: L'ermeneutica cristiana antica e le sue trasformazioni*. Bologna, 1987.

Burghardt, W. J. "On Early Christian Exegesis." *Theological Studies* 2 (1950):78–116.

Daniélou, J. "Herméneutique judéo-chrétienne." In *Ermeneutica e tradizione* (Archivio di filosofia). Padua, 1963. 255–261.

————. *Sacramentum futuri: Etudes sur les origines de la typologie biblique*. Paris, 1950.

De Boer, W. "Hermeneutic Problems in Early Christian Literature." *Vigiliae christianae* 1 (1947):150–167.

De Lubac, H. "Typologie et allégorisme." *Recherches de science religieuse* 34 (1947):180–266.

Doeve, J. W. *Jewish Hermeneutics in the Synoptic Gospels and Acts.* Leiden, 1954.

Grant, R. M. *L'interprétation de la Bible des origines chrétiennes à nos jours.* Paris, 1967.

Rost, H. *Die Bibel in den ersten Jahrhunderten.* Westheim, 1946.

Tetz, M. "H'Agia Graphe e auten ermeneuousa: Zur altkirchlichen Frage nach der Klarheit der Heiligen Schrift." In *Theologie in Geschichte und Kunst: Festschrift für W. Elliger,* ed. S. Hermann and O. Sohngen. Witten, 1968. 206–213.

Patristics

Alexandre, M. "La théorie de l'exégèse dans le 'De hominis opificio' et l'"In Hexaemeron.'" In *Ecriture et culture philosophique dans la pensée de Grégoire de Nysse,* ed. M. Harl. Leiden, 1971.

Allgeier, A. "Der Einfluß des Manichäismus auf die exegetische Fragestellung bei Augustin." In *Aurelius Augustinus: Festschrift der Görresgesellschaft.* 1930. 1–13.

Altraner, B. *Patrologia.* Turin, 1968.

Augustin. "De Doctrina Christiana." In *Corpus Christianorum: Series latina,* vol. 32, ed. I. Martin. Turnholt, 1954, 1962.

———. "De Trinitate." In *Oeuvres de Saint-Augustin,* vol. 15–16. Paris, 1955.

Basevi, C. *San Agustín: La interpretación del Nuevo testamento. Criterios exegéticos propuestos per S. Agustín en el "De Doctrina Christiana," en el "Contra Faustum" y en el "De consensu Evangelis rarum."* Pamplona, 1983.

Brunner, P. "Charismatische und methodische Schriftauslegung nach Augustinus Prolog zu *De doctrina christiana.*" *Kerygma und Dogma* 1 (1955):59–69, 85–103.

Canévet, M. *Grégoire de Nysse et l'herméneutique biblique: Etude des rapports entre le language et la connaissance de Dieu.* Paris, 1983.

Charlier, C. "Exégèse patristique et exégèse scientifique." *Esprit et vie* (1949):52–69.

Daniélou, J. "La démythisation dans l'école d'Alexandrie." *Archivio di filosofia* (1961):45–49.

———. *Origène.* Paris, 1948.

———. "Origène comme exégète de la Bible." *Studia patristica* 1 (1957):280–290.

De Lubac, H. *Histoire et esprit: L'intelligence de l'Ecriture d'après Origène.* Paris, 1950.

Duchrow, U. *Sprachverständnis und biblisches Hören bei Augustinus.* Tübingen, 1965.

Fahey, A. *Cyprian and the Bible: A Study in Third-Century Exegesis.* Tübingen, 1971.

Gögler, R. *Zur Theologie des biblischen Wortes bei Origenes.* Düsseldorf, 1963.

Gruber, W. *Die pneumatische Exegese bei den Alexandrinern: Ein Beitrag zur Noematik der Heiligen Schrift.* Graz, 1957.

Guillert, J. "Les exégèses d'Alexandrie et d'Antioche: Conflit ou malentendu." *Recherches de science religieuse* 34 (1947):267–302.

Gusie, T. W. "Patristic Hermeneutics and the Meaning of Tradition." *Theological Studies* 32 (1971):647–658.

Hanson, R. P. C. *Allegory and Event: A Study of the Sources and Significance of Origen's Interpretation of Scripture.* Richmond, 1932; London, 1958.

Harl, M. "Origène et les interprétations patristiques grecques de l'obscurité biblique." *Vigiliae christianae* 36 (1982):334–371.

Heinemann, I. "Palästinensische und alexandrinische Schriftsforschung." *Der Morgen* 9 (1933):122–137.

Horn, H.-J. "Zur Motivation der allegorischen Schriftexegese bei Clemens von Alexandrien." *Hermes* 97 (1969).

Istace, G. "Le livre 1er du 'De Doctrina christiana' de Saint Augustin: Organisation synthétique et méthode de mise en oeuvre." *Ephemerides: Theologicae Lovanienses* 32 (1956):289–330.

Karpp, H. *Die Bedeutung der antiochenischen Schule auf dem exegetischen Gebiete.* Weissenburg, 1866.

———. "Über theoria und allegoria nach den verlorenen hermeneutischen Schriften der Antiochener." *Theologische Quartalschrift* 32 (1880):531–582.

Kuss, O. "Zur Hermeneutik Tertullians." In *Neutestamentliche Aufsätze: Festschrift für J. Schmidt.* Regensburg, 1963. 138–160.

Kuypers, K. *Der Zeichen- und Wortbegriff im Denken Augustinus.* Amsterdam, 1934.

La Bonnardiére, A. M., ed. *Saint Augustin et la Bible.* Paris, 1986.

Laistern, M. L. W. "Antiochene Exegesis in Western Europe during the Middle Ages." *Harvard Theological Review* 40 (1947):19–32.

Läuchli, S. "Die Frage nach der Objektivität der Exegese in Origenes." *Theologische Zeitschrift* 10 (1954):175–197.

Magnanini, P. "La Teoria degli Antiocheni." In *Scritti in onore di S. Ecc. Mons. G. Battaglia.* 1957. 221–242.

Morat, E. *La notion augustinienne de l'herméneutique.* Clermont-Ferrand, 1906.

Mortley, R. *Connaissance religieuse et herméneutique chez Clément d'Alexandrie.* Leiden, 1973.

Neuschöpfer, B. *Origenes als Philologe.* Basel, 1987.

Oikonomou, E. B. "Hermeneutical Logotypes: The Basic Elements of Patristic Hermeneutics." *Theologia* 53 (1982):627–671.

Origenes. *Traité des principes.* Paris, 1976.

———. *Vier Bücher von den Prinzipien (Peri Archon; De principiis): Zweisprachige Ausgabe.* 2d ed., ed. H. Görgemanns and H. Kapp. Darmstadt, 1985.

Payne, J. B. "Biblical Problems and Augustine's Allegorizing." *Westminster Theological Journal* 14 (1951–1952):46–64.

Pontet, M. *L'exégèse de S. Augustin prédicateur.* Paris, 1946.

Prete, B. "I principi esegetici di Sant'Agostino." *Sapienza* 8 (1955):522–594.

Ranson, P., ed. *Saint Augustin.* Lausanne, 1988.

Rahner, K. "Le début d'une doctrine des cinq sens spirituels chez Origène." *Revue d'ascétique et de mystique* 13 (1932):113–145.

Ripanti, G. *Agostino teorico dell'interpretazione.* Brescia, 1980.

Schäublin, C. "Augustin, De utilitate redendi: Über das Verhältnis des Interpreten zum Text." *Vigiliae christianae* 43 (1989):53–68.

———. *Untersuchungen zur Methode und Herkunft der antiochenischen Exegese.* Cologne, 1974.

Schildenberger, J. "Gegenwartsbedeutung exegetischer Grundsätze des Hl. Augustinus." In *Augustinus Magister: II Études Augustiniennes.* Paris, 1954. 677–690.

Simonetti, M. *Lettera eo allegoria: Un contributo alla Storia dell'esegesi patristica.* Rome, 1985.

Strauss, G. *Schriftgebrauch, Schriftauslegung und Schriftbeweis bei Augustin.* Tübingen, 1959.

Tardieu, M., ed. *Les règles de l'interprétation.* Paris, 1987.

Ternant, P. "La Theoria d'Antioche dans le cadre des sens de l'Ecriture." *Biblica* 34 (1953):135–158, 354–383, 456–486.

Tissot, Y. "Allégories patristiques de la parabole lucanienne des deux fils, Luc 15,11–32." In *Exegesis: Problèmes de méthode et exercices de lecture,* ed. F. Bovon and G. Rouiller. 243–272.

Tyconius. "Liber de septum regulis." In *Patrologiae cursus completus.* 221 vols., ed. J. P. Migne. Paris, 1844–1864. 19:15–66.

Ullmann, W. "Hermeneutik und Semantik in der Bibeltheologie des Origenes: Dargestellt anhand von Buch 10 seines Johanneskommentares." *Studia patristica* 17 (1982):966–977.

Vacari, A. "La theoria nella scuola esegetica d'Antiochia." *Biblica* 1 (1920):3–36.

Viciano, A. "'Homeron ex Homerou saphenizein': Principios hermenéuticos de Teodoreto de Ciro en su Comentario a las Epístolas paulinas." *Scripta Theologica* 21 (1989):13–61.

Vogels, J. H. "Die Heilige Schrift bei Augustinus." In *Aurelius Augustinus: Festschrift der Görresgesellschaft.* 1930. 411–421.

Late Middle Ages

Apel, K.-O. *Die Idee der Sprache in der Tradition des Humanismus von Dante bis Vico.* Bonn, 1963.

Aquinas, T. *Summa theologica,* I.1.10.

Bacher, W. "Die jüdische Bibelexegese vom Anfang des zehnten bis zum Ende des fünfzehnten Jahrhunderts." In *Die jüdische Literatur seit Abschluss des Kanons,* ed. J. Winter and A. Wünsche. Trier, 1894–1896. 2:239–339.

Brinkmann, H. *Mittelalterliche Hermeneutik.* Tübingen, 1980.

De Lubac, H. *Exégèse médiévale: Les quatre sens de l'Ecriture.* 4 vols. Paris, 1959–1964.

———. "Les humanistes chrétiens du XVe-XVIe siècle et l'herméneutique traditionnelle." In *Ermeneutica e tradizione* (Archivio di filosofia). Padua, 1963. 173–177.

Fessard, G. "Le Fondement de l'Herméneutique selon la XIII Règle d'orthodoxie des Exercices spirituels d'Ignace de Loyola." In *Ermeneutica e tradizione* (Archivio di filosofia). Padua, 1963. 203–219.

Fischer, M. "Des Nikolaus von Lyra Postillae perpetuae in Vetus et Nov. Test. in ihrem eigentümlichen Unterschied von der gleichzeitigen Schriftauslegung." *Jahrbücher für protestantische Theologie* 15 (1889):430–471.

Glunz, H. H. *Die Literaturästhetik des europäischen Mittelalters.* Bochum, 1937. (Rpt. Frankfurt, 1963.)

Guth, K. "Zum Verhältnis von Exegese und Philosophie im Zeitalter der Frühscholastik." *Recherches de théologie ancienne et médiévale* 38 (1971):121–136.

Pépin, J. *Dante et la tradition de l'allégorie.* Montreal, 1970.

Scholem, G. *Die jüdische Mystik in ihren Hauptströmungen.* Zurich, 1958.

Smalley, B. *The Study of the Bible in the Middle Ages.* Oxford, 1952.

Spicq, C. *Esquisse d'une histoire de l'exégèse latine au Moyen Age.* Paris, 1944.

———. "Exégèse mediévale en Occident." *Supplément au dictionnaire de la Bible* 4 (1949):608–627.

Strack, H., and P. Billerbeck. *Kommentar zum Neuen Testament aus Talmud und Midrasch,* 6 vols. Munich, 1922.

B) FROM THE REFORMATION TO THE NINETEENTH CENTURY

Early Protestant Hermeneutics

Beisser, F. *Claritas scripturae bei Martin Luther.* Göttingen, 1966.

Bornkamm, H. *Luther und das Alte Testament.* Tübingen, 1948.

Dannhauer, J. C. *Hermeneutica sacra sive methodus exponendarum sacrarum literarum.* Augsburg, 1654.

———. *Idea boni interpretis.* Strasbourg, 1630.

Ebeling, G. "Die Anfänge von Luthers Hermeneutik." *Zeitschrift für Theologie und Kirche* 48 (1951):174–230.

———. "Evangelische Evangelienauslegung: Eine Untersuchung zu Luthers Hermeneutik." In *Religion in Geschichte und Gegenwart.* Darmstadt, 1962.

Ficker, J. *Anfänge reformatorischer Bibelauslegung: Luthers Vorlesung über den Römerbrief mit besonderer Rücksicht auf die Frage der Heilsgewißheit.* Foreword to *Luthers Gesammelte Werke I,* 1. Weimar, 1980.

Flacius Illyricus, M. *Clavis scripturae sacrae.* Basel, 1567; Frankfurt, 1719.

———. *De ratione cognoscendi sacras literas.* 1719. In *Über den Erkenntnisgrund der heiligen Schrift,* ed. L. Geldsetzer. Düsseldorf, 1968.

———. "Nachdruck der 1719er Ausgabe." In *Über den Erkenntnisgrund der heiligen Schrift,* ed. L. Geldsetzer. Düsseldorf, 1968.

Franzmann, M. A. "Seven Theses on Reformation Hermeneutics." *Concordia Theological Monthly* 40:4 (1969):235–246.

Hahn, F. "Luthers Auslegungsgrundsätze und ihre theologischen Voraussetzungen." *Zeitschrift für systematische Theologie* (1934–1935):165–218.

Henrici, P. "Herméneutique, oecuménisme et religion: Le cas Leibniz." *Archivio di filosofia* (1968):553–561.

Hermann, R. *Von der Klarheit der heiligen Schrift: Untersuchungen über Luthers Lehre von der Schrift.* Tübingen, 1958.

Horning, W. *Der Straßburger Universitätsprofessor, Munsterprediger und Präsident des Kirchenkonvents Dr. Johann Conrad Dannhauer geschildert nach benützten Druckschriften und Manuskripten aus dem 17. Jahrhundert.* Strasbourg, 1883.

Kimmerle, H. "'Typologie der Grundformen des Verstehens von der Reformation bis zu Schleiermacher." *Zeitschrift für Theologie und Kirche* 67 (1970):162–182.

Kraus, J. H. *Geschichte der historisch-kritischen Erforschung des Alten Testaments von der Reformation bis zur Gegenwart.* 2d ed. Neukirchen, 1956, 1969.

Lücke, F. *Grundriß der neutestamentlichen Hermemeutik und ihrer Geschichte.* Göttingen, 1817.

Luther, M. *Luthers Gesammelte Werke (Weimarer Ausgabe).* 66 vols. Weimar, 1833ff.

Meinhold, P. *Luthers Sprachphilosophie.* Berlin, 1958.

Melanchthon, P. *Rhetorik.* ed. J. Knape. Tübingen, 1993.

Moldaenke, G. *Schriftverständnis und Schriftdeutung im Zeitalter der Reformation,* vol. 1: *Matthias Flacius Illyricus.* Stuttgart, 1936.

Montgomery, J. W. "Lutherische Hermeneutik—und Hermeneutik heute." *Lutherischer Rundblick* 15:1 (1967):2–32.

Rosenzweig, F. *Die Schrift und Luther.* Berlin, 1926.

Scholder, K. *Ursprünge und Probleme der Bibel-Kritik im 17. Jahrhundert: Ein Beitrag der historische-kritischen Theologie.* Munich, 1966.

Schwartz, A. von. *Die theologische Hermeneutik des Matthias Flacius Illyricus.* Munich, 1933.

The Enlightenment

Aliprandi, G. G. B. *Vico e la Scrittura.* Turin, 1949.

Altwicker, N., ed. *Texte zur Geschichte des Spinozismus.* Darmstadt, 1971.

Bartuschat, W. "Zum Problem der Auslegung bei Leibniz." In *Hermeneutik und Dialektik,* ed. R. Bubner, K. Cramer, and R. Wiehl. Tübingen, 1970. 2:219–240.

Baumgarten, S. J. *Ausführlicher Vortrag der Biblischen Hermeneutik.* Ed. J. C. Bertram. Halle, 1769.

———. *Unterricht von der Auslegung der Heiligen Schrift: Compendium der biblischen Hermeneutik.* Halle, 1742.

Beetz, M. "Nachgeholte Hermeneutik: Zum Verhältnis von Interpretations- und Logiklehren in Barock und Aufklärung." *Deutsche Vierteljahresschrift für Literaturwissenschaft und Geistesgeschichte* 55 (1981):591–688.

Bergmann, E. *Die Begründung der deutschen Aesthetik durch A. G. Baumgarten und G. F. Meier.* Leipzig, 1911.

Betti, E. "I principi di scienza nuova di G. B. Vico e la teoria della interpretazione storica." *Nuova rivista de diritto commerciale* 10 (1957):48–59.

Blanke, H. W. "Georg Andreas Wills Einleitung in die historische Gelahrtheit (1766) und die Anfänge moderner Historik-Vorlesungen in Deutschland." *Dilthey-Jahrbuch* 2 (1984):193–222.

Blanke, H. W., and D. Fleischer. "Allgemeine und historische Wahrheiten: Chladenius und der Verwissenschaftlichungsprozeß der Historie." *Dilthey-Jahrbuch* 5 (1988):258–270.

Blumenberg, H. *Die Legitimität der Neuzeit.* Frankfurt, 1966.

Büss, E. *Die Geschichte des mythischen Erkennens.* Munich, 1953.

Chladenius, J. M. *Allgemeine Geschichtswissenschaft.* Leipzig, 1752.

———. *Einleitung zur richtigen Auslegung vernünftiger Reden und Schriften.* Leipzig, 1742. (Rpt. Düsseldorf, 1969.)

———. *Vernünftige Gedanken von dem Wahrscheinlichen und desselben gefährliche Missbräuche.* Leipzig, 1748.

Ernesti, J. A. "De Origene: Interpretationis sacrorum librorum grammaticae auctore." In *Opuscula philologico-critica.* Leipzig, 1764.

———. *Institutio interpretis Novi Testamenti.* Leipzig, 1792.

Freidrich, C. "Johann Martin Chladenius: Die Allgemeine Hermeneutik und das Problem der Geschichte." In *Klassiker der Hermeneutik,* ed. U. Nassen. 43–75.

———. *Sprache und Geschichte: Untersuchungen zur Hermeneutik von Johann Martin Chladenius.* Meisenheim, 1978.

Geldsetzer, L. "Einleitung." In *G. F. Meier: Versuch einer allgemeinen Auslegungskunst.* Düsseldorf, 1965.

———. "Einleitung." In *J. M. Chladenius: Einleitung zur richtigen Auslegung vernünftiger Reden und Schriften.* Düsseldorf, 1969. ix–xxix.

Griffero, T. "Chladenius: L'ermeneutica . . . prospettivismo e obiettivismo." *Rivista di estetica,* n.s., 23 (1986):3–31.

———. "Ciò che l'autore non sa." In *Ciò che l'autore non sa.* Milan, 1988.

Hasso Jaeger, H.-E. "Studien zur Frühgeschichte der Hermeneutik." *Archiv für Begriffsgeschichte* 18 (1974):35–84.

Henn, C. "'Sinnreiche Gedanken': Zur Hermeneutik des Chladenius." *Archiv für Geschichte der Philosophie* 58 (1976):240–264.

Hess, J. J. "Gränzenbestimmung dessen, was in der Bibel Mythos, Anthropopathie, personificierte Darstellung, Poesie, Vision, was würkliche Geschichte ist." In his *Bibliothek der heiligen Geschichte.* 2 vols. Zurich, 1791. 2:153–254.

Husik, I. "Maimonides and Spinoza on the Interpretation of the Bible." *Supplement to the Journal of the American Oriental Society* 1 (1935):22–40.

Lange, S. G. *Leben Georg Friedrich Meiers.* Halle, 1778.

Leibniz, G. W. F. *Philosophische Schriften,* vol. 7, ed. C. I. Gerhardt. Berlin, 1875–1890.

Lübbe, H. *Säkularisierung: Geschichte eines ideenpolitischen Begriffs.* Freiburg, 1965.

Meier, G. F. *Versuch einer allgemeinen Auslegungskunst.* Halle, 1757. (Rpt. Düsseldorf, 1965.)

Müller, H. *Johann Martin Chladenius (1710–1759).* Berlin, 1917. (Rpt. Vaduz, 1965.)

Piepmeier, R. "Baruch de Spinoza: Vernünftanspruch und Hermeneutik." In *Klassiker der Hermeneutik,* ed. U. Nassen. 9–42.

Semler, J. S. *Abhandlung von freier Untersuchung des Canon,* 4 vols. Halle, 1771–1775.

———. *Neuer Versuch zur Beförderung der Kirchlichen Hermeneutik.* Halle, 1788.

———. *Vorbereitung zur theologischen Hermeneutik,* 4 vols. Halle, 1760–1769.

Spinoza, B. *Tractatus theologico-politicus.* Ed. G. Gawlick. Hamburg, 1976. (Rpt. in the Latin and German edition by G. Gawlick and F. Niewöhner, Darmstadt, 1979.)

Strauss, L. *Die Religionskritik Spinozas als Grundlage seiner Bibelwissenschaft: Untersuchungen zu Spinozas theologischpolitischem Traktat.* Berlin, 1930. (Rpt. Darmstadt, 1981.)

Tagliacozzo, G., and D. P. Verene, eds. *Giambattista Vico's Science of Humanity.* Baltimore, 1976.

Warnach, V., ed. *Hermeneutik als Weg heutiger Wissenschaft: Ein Forschungsgespräch.* Salzburg, 1971.

Weinsheimer, J. *Eighteenth-Century Hermeneutics: Philosophy of Interpretation in England from Locke to Burke.* New Haven, 1993.

Zac, S. *Spinoza et l'interprétation de l'écriture.* Paris, 1965.

Pietist Hermeneutics

Dilthey, W. "Die hermeneutische Lehre des Pietismus von den Affekten." In his *Leben Schleiermachers,* in *Gesammelte Schriften* 14, 1.

Francke, A. H. *Manductio ad lectionem Scripturae Sacrae.* Halle, 1693.

———. *Praelectiones hermeneuticae ad viam dextre indagandi et exponendi sensum Sacrae Scripturae.* Halle, 1717–1723.

———. *Werke in Auswahl.* Ed. E. Peschke. Wittenberg, 1969.

Greschat, M., ed. *Zur neueren Pietismusforschung.* Darmstadt, 1977.

Kaiser, O. "Kants Answeisung zur Auslegung der Bibel: Ein Beitrag zur Geschichte der Hermeneutik." *Neue Zeitschrift für systematische Theologie und Religionsphilosophie* 11 (1969):125–138.

Meyer, G. *Der Hallenser P. August Hermann Francke in seinem Verhältnis zum Protestantismus.* Berlin, 1970.

Peterson, E. "Das Problem der Bibelauslegung im Pietismus des 18. Jahrhunderts." *Zeitschrift für systematische Theologie* (1923):468–481.

Pietismus und Bibel. Wittenberg, 1970.

Rambach, J. J. "Dissertatio theologica de idoneo sacrarum literarum interprete." In *Miscellanea sacra,* pt. 3, ed. J. F. Buddeus. Leipzig, 1730.

————. *Erläuterungen über seine eigene Institutiones hermeneuticae sacrae, aus der eigenen Handschrift des seligen Verfassers.* Ed. E. F. Neubauer. Giessen, 1738.

————. *Exercitationes hermeneuticae sive pars altera institutionum hermeneuticarum sacrarum.* Bremen, 1728.

————. *Institutiones hermeneuticae sacrae.* Jena, 1723.

Ratschow, C. H. *Lutherische Dogmatik zwischen Reformation und Aufklärung.* 2 vols. Gütersloh, 1964–1966.

Schleiermacher and Romantic Hermeneutics

Ast, G. A. F. *Entwurf der Universalgeschichte.* Landshut, 1808.

————. "Epochen der griechischen Philosophie." 1805. (Rpt. in E. Behler, *Kritische Friedrich-Schlegel-Ausgabe.* Munich, 1958.)

————. *Grundlinien der Grammatik, Hermeneutik und Kritik.* Landshut, 1808.

————. *Grundriss der Philologie.* Landshut, 1808.

————. *Lexicon Platonicum.* 3 vols. Leipzig, 1835–1838.

————. *Über den Geist des Altertums und dessen Bedeutung für unser Zeitalter.* Landshut, 1805. (Rpt. in *Dokumente des Neuhumanismus.* Berlin, 1831.)

Schlegel, F. "Philosophie der Philologie." Introduction by Josef Körner. *Logos* 17 (1928):1–72.

Schleiermacher, F. E. D. "Allgemeine Hermeneutik von 1809–10." Ed. W. Virmond. *Schleiermacher-Archiv* 1 (1985):1269–1310.

————. *Dialektik.* Ed. R. Odebrecht. Leipzig, 1942. (Rpt. Darmstadt, 1988.)

————. *Hermeneutik.* Ed. H. Kimmerle. Heidelberg, 1959, 1974.

————. *Hermeneutik und Kritik.* Ed. M. Frank. Frankfurt, 1977.

————. *Hermeneutik und Kritik, mit besonderer Beziehung auf das Neue Testament.* Ed. F. Lücke. Berlin, 1838. (Rpt. Darmstadt, 1988).

————. *Werke.* Ed. O. Braun and J. Bauer. Leipzig, 1910; Aalen, 1967.

Secondary Literature

Avni. *The Bible and Romanticism.* The Hague, 1969.

Behler, E. "Friedrich Schlegels Theorie des Verstehens: Hermeneutik oder Dekonstruktion?" In *Die Aktualität der Frühromantik,* ed. E. Behler and J. Hörisch. Paderborn, 1988. 141–160.

Bianco, F. "Schleiermacher e la fondazione dell'ermeneutica moderna." *Archivio di filosofia* (1968):609–628.

Birus, H. "Schleiermachers Begriff der 'Technischen Interpretation.'" *Schleiermacher-Archiv* 1 (1985):591–600.

———. "Zwischen den Zeiten: Friedrich Schleiermacher als Klassiker der neuzeitlichen Hermeneutik." In his *Hermeneutische Positionen*. 15–58.

Despland, M. "L'herméneutique de Schleiermacher dans son contexte historique et culturel." *Studies in Religion/Sciences religieuses* 12 (1983):35–50.

Flashar, H. "Die methodisch-hermeneutischen Ansätze von Friedrich August Wolf und Friedrich Ast: Traditionelle und neue Begründungen." In *Philologie und Hermeneutik im 19. Jahrhundert,* ed. H. Flashar, K. Gründer, and A. Horstmann 21–31.

Flashar, H., K. Gründer, and A. Horstmann, eds. *Philologie und Hermeneutik im 19. Jahrhundert: Zur Geschichte und Methodologie der Geisteswissenschaften.* Göttingen, 1979.

Forstmann, H. J. "The Understanding of Language by Friedrich Schlegel and Schleiermacher." *Soundings* 51 (1968):146–165.

Frank, M. *Einleitung zu Schleiermacher: Hermeneutik und Kritik.* Frankfurt, 1977. 7–67.

———. *Das individuelle Allgemeine: Textstrukturierung und -interpretation nach Schleiermacher.* Frankfurt, 1977.

———. "Partialität oder Universalität der 'Divination.'" *Deutsche Vierteljahresschrift für Literaturwissenschaft und Geistesgeschichte* 58 (1984):238–249.

———. "Der Text und sein Stil: Schleiermachers Sprachtheorie." In his *Das Sagbare und das Unsagbare.* 13–35.

Gipper, H. "L'ermeneutica dello spirito di Ast." *Wirkendes Wort* 15 (1965):39–61.

Hentschke, A., and U. Muhlack. *Einführung in die Geschichte der klassischen Philologie.* Darmstadt, 1972.

Hinrichs, W. "Standpunktfrage und Gesprächsmodell: Das vergessene Elementarproblem der hermeneutisch-dialektischen Wissenschaftstheorie seit Schleiermacher." *Schleiermacher-Archiv* 1 (1985):513–538.

Horstmann, A. "Die Forschung in der klassischen Philologie des 19. Jahrhunderts." In *Konzeption und Begriff der Forschung in den Wissenschaften des 19. Jahrhunderts: Studien zur Wissenschaftstheorie.* Meisenheim, 1978. 12:27–57.

———. "Die 'Klassische Philologie' zwischen Humanismus und Historismus: Friedrich August Wolf und die Begründung der modernen Altertumswissenschaft." *Berichte zur Wissenschaftsgeschichte* 1 (1978):51–70.

Hübener, W. "Schleiermacher und die hermeneutische Tradition." *Schleiermacher-Archiv* 1 (1985):561–574.

Huge, E. *Poesie und Reflexion in der Ästhetik des frühen Friedrich Schlegel.* Stuttgart, 1971.

Kimmerle, H. "Die Hermeneutik Schleiermachers im Zusammenhang seines spekulativen Denkens." Ph.D. diss., University of Heidelberg, 1957.

———. "Typologie der Grundformen des Verstehens von der Reformation bis zu Schleiermacher." *Zeitschrift für Theologie und Kirche* 67 (1970):162–182.

———. "Das Verhältnis Schleiermachers zum transzendentalen Idealismus." *Kantstudien* 51 (1959–1960):410–426.

Koppel, M. *Schellings Einfluss auf die Naturphilosophie Görres.* Würzburg, 1930.

Patsch, H. "Friedrich August Wolf und Friedrich Ast: Die Hermeneutik als Appendix der Philologie." In *Klassiker der Hermeneutik,* ed. U. Nassen. 76–107.

———. "Friedrich Schlegels 'Philosophie der Philologie' und Schleiermachers frühe Entwürfe zur Hermeneutik: Zur Frühgeschichte der romantischen Hermeneutik." *Zeitschrift für Theologie und Kirche* 63 (1966):432–472.

Pleger, W. H. *Schleiermachers Philosophie.* Berlin, 1988.

Pohl, K. "Die Bedeutung der Sprache für den Erkenntnisakt in der 'Dialektik' F. Schleiermachers." *Kantstudien* 46 (1954–1955):302–332.

Potepa, M. "Hermeneutik und Dialektik bei Schleiermacher." *Schleiermacher-Archiv* 1 (1985):485–498.

Rieger, R. *Interpretation und Wissen: Zur philosophischen Begründung der Hermeneutik bei Friedrich Schleiermacher und ihrem geschichtlichen Hintergrund.* Berlin, 1981. 171–189.

Scholtz, G. *Die Philosophie Schleiermachers.* Darmstadt, 1984.

———. "Schleiermachers Dialektik und Diltheys erkenntnistheoretische Logik." *Dilthey-Jahrbuch* 2 (1984):171–189.

Schultz, W. "Die Grundlagen der Hermeneutik Schleiermachers: Ihre Auswirkungen und ihre Grenzen." *Zeitschrift für Theologie und Kirche* 50 (1953):158–184.

———. "Die unendliche Bewegung in der Hermeneutik Schleiermachers und ihre Auswirkung auf die hermeneutische Situation der Gegenwart." *Zeitschrift für Theologie und Kirche* 65 (1968):23–52.

Szondi, P. "L'herméneutique de Schleiermacher." *Poétique* 1 (1970):141–155.

Torrance, J. B. "Interpretation and Understanding in Schleiermacher's Theology: Some Critical Questions." *Scottish Journal of Theology* 21 (1968):268–282.

Torrance, T. F. "Hermeneutics according to F. E. D. Schleiermacher." *Scottish Journal of Theology* 21 (1968):257–267.

Vattimo, G. *Schleiermacher filosofo dell'interpretazione.* Milan, 1968.

Vercellone, F. "Ast." *Il pensiero ermeneutico.* Genoa, 1986. 93–95.

Virmond, W. "Neue Textgrundlagen zu Schleiermachers früher Hermeneutik." *Schleiermacher-Archiv* 1 (1985):575–590.

Wobbermin, G. "Schleiermachers Hermeneutik in ihrer Bedeutung für seine religionswissenschaftliche Arbeit." *Nachrichten von der Gesellschaft der Wissenschaften zu Göttingen* (1930).

Philological and Historical Hermeneutics in the Nineteenth Century

Becker, L. "Droysens Geschichtsauffassung." Ph.D. diss., University of Heidelberg, 1929.

Behler, E. "Friedrich Schlegels Theorie des Verstehens: Hermeneutik oder Dekonstruktion?" In *Die Aktualität der Frühromantik,* ed. E. Behler and J. Hörisch. Paderborn, 1988. 141–160.

Blanke, H. W. "Georg Andreas Wills Einleitung in die historische Gelahrtheit (1766) und die Anfänge moderner Historik-Vorlesungen in Deutschland." *Dilthey-Jahrbuch* 2 (1984):193–222.

Blanke, H. W., D. Fleischer, and J. Rüsen. "Historik als akademische Praxis: Eine Dokumentation der geschichtstheoretischen Vorlesungen an deutschsprachigen Universitäten von 1750 bis 1900." *Dilthey-Jahrbuch* 1 (1983):182–255.

Böckh, A. *Enzyklopädie und Methodenlehre der philologischen Wissenschaften.* Ed. E. Bratuschek. Leipzig, 1877, 2d ed. 1886; Darmstadt, 1966.

———. *Gesammelte kleine Schriften.* 7 vols., ed. F. Ascherson, E. Bratuschek, and P. Eichloht. Leipzig, 1858–1884.

Danz, J. "August Böckh: Die Textinterpretation als Verstehen des subjektiven Objektiven." In *Klassiker der Hermeneutik,* ed. U. Nassen. 131–172.

Droysen, J. G. *Grundriß der Historik.* Berlin, 1868; 3d. ed. 1882.

———. *Historik: Vorlesungen über die Enzyklopädie und Methodologie der Geschichte.* Ed. R. Hübner. Munich, 1937; Darmstadt, 1977.

———. *Texte zur Geschichtstheorie.* Ed. G. Birtsch and J. Rüsen. Göttingen, 1972.

Grover, J. A. "August Boeckh's Hermeneutic and Its Relationship to Contemporary Scholarship." Ph.D. diss., Stanford University, 1973.

Hoffmann, M. *August Böckh: Lebensbeschreibung und Auswahl aus seinem wissenschaftlichen Briefwechsel.* Leipzig, 1901.

Landfester, M. "Ulrich Wilamowitz-Moellendorff und die Hermeneutische Tradition des 19. Jahrhundert." In *Philologie und Hermeneutik im 19. Jahrhundert,* ed. H. Flashar, K. Gründer, and A. Horstmann. 156–180.

MacLean, M. J. "Johann Gustav Droysen and the Development of Historical Hermeneutics." *History and Theory* 21 (1982):347–365.

Muhlack, U. "Zum Verhältnis klassischer Philologie und Geschichtswissenschaft im 19. Jahrhundert." In *Philologie und Hermeneutik im 19. Jahrhundert,* ed. H. Flashar, K. Gründer, and A. Horstmann. 225–239.

Overbeck, F. *Über Entstehung und Recht einer historischen Betrachtung der neutestamentlichen Schrift in der Theologie.* Basel, 1872.

Pflaum, J. G. J. G. *Droysens Historik in ihrer Bedeutung für die moderne Geschichtswissenschaft.* Gotha, 1907.

Pflug, G. "Hermeneutik und Kritik: August Böckh in der Tradition des Begriffspaars." *Archiv für Begriffsgeschichte* 18 (1975):138–196.

Rinhe-Fink, L. *Geschichtlichkeit: Ihr terminologischer und begrifflicher Ursprung bei Hegel, Haym, Dilthey und Yorck.* Göttingen, 1964.

Rüsen, J. *Begriffene Geschichte: Genesis und Begründung der Geschichtstheorie J. G. Droysens.* Paderborn, 1969.

Schnädelbach, H. *Geschichtsphilosophie nach Hegel: Die Probleme des Historismus.* Freiburg, 1974.

Spieler, K.-H. *Untersuchungen zu Johann Gustav Droysens "Historik."* Berlin, 1970.

Steinthal, H. *Die Arten und Formen der Interpretation.* 1878. (Rpt. in *Seminar: Philosophische Hermeneutik,* ed. H.-G. Gadamer and G. Boehm. 532–542.)

———. "Darstellung und Kritik der Böckhschen Encyclopädie und Methodologie der Philologie." *Zeitschrift für Völkerpsychologie und Sprachwissenschaft* 11 (1880):303–326. (Rpt. in his *Kleine sprachtheoretische Schriften,* ed. W. Bumann. Hildesheim, 1970. 564–605.)

Stierle, K. "Altertumswissenschaftliche Hermeneutik und die Entstehung der Neuphilologie." In *Philologie und Hermeneutik im 19. Jahrhundert,* ed. H. Flashar, K. Gründer, and A. Horstmann. 260–288.

Strohschneider-Kohrs, I. "Textauslegung und hermeneutischer Zirkel: Zur Innovation des Interpretationsbegriffs August Böckh." In *Philologie und Hermeneutik im 19. Jahrhundert,* ed. H. Flashar, K. Gründer, and A. Horstmann.

Vercellone, F. "L'ermeneutica nell'Encyklopädie di August Boeckh." In his *L'ermeneutica e l'immagine dell'antico.* Turin, 1988.

Vogt, E. "Der Methodenstreit zwischen Herman und Böckh und seine Bedeutung für die Geschichte der Philologie." In *Philologie und Hermeneutik im 19. Jahrhundert,* ed. H. Flashar, K. Gründer, and A. Horstmann. 103–121.

Wolf, F. A. *Darstellung der Altertumswissenschaft nach Begriff, Umfang, Zweck und Wert.* Ed. S. F. W. Hoffmann. Leipzig, 1830.

———. *Museum der Altertumswissenschaften.* Berlin, 1807. (Rpt. Weinheim, 1986.)

———. *Vorlesungen über die Enzyklopädie der Altertumswissenschaften.* Ed. J. D. Gürtler. Leipzig, 1831.

Dilthey

Dilthey, W. *Gesammelte Schriften.* 20 vols. Stuttgart, 1914ff.

———. "Der Aufbau der geschichtlichen Welt in den Geisteswissenschaften." In 7 (4th ed., 1958).

———. *Einleitung in die Geisteswissenschaften.* In 1 (1962).

———. "Die Entstehung der Hermeneutik." In 5 (4th ed., 1964):317–331.

———. "Das hermeneutische System Schleiermachers in der Auseinandersetzung mit der älteren protestantischen Hermeneutik." In 14, 2 (1966):595–787.

———. *Der junge Dilthey: Ein Lebensbild in Briefen und Tagebüchern, 1852–1870.* 2d ed., ed. C. [Dilthey] Misch. Leipzig, 1960.

Secondary Literature

Acham, K. "Diltheys Beitrag zur Theorie der Kultur- und Sozialwissenschaften." *Dilthey-Jahrbuch* 3 (1985):9–51.

Anz, H. "Hermeneutik der Individualität: Wilhelm Diltheys hermeneutische Position und ihre Aporien." In *Hermeneutische Positionen,* ed. H. Birus. 59–88.

Bianco, F. "Dilthey e il problema del relativisimo." In *Wilhelm Dilthey,* ed. G. Cacciatore and G. Cantillo.

————. *Dilthey e la genesi della critica storica della ragione.* Milan, 1971.

————. *Introduzione a Dilthey.* Rome, 1985.

————. ed. *Dilthey e il pensiero del Novecento.* Milan, 1985.

Boeder, H. "Dilthey 'und' Heidegger: Zur Geschichtlichkeit des Menschen." In *Dilthey und der Wandel des Philosophiebegriffs seit dem 19. Jahrhundert,* ed. E. W. Orth. 161–177.

Bollnow, O. F. *Dilthey: Eine Einführung in seine Philosophie.* 1936; 4th ed. Schaffhausen, 1980.

————. "Festrede zu Wilhelm Diltheys 150. Geburtstag." *Dilthey-Jahrbuch* 2 (1984):28–50.

————. *Studien zur Hermeneutik.* 2 vols. Freiburg, 1982, 1983.

Bulhof, I. N. *Wilhelm Dilthey: A Hermeneutic Approach to the Study of History and Culture.* The Hague, 1980.

Cacciatore, G. "Dilthey e la storiografia tedesca dell'Ottocento." *Studi storici* 24 (1983):55–89.

————. *Scienza e filosofia in Dilthey,* vol. 2. Naples, 1976.

————. *Vita e forme della scienza storica: Saggi sulla storiografia di Dilthey.* Naples, 1985.

Cacciatore, G., and G. Cantillo, eds. *Wilhelm Dilthey: Critica della metafisica e ragione storica.* Bologna, 1986.

Cantillo, G. "Conoscenza storica e teoria della storia: Dilthey e Droysen." *Studi storici* 24 (1983):91–126.

Cüppers, K. *Die erkenntnistheoretischen Grundgedanken Wilhelm Diltheys.* Leipzig, 1933.

Dilthey-Jahrbuch für Philosophie und Geschichte der Geisteswissenschaften. Ed. F. Rodi. 1983ff.

Diwald, H. *Wilhelm Dilthey: Erkenntnistheorie und Philosophie der Geschichte.* Göttingen, 1963.

Ermarth, M. "Historical Understanding in the Thought of Wilhelm Dilthey." *History and Theory* 20 (1981):323–334.

————. "The Transformation of Hermeneutics." *Monist* 64 (1981):175–194.

————. *Wilhelm Dilthey: The Critique of Historical Reason.* Chicago, 1978.

Hermann, U. *Bibliographie Wilhelm Dilthey: Quellen und Literatur.* Weinheim, 1960.

Holborn, H. "Wilhelm Dilthey and the Critique of Historical Reason." *Journal of the History of Ideas* 11 (1950):93–118.

Hufnagel, E. "Wilhelm Dilthey: Hermeneutik als Grundlegung der Geisteswissenschaften." In *Klassiker der Hermeneutik,* ed. U. Nassen. 173–206.

Ineichen, H. *Erkenntnistheorie und geschichtlich-gesellschaftliche Welt: Diltheys Logik der Geisteswissenschaften.* Frankfurt, 1975.

Jensen, B. E. "The Recent Trend in the Interpretation of Dilthey." *Philosophy of the Social Sciences* 8 (1978):419–438.

————. "The Role of Intellectual History in Dilthey's Kritik der historischen Vernunft." *Dilthey-Jahrbuch* 2 (1984):65–91.

Johach, H. "Diltheys Philosophie des Subjekts und die Grundlegung der Geistes- und Sozialwissenschaften: Zur Aktualität der Einleitung in die Geisteswissenschaften." *Dilthey-Jahrbuch* 2 (1984):92–127.

Kerckhoven, G. van. "Die Grundansätze von Husserls Konfrontation mit Dilthey im Lichte der geschichtlichen Selbstzeugnisse." In *Dilthey und der Wandel des Philosophiebegriffs seit dem 19. Jahrhundert,* ed. E. W. Orth. 134–160.

Kornbichler, T. *Deutsche Geschichtsschreibung im 19. Jahrhundert: Wilhelm Dilthey und die Begründung der modernen Geschichtswissenschaft.* Pfaffenweiler, 1984.

Krausser, P. *Kritik der endlichen Vernunft: Wilhelm Diltheys Revolution der allgemeinen Wissenschafts- und Handlungstheorie.* Frankfurt, 1968.

Landgrebe, L. "Wilhelm Diltheys Theorie der Geisteswissenschaften." *Jahrbuch für Philosophie und Phänomenologische Forschung* 9 (1928):237–366.

Lessing, H.-U. "Briefe an Dilthey anläßlich der Veröffentlichung seiner 'Ideen über eine beschreibende und zergliedernde Psychologie.'" *Dilthey-Jahrbuch* 3 (1985):193–234.

————. "Dilthey und Lazarus." *Dilthey-Jahrbuch* 3 (1985):57–82.

————. *Die Idee einer Kritik der historischen Vernunft: Wilhelm Diltheys erkenntnistheoretisch-logisch-methodologische Grundlegung der Geisteswissenschaften.* Freiburg, 1984.

————. "Die zeitgenössischen Rezensionen von Diltheys Einleitung in die Geisteswissenschaften (1883 bis 1885)." *Dilthey-Jahrbuch* 1 (1983):91–181.

Linge, D. E. "Dilthey and Gadamer: Two Theories of Historical Understanding." *Journal of the American Academy of Religion* 41 (1973):536–553.

Makkreel, R. A. *Dilthey: Philosopher of the Human Studies.* Princeton, 1975.

————. "Dilthey und die interpretierenden Wissenschaften: Die Rolle von Erklären und Verstehen." *Dilthey-Jahrbuch* 1 (1983):57–73.

————. *Introduction to W. Dilthey: Descriptive Psychology and Historical Understanding.* The Hague, 1977.

Marini, G. *Dilthey e la comprensione del mondo umano.* Milan, 1965.

Oehler, K. "Dilthey und die klassische Philologie." In *Philologie und Hermeneutik im 19. Jahrhundert,* ed. H. Flashar, K. Gründer, and A. Horstmann. 181–198.

Orth, E. W., ed. *Dilthey und der Wandel des Philosophiebegriffs seit dem 19. Jahrhundert.* Freiburg, 1984.

————. *Dilthey und die Philosophie der Gegenwart.* Freiburg, 1985.

Rand, C. G. "Two Meanings of Historicism in the Writings of Dilthey, Troeltsch, and Meinecke." *Journal of the History of Ideas* 21 (1964):503–518.

Rickert, H. *Die Philosophie des Lebens: Darstellung und Kritik der philosophischen Modeströmungen unserer Zeit.* Tübingen, 1920.

Rickman, H. P. *Wilhelm Dilthey: Pioneer of the Human Study.* Berkeley, 1979.

Riedel, M. "Das erkenntnistheoretische Motiv in Diltheys Theorie der Geisteswissenschaften." In *Hermeneutik und Dialektik,* ed. R. Bubner, K. Cramer, and R. Wiehl.

———. *Erklären oder Verstehen? Zur Theorie und Geschichte der hermeneutischen Wissenschaften.* Stuttgart, 1978.

Rodi, F. "Diltheys Kritik der historischen Vernunft—Programm oder System?" *Dilthey-Jahrbuch* 3 (1985):140–165.

———. *Morphologie und Hermeneutik: Zur Methode Diltheys Ästhetik.* Stuttgart, 1969.

———. "Zum Gegenwärtigen Stand der Dilthey-Forschung." *Dilthey-Jahrbuch* 1 (1983):260–267.

Rodi, F., and H.-U. Lessing, eds. *Materialien zur Philosophie Wilhelm Diltheys.* Frankfurt, 1984.

Scholtz, G. "Schleiermachers Dialektik und Diltheys erkenntnistheoretische Logik." *Dilthey-Jahrbuch* 2 (1984):171–189.

Seebohm, T. M. "Boeckh and Dilthey: The Development of Methodical Hermeneutics." *Man and World* 17 (1984):325–346.

Sommerfeld, H. *Wilhelm Dilthey und der Positivismus: Eine Untersuchung zur "Einleitung in die Geisteswissenschaften."* Berlin, 1926.

Strube, W. "Analyse der Textinterpretation." *Dilthey-Jahrbuch* 5 (1988):141–163.

Tuttle, H. N. *Wilhelm Dilthey's Philosophy of Historical Understanding: A Critical Analysis.* Leiden, 1969.

Young, T. J. "The Hermeneutical Significance of Dilthey's Theory of World-Views." *International Philosophical Quarterly* 23 (1983):125–140.

Zöckler, C. *Dilthey und die Hermeneutik: Diltheys Begründung der Hermeneutik als "Praxiswissenschaft" und die Geschichte ihrer Rezeption.* Stuttgart, 1975.

The Dilthey School

Aron, R. *Essai sur la théorie de l'histoire dans l'Allemagne contemporaine.* Paris, 1938. Under a new title in the second edition: *La philosophie critique de l'histoire: Essai sur une théorie allemande de l'histoire.* Paris, 1950.

Bollnow, O. F. *Studien zur Hermeneutik,* vol. 2: *Zur hermeneutischen Logik bei Georg Misch und Hans Lipps.* Freiburg, 1983.

———. "Über das kritische Verstehen." *Deutsche Vierteljahrsschrift für Literaturwissenschaft und Geistesgeschichte* 22 (1944):1–29.

———. "Verstand und Leben: Die Philosophie des jungen Nohl." *Dilthey-Jahrbuch* 4 (1986–1987):228–265.

Kohls, E.-W. "Einen Autor beser verstehen als er sich selbst verstanden hat: Zur Problematik der neueren Hermeneutik und Methodik am Beispiel Wilhelm Dilthey, Adolf Harnack und Ernst Troeltsch." *Theologische Zeitschrift* 26 (1970):321–337.

——. *Vorwärts zu den Tatsachen: Zur Überwindung der heutigen Hermeneutik seit Schleiermacher, Dilthey, Harnack und Troeltsch*. Basel, 1973.

Lipps, H. *Untersuchungen zu einer hermeneutischen Logik*. Frankfurt, 1938. (Rpt. in his *Werke*, vol. 2, 2d ed. Frankfurt, 1975.)

——. *Die Verbindlichkeit der Sprache*. 4th ed., ed. E.-M. v. Busse. Frankfurt, 1977.

Meinecke, F. *Die Entstehung des Historismus*. 2d ed. Munich, 1946.

——. *Ernst Troeltsch und das Problem des Historismus*. 1923. (Rpt. in his *Schaffender Spiegel: Studien zur deutschen Geschichtsschreibung und Geschichtsauffassung*. Stuttgart, 1948.)

Misch, G. *Lebensphilosophie und Phänomenologie: Eine Auseinandersetzung der Diltheyschen Richtung mit Heidegger und Husserl*. 1930; 3d ed. Darmstadt, 1967.

Rodi, F. *Erkenntnis des Erkannten: Zur Hermeneutik des 19. und 20. Jahrhunderts*. Frankfurt, 1990.

Rothacker, E. "Die dogmatische Denkform in den Geisteswissenschaften und das Problem des Historismus." In *Abhandlungen der Akademie der Wissenschaften und der Literatur in Mainz*. Mainz, 1954. (Rpt. in *Seminar: Philosophische Hermeneutik*, ed. H.-G. Gadamer and G. Boehm. 221–238.)

——. *Einleitung in die Geisteswissenschaften*. 2d ed. Tübingen, 1930.

——. "Historismus." *Schmollers Jahrbuch* 62 (1938):388–399.

——. "Logik und Systematik der Geisteswissenschaften." In *Handbuch der Philosophie*, vol. 2: *Natur, Geist, Gott*, ed. A Bauemler and M. Schroter. Munich, 1927; 3d ed. Bonn, 1948.

——. *Das Verstehen in den Gesteswissenschaften*. 1925.

Spranger, E. *Der Sinn der Voraussetzungslosigkeit in den Geisteswissenschaften 1929*. 3d ed. Heidelberg, 1964.

——. "Zur Theorie des Verstehens und zur geisteswissenschaftlichen Psychologie." In *Festschrift für J. Volkelt*. Munich, 1918. 357–403.

Troeltsch, E. *Der Historismus und seine Probleme*. Tübingen, 1922. (Rpt. Aalen, 1961.)

——. *Der Historismus und seine Überwindung*. Berlin, 1924. (Rpt. Aalen, 1966.)

Nietzsche

Nietzsche, F. *Sämtliche Werke: Kritische Studienausgabe in 15 Bänden*. ed. G. Colli and M. Montinari. Munich, 1980.

Secondary Literature

Allison, D. "Destruction/Deconstruction in the Text of Nietzsche." *Boundary 2* 8 (1979):197–222.

Behler, E. *Derrida-Nietzsche, Nietzsche-Derrida*. Munich, 1988.

Bertmann, M. A. "Hermeneutic in Nietzsche." *Journal of Value Inquiry* 7 (1973):254–260.

Birus, H. "Wir Philologen: Überlegung zu Nietzsches Begriff der Interpretation." *Revue Internationale de Philosophie* 151 (1984):373–395.

Deleuze, G. *Nietzsche et la philosophie.* Paris, 1962.

Derrida, J. *L'ecriture et la différence.* Paris, 1967.

Figl, J. *Interpretation als philosophisches Prinzip.* Berlin, 1982.

———. "Nietzsche und die philosophische Hermeneutik des 20. Jahrhunderts: Mit besonderer Berücksichtigung Diltheys, Heideggers und Gadamers." *Nietzsche-Studien* 10–11 (1981–1982):408–430.

Fink, E. *Nietzsches Philosophie.* 3d ed. Stuttgart, 1973.

Foucault, M. "Nietzsche, Freud, Marx." In *Nietzsche: Cahiers de Royaumont.* Paris, 1967. 183–200.

———. "Nietzsche, la généalogie, l'histoire." In *Hommages à Jean Hyppolite.* Paris, 1971. 145–172.

Gerhardt, V. *Pathos und Distanz: Studien zur Philosophie Nietzsches.* Stuttgart, 1988.

———. "Die Perspektive des Perspektivismus." *Nietzsche-Studien* 18 (1989):260–281.

Graybeal, J. "Nietzsche's Fiddle." *Philosophy Today* 32 (1988):232–243.

Habermas, J. *Nachwort zu F. Nietzsche: Erkenntnistheoretische Schriften.* Frankfurt, 1968.

Hamacher, W. "Das Versprechen der Auslegung: Überlegungen zum hermeneutischen Imperativ bei Kant und Nietzsche." In *Spiegel und Gleichnis: Festschrift für Jacob Taubes,* ed. N. W. Bolz and W. Hübener. Würzburg, 1983. 252–273.

Heidegger, M. *Nietzsche.* 2 vols. Pfullingen, 1961.

Krell, D. F. "'Ashes, ashes, we all fall . . .': Encountering Nietzsche." In *Dialogue and Deconstruction,* ed. P. Michelfelder and R. E. Palmer. 222–232.

Krell, D. F., and D. Wood, eds. *Exceedingly Nietzsche: Aspects of Contemporary Nietzsche Interpretation.* New York, 1988.

Müller-Lauter, W. *Nietzsche: Seine Philosophie der Gegensätze und die Gegensätze seiner Philosophie.* Berlin, 1971.

———. "Nietzsches Lehre vom Willen zur Macht." *Nietzsche-Studien* 3 (1974):1–60.

Pöschl, V. "Nietzsche und die klassische Philologie." In *Philologie und Hermeneutik im 19. Jahrhundert,* ed. H. Flashar, K. Gründer, and A. Horstmann. 141–155.

Risser, J. "The Disappearance of the Text: Nietzsche's Double Hermeneutic." *Research in Phenomenology* 15 (1985):113–142.

Salaquarda, J., ed. *Nietzsche.* Darmstadt, 1980.

Schrift, A. *Nietzsche and the Question of Interpretation: Between Hermeneutics and Deconstruction.* London, 1990.

———. "Nietzsche's Hermeneutic Significance." *Auslegung* 10 (1983):39–47.

3. Philosophical Hermeneutics in the Twentieth Century

A) HEIDEGGER

Heidegger, M. *Gesamtausgabe.* Frankfurt, 1975–.

———. "Anmerkungen zu Karl Jaspers' Psychologie der Weltanschauung." In *Wegmarken.* 2d enl. ed. Frankfurt, 1978.

———. *Being and Time.* Trans. John Macquarrie and Edward Robinson. New York, 1962.

———. *Die Grundprobleme der Phänomenologie.* Ed. F. W. v. Herrmann. In *GA* 24 (1975).

———. *Logik: Die Frage nach der Wahrheit.* Ed. W. Biemel. In *GA* 21 (1976).

———. *Nietzsche.* 2 vols. Pfullingen, 1961.

———. *Ontologie (Hermeneutik der Faktizität).* Ed. K. Bröcker-Oltmans. In *GA* 63 (1988).

———. "Phänomenologische Interpretation zu Aristoteles (Anzeige der hermeneutischen Situation)." Ed. H.-U. Lessing. *Dilthey-Jahrbuch* 6 (1989):235–276.

———. *Prolegomena zur Geschichte des Zeitbegriffs.* Ed. P. Jaeger. In *GA* 20 (1979).

———. *Sein und Zeit.* 1927. 14th ed. Tübingen, 1977.

———. *Unterwegs zur Sprache.* Pfullingen, 1959.

Secondary Literature

Bernasconi, R. "Bridging the Abyss: Heidegger and Gadamer." *Research in Phenomenology* 16 (1986):1–24.

———. *The Question of Language in Heidegger's History of Being.* Atlantic Highlands, N.J., 1985.

Caputo, J. D. "Hermeneutics as the Recovery of Man." *Man and World* 15 (1982):343–367. (Rpt. in *Hermeneutics and Modern Philosophy,* ed. B. R. Wachterhauser. 416–445.)

———. "Husserl, Heidegger, and the Question of a 'Hermeneutic' Phenomenology." *Husserl Studies* 1 (1984):157–178.

Carr, D. *Phenomenology and the Problem of History.* Evanston, Ill., 1974.

De Santiago Guervos, L. E. "La radicalización ontológica de la hermenéutica en Heidegger." *Pensamiento: Revista de investigación e información filosófica* 44 (1988):49–66.

Figal, G. *Martin Heidegger: Phänomenologie der Freiheit.* Frankfurt, 1988.

———. "Selbstverstehen in instabiler Freiheit: Die hermeneutische Position Martin Heideggers." In *Hermeneutische Positionen,* ed. H. Birus. 89–119.

Gadamer, H.-G. "Heideggers 'theologische' Jugendschrift." *Dilthey-Jahrbuch* 6 (1989).

Gethmann, C. F. "Philosophie als Vollzug und als Begriff: Heideggers Identitäts-philosophie des Lebens in der Vorlesung vom Wintersemester 1921/22 und ihr Verhältnis zu Sein und Zeit." *Dilthey-Jahrbuch* 4 (1986–1987):27–53.

———. *Verstehen und Auslegung: Das Methodenproblem in der Philosophie Martin Heideggers.* Bonn, 1974.

Gethmann-Siefert, A., ed. *Philosophie und Poesie: Otto Pöggeler zum 60. Geburtstag.* 2 vols. Stuttgart, 1988.

Gethmann-Seifert, A., and O. Pöggeler, eds. *Heidegger und die praktische Philosophie.* Frankfurt, 1988.

Grondin, J. "Die Hermeneutik der Faktizität als ontologische Destruktion und Ideologiekritik." In *Zur philosophischen Aktualität Heideggers,* ed. D. Pappenfuss and O. Pöggeler. Frankfurt, 1990–1991. 1:163–178.

———. "Le sens du titre *Etre et temps.*" *Dialogue* 25 (1986):709–725. (Rpt. in his *L'horizon herméneutique de la pensée contemporaine* [Paris, 1993].)

———. *Le tournant dans la pensée de Martin Heidegger.* Paris, 1987.

Hermann, F.-W. von. *Phänomenologie des Daseins,* vol. 1. Frankfurt, 1987.

———. *Subjekt und Dasein: Interpretationen zu "Sein und Zeit."* Frankfurt, 1974.

Hogemann, F. "Heideggers Konzeption der Phänomenologie in den Vorlesungen aus dem Wintersemester 1919/20 und dem Sommersemester 1920." *Dilthey-Jahrbuch* 4 (1986–1987):54–71.

Jäger, H. *Gott: Nochmals Martin Heidegger.* Tübingen, 1978.

Jamme, C. "Heideggers frühe Begründung der Hermeneutik." *Dilthey-Jahrbuch* 4 (1986–1987):72–90.

Jamme, C., and O. Pöggeler, eds. *Phänomenologie im Widerstreit: Zum 50. Todestag Edmund Husserls.* Frankfurt, 1989.

Jankowitz, W. G. *Philosophie und Vorurteil.* Meisenheim, 1975.

Kelkel, A. L. *La légende de l'être: Language et poésie chez Heidegger.* Paris, 1980.

Kisiel, T. "Das Entstehen des Begriffsfeldes 'Faktizität' im Frühwerk Heideggers." *Dilthey-Jahrbuch* 4 (1986–1987):91–120.

———. "The Happening of Tradition: The Hermeneutics of Gadamer and Heidegger." *Man and World* 2 (1969):358–385.

———. "Why the First Draft of *Being and Time* Was Never Published." *Journal of the British Society for Phenomenology* 20 (1989):3–22.

Kockelmans, J. J. "Destructive Retrieve and Hermeneutic Phenomenology in *Being and Time.*" *Research in Phenomenology* 7 (1977):106–137.

———. *On Heidegger and Language.* Evanston, Ill., 1972.

Maraldo, J. C. *Der hermeneutische Zirkel: Untersuchungen zu Schleiermacher, Dilthey und Heidegger.* Freiburg, 1974.

Marx, W. *Heidegger und die Tradition.* Stuttgart, 1961.

Murray, M., ed. *Heidegger and Modern Philosophy: Critical Essays.* New Haven, 1978.

Pöggeler, O. *Der Denkweg Martin Heideggers.* 2d ed. Pfullingen, 1983.

———. *Heidegger und die hermeneutische Philosophie.* Freiburg, 1983.

———. "Heideggers Begegnung mit Dilthey." *Dilthey-Jahrbuch* 4 (1986–1987):121–160.

———. "Heideggers Neubestimmung der Phänomenologie." In *Neuere Entwicklungen des Phänomensbegriffs.* Freiburg, 1980. 124–162.

———, ed. *Heidegger: Perspektiven zur Deutung seines Werks.* Cologne, 1969.

———, ed. *Hermeneutische Philosophie.* Munich, 1972.

Regina, U. "Anticipazioni valutatuve e apertura ontologica nelle teorie ermeneutiche di M. Heidegger, R. Bultmann, H.-G. Gadamer." In *Interpretazione e valori,* ed. G. Galli. Turin, 1982. 139–172.

Riedel, M. "Die akroamatische Dimension der Hermeneutik." In *Philosophie und Poesie,* ed. A. Gethmann-Siefert.

———. "Naturhermeneutik und Ethik im Denken Heideggers." *Heidegger Studien* 5 (1989):153–172.

———. "Zwischen Plato und Aristoteles: Heideggers doppelte Exposition der Seinsfrage und der Ansatz von Gadamers hermeneutischer Gesprächsdialektik." *Allgemeine Zeitschrift für Philosophie* 11 (1986):1–28.

Rodi, F. "Die Bedeutung Diltheys für die Konzeption von *Sein und Zeit:* Zum Umfeld von Heideggers Kasseler Vorträgen (1921)." *Dilthey-Jahrbuch* 4 (1986–1987):161–176.

Sass, H. H. *Heidegger-Bibliographie.* Meisenheim, 1968.

Schulz, W. "Die Aufhebung der Metaphysik in Heideggers Denken." In *Heideggers These vom Ende der Philosophie,* ed. M. F. Fresco. Bonn, 1989. 33–48.

———. "Über den philosophiegeschichtlichen Ort Martin Heideggers." *Philosophische Rundschau* 1 (1953–1954):211–232.

Sheehan, T. "Heidegger's Lehrjahre." In *The Collegium Phaenomenologicum: The First Ten Years.* Dordrecht, 1988. 77–137.

———. *Time and Being,* 1925–27." In *Thinking about Being: Aspects of Heidegger's Thought,* ed. W. Shahan and J. N. Mohanty. Norman, Okla., 1984. 177–219.

Sinn, D. "Heideggers Spätphilosophie." *Philosophische Rundschau* 14 (1967):81–182.

Thurnher, R. "Heideggers *Sein und Zeit* als philosophisches Programm." *Allgemeine Zeitschrift für Philosophie* 11 (1986):29–52.

———. "Hermeneutik und Verstehen in Heideggers *Sein und Zeit.*" *Salzburger Jahrbuch für Philosophie* 28–29 (1984–1985):101–114.

Tugendhat, E. *Der Wahrheitsbegriff bei Husserl und Heidegger.* 2d ed. Berlin, 1970.

Vattimo, G. *Introduzione a Heidegger.* 3d ed. Rome, 1982.

Volpi, F. "La trasformazione della fenomenologica da Husserl a Heidegger." *Teoria* (1984):125–162.

Waehlens, A. de. "Quelques problèmes ontologiques de l'herméneutique." In *Ermeneutica e tradizione* (Archivio di filosofia). Padua, 1963. 43–53.

Wilson, T. J. *Sein als Text: Vom Textmodell als Martin Heideggers Denkmodell. Eine funktionalistische Interpretation.* Freiburg, 1981.

Wiplinger, F. *Wahrheit und Geschichtlichkeit: Eine Untersuchung über die Frage nach dem Wesen der Wahrheit im Denken Heideggers.* Freiburg, 1961.

Zarader, M. *Heidegger et les paroles de l'origine.* Paris, 1986.

B) GADAMER

Gadamer, H.-G. *Gesammelte Werke.* Tübingen, 1986ff.

Vol. 1: *Hermeneutik I: Wahrheit und Methode. Grundzüge einer philosophischen Hermeneutik.* 1960, 1986.

Vol. 2: *Hermeneutik II: Wahrheit und Methode. Ergänzungen, Register.* 1986.

Vol. 3: *Neuere Philosophie I: Hegel—Husserl—Heidegger.* 1987.

Vol. 4: *Neuere Philosophie II; Probleme—Gestalten.* 1987.

Vol. 5: *Griechische Philosophie I.* 1985.

Vol. 6: *Griechische Philosophie II.* 1985.

Vol. 7: *Griechische Philosophie III: Plato im Dialog.* 1990.

Vol. 8: *Ästetik und Poetik I: Kunst aus Aussage.* 1993.

Vol. 9: *Ästetik und Poetik II: Hermeneutik im Vollzug.* 1993.

Vol. 10: *Nachträge und Verzeichnisse.* 1994.

———. "Dekonstruktion und Hermeneutik," In *Philosophie und Poesie,* ed. A. Gethmann-Siefert. 1:3–16.

———. *Das Erbe Europas: Beiträge.* Frankfurt, 1989.

———. *Das Erbe Hegels.* Frankfurt, 1979.

———. "Erinnerungen an Heideggers Anfänge." *Dilthey-Jahrbuch* 4 (1986–1987): 13–26.

———. "Die Kunst, unrecht haben zu können: Gespräch mit dem Philosophen Hans-Georg Gadamer." *Süddeutsche Zeitung,* no. 34 (February 10–11, 1990): 16.

———. "Grenzen der Sprache." *Evolution und Sprache: Über Entstehung und Wesen der Sprache, Herrenalber Texte* 66 (1985):89–99.

———. *Kleine Schriften.* Tübingen, 1967–1977. Vol. 1: *Philosophische Hermeneutik.* 1967; vol. 2: *Interpretationen.* 1967; vol. 3: *Idee und Sprache: Platon, Husserl, Heidegger.* 1972; Vol. 4: *Variationen.* 1977.

———. *Le Problème de la conscience historique.* Paris, 1963.

———. "The Science of the Life-World." In *The Later Husserl and the Idea of Phenomenology,* ed. A.-T. Tymieniecka. Dordrecht, 1972.

Gadamer, H.-G., and R. Koselleck. *Hermeneutik und Historik.* Heidelberg, 1987.

Secondary Literature

Ambrosio, F. "Gadamer, Plato, and the Discipline of Dialogue." *International Philosophical Quarterly* 27 (1987):17–32.

Arthur, C. E. "Gadamer and Hirsch: The Canonical Work and the Interpreter's Intention." *Cultural Hermeneutics* 4 (1976–1977):183–197.

Basso, M. L. "'Comprensione' o 'critica'? Appunti in margine ad 'Ermeneutica e critica dell'ideologia' di H.-G. Gadamer." *Filosofia Ogge* 5 (1982):429–456.

Becker, J. *Begegnung: Gadamer und Lévinas.* Frankfurt, 1981.

———. *Der "Hermeneutische Zirkel" bei Gadamer und die "Alteritas" bei Lévinas, zu verstehen als ein ethisches Ereignis.* Rome, 1978.

Becker, O. "Die Fragwürdigkeit der Transzendierung der ästhetischen Dimension der Kunst." *Philosophische Rundschau* 10 (1962):225–238.

Bellino, C. *La praticità della ragione ermeneutica: Ragione e morale in Gadamer.* Bari, 1984.

Bernstein, J. J. "From Hermeneutics to Praxis." *Review of Metaphysics* 35 (1982):823–845. (Rpt. in *Hermeneutics and Modern Philosophy,* ed. B. R. Wachterhauser. 87–110.)

———. "What Is the Difference That Makes a Difference? Gadamer, Habermas, and Rorty." In *Hermeneutics and Modern Philosophy,* ed. B. R. Wachterhauser. 343–376.

Bianco, F. "I limiti dell'esperienza ermeneutica." In *Il conflitto delle ermeneutiche,* ed. A. Molonaro. 23–55.

Bontekoe, R. "A Fusion of Horizons: Gadamer and Schleiermacher." *International Philosophical Quarterly* 27 (1987):3–16.

Bronk, *Rozumienie dzieje jezyk: Filozoficzna hermeneutiyka H.-G. Gadamera.* Lublin, 1988.

Carrington, R. S. "A Comparison of Royce's Key Notion of the Community of Interpretation with the Hermeneutics of Gadamer and Heidegger." *Transactions of the Charles S. Peirce Society* 20 (1984):279–302.

Cota Marcal, A. "Das Problem einer transzendentalen Hermeneutik in Wahrheit und Methode von H.-G. Gadamer." Ph.D. diss., University of Frankfurt, 1977.

Da Re, A. *L'ermeneutica di Gadamer e la filosofia pratica.* Rimini, 1982.

———. "Retorica ed ermeneutica in H.-G. Gadamer." *Verifiche* 2 (1982):227–248.

Davey, N. "Baumgarten's Aesthetics: A Post-Gadamerian Reflection." *British Journal of Aesthetics* 29:2 (1989):101–115.

Dockhorn, K. "Hans-Georg Gadamer: Wahreit und Methode." *Göttingsche Gelehrte Anzeigen* 218 (1966):169–206.

Dreyfus, H. "Holism and Hermeneutics." *Review of Metaphysics* 34 (1980):389–421.

Feil, E. "Die 'Neue Hermeneutik' und ihre Kritiker: Habermas und Albert contra Gadamer." *Herder Korrespondenz* 28 (1974):198–202.

Fruchon, P. "Compréhension et verité dans les sciences de l'esprit." *Archives de philosophie* 29 (1966):281–301.

———. "Herméneutique, language et ontologie: Un discernement du platonisme chez H.-G. Gadamer." *Archives de philosophie* 36 (1973):529–568; 37 (1974): 223–242, 353–375, 533–571.

———. "Pour une herméneutique philosophique." *Revue de métaphysique et de morale* 82 (1977):550–566.

———. "Ressources et limites d'une herméneutique philosophique." *Archives de philosophie* 30 (1967):411–438.

Garcia Roca, J. *La ontología hermenéutica: Significación y límites. El pensamiento de Hans-Georg Gadamer.* Valencia, 1979.

Garrett, J. E. "Hans-Georg Gadamer on 'Fusion of Horizons.'" *Man and World* 11 (1978):392–400.

Graeser, A. "Über 'Sinn' und 'Bedeutung' bei Gadamer." *Zeitschrift für philosophische Forschung* 38 (1984):436–445.

Gram, M. S. "Gadamer on Hegel's Dialectic: A Review Article." *Thomist* 43 (1979):322–330.

Griswold, C. "Gadamer and the Interpretation of Plato." *Ancient Philosophy* 2 (1981):121–128.

Grondin, J. "La conscience du travail de l'histoire et la problème de la vérité en herméneutique." *Archives de philosophie* 44 (1981):435–453.

———. "Herméneutique et relativisme." In his *L'horizon herméneutique de la pensée contemporaine* Paris, 1993.

———. *Hermeneutische Wahrheit? Zum Wahrheitsbegriff Hans-Georg Gadamers.* Königstein, 1982.

———. "Zur Entfaltung eines hermeneutischen Wahrheitsbegriffs." *Philosophisches Jahrbuch* 90 (1983):145–153.

Hans, J. S. "H.-G. Gadamer and Hermeneutic Phenomenology." *Philosophy Today* 22 (1978):3–19.

———. "Hermeneutics, Play, Deconstruction." *Philosophy Today* 24 (1980):299–317.

Heckman, S. "Action as a Text: Gadamer's Hermeneutics and the Social Scientific Analyses of Action." *Journal for the Theory of Social Behavior* 14 (1984):333–354.

Hinman, L. "Gadamer's Understanding of Hermeneutics." *Philosophy and Phenomenological Research* 40 (1980).

———. "Quid facti or quid juris? The Fundamental Ambiguity of Gadamer's Understanding of Hermeneutics." *Philosophy and Phenomenological Research* 40 (1980).

Hirsch, E. D. "Truth and Method in Interpretation." *Review of Metaphysics* 18 (1965):488–507.

Hogan, J. "Gadamer and the Hermeneutical Experience." *Philosophy Today* 20 (1976):3–12.

Hottois, G. *L'inflation du langage dans la philosophie contemporaine.* Brussels, 1979.

Hoy, D. C. *The Critical Circle: Literature, History, and Philosophical Hermeneutics.* Berkeley, 1978.

Ingram, D. "Hermeneutics and Truth." *Journal of the British Society for Phenomenology* 15 (1984):62–76.

———. "The Possibility of a Communication Ethic Reconsidered: Habermas, Gadamer and Bourdieu on Discourse." *Man and World* 15 (1982):149–161.

———. "Truth, Method and Understanding in the Human Sciences: The Gadamer/Habermas Controversy." Ph.D. diss., University of California, San Diego, 1980.

Innis, R. E. "Hans-Georg Gadamer's Truth and Method: A Review Article." *Thomist* 40 (1976):311–321.

Johnson, P. "The Task of the Philosopher: Kierkegaard/Heidegger/Gadamer." *Philosophy Today* 28 (1984):3–19.

Kelly, M. "Gadamer and Philosophical Ethics." *Man and World* 21 (1988):327–346.

Kirkland, F. M. "Gadamer and Ricoeur: The Paradigm of the Text." *Graduate Faculty Philosophy Journal* 6 (1977):131–144.

Kisiel, T. "Repetition in Gadamer's Hermeneutics." *Analecta Husserliana* 2 (1972):196–203.

Knapke, M. L. "The Hermeneutical Focus of Heidegger and Gadamer: The Nullity of Understanding." *Kinesis* 12 (1981):3–18.

Krämer, H. J. "Anmerkungen zur philosophischen Hermeneutik." In *Kulturwissenschaften: Festgabe für W. Perpeet zum 65. Geburtstag.* Bonn, 1980. 263–274.

Kuhn, H. "Wahrheit und geschichtliches Verstehen: Bemerkungen zu H.-G. Gadamers philosophischer Hermeneutik." *Historische Zeitschrift* 193 (1961):376–389.

Lang, P. C. *Hermeneutik, Ideologiekritik, Ästhetik: Über Gadamer und Adorno sowie Fragen einer aktuellen Ästhetik.* Königstein, 1981.

Larmore, C. "Tradition, Objectivity, and Hermeneutics." In *Hermeneutics and Modern Philosophy,* ed. B. R. Wachterhauser. 137–167.

Lawrence, F. "Gadamer and Lonergan: A Dialectical Comparison." *International Philosophical Quarterly* 20 (1980):25–47.

———. "Self-knowledge in History in Gadamer and Lonergan." In *Language, Truth and Meaning: Papers from the International Lonergan Congress 1970,* ed. Philip McShane. Notre Dame, Ind., 1972. 167–217.

———. "*Truth and Method* by Hans-Georg Gadamer." *Religious Studies Review* 3:1 (1977):35–44.

Linge, D. E. "Dilthey and Gadamer: Two Theories of Historical Understanding." *Journal of the American Academy of Religion* 41 (1973):536–553.

Lohmann, J. "Gadamers *Wahrheit und Methode.*" *Gnomon* 38 (1965):709–718.

MacIntyre, A. "Contexts of Interpretation: Reflections on Hans-Georg Gadamer's *Truth and Method.*" *Boston University Journal* 24 (1976):41–46.

MacKenzie, I. "Gadamer's Hermeneutics and the Uses of Forgery." *Journal of Aesthetics and Art Criticism* 45 (1986):41–42.

Márcus, G. "Diogenes Laertius contra Gadamer: Universal or Historical Hermeneutics?" In *Life after Postmodernism: Essays on Value and Culture,* ed. J. Fekete. New York, 1987. 140–162.

Misgeld, D. "On Gadamer's Hermeneutics." *Philosophy of the Social Sciences* 9 (1979):221–239.

Mitscherling, J. "Philosophical Hermeneutics and 'The Tradition.'" *Man and World* 22 (1989):247–250.

Möller, J. "Hans-Georg Gadamer, *Wahrheit und Methode.*" *Tübinger Theologische Quartalschrift* 141 (1961):467–471.

Negrin, L. "Two Critiques of the Autonomy of Aesthetic Consciousness: A Comparison of Benjamin and Gadamer." *Philosophy and Social Criticism* 13–14 (1987):343–366.

Peters, T. "Truth in History: Gadamer's Hermeneutics and Pannenberg's Apologetical Method." *Journal of Religion* 55 (1975):36–56.

Pöggeler, O. "H.-G. Gadamer, *Wahrheit und Methode.*" *Philosophischer Literaturanzeiger* 16 (1963):6–16.

Pohl, F.-W. "Verabsolutierung der Vermittlung: Idealistische Positionen in der philosophischen Hermeneutik Hans-Georg Gadamers." Ph.D. diss., University of Hanover, 1981.

Privoznik, G. "La vérità nella comprensione della storia: Nota sull'ermeneutica di H.-G. Gadamer." *Salesianum* 34 (1972):117–140.

Ravera, M. "Elementi per un confronto di due teorie ermeneutiche: Il concetto di 'tradizione' in Pareyson e in Gadamer." In *Estetica ed ermeneutica*. Naples, 1981.

Renaud, M. "Réflexions théologiques sur l'herméneutique de Gadamer." *Revue théologique de Louvain* 3 (1972):426–448.

Riedel, M. "Gadamers dialektische Hermeneutik und der 'Schritt zurück' zum Ethos der Dialektik." *Allgemeine Zeitschrift für Philosophie* 15 (1990):43–49.

Ripanti, G. *Gadamer.* Assisi, 1978.

Sansonetti, G. *Il pensiero di Hans-Georg Gadamer.* Brescia, 1988.

———. "Gli 'studi platonici' di H.-G. Gadamer." *Studi Urbinati* 60 (1987):41–78.

Schmidt, L. K. *The Epistemology of Hans-Georg Gadamer: An Analysis of the Legitimization of Vorurteile.* Frankfurt, 1987.

Schmied, G. "Gadamer sozialwissenschaftlich gelesen: Hans-Georg Gadamers *Wahrheit und Methode* und die verstehende Soziologie." *Theologie und Philosophie* 62:3 (1987):423–445.

Schuckman, P. "Aristotle's Phronesis and Gadamer's Hermeneutics." *Philosophy Today* 23 (1979):41–50.

Schultz, W. "Anmerkungen zur Hermeneutik Gadamers." In *Hermeneutik und Dialektik,* ed. R. Bubner, K. Cramer, and R. Wiehl. 1:305–316.

———. "Philosophische und theologische Hermeneutik im Gespräch: Kritische Anmerkungen zu Gadamers *Wahrheit und Methode.*" *Neue Zeitschrift für systematische Theologie und Religionsphilosophie* 14 (1972):214–232.

Schwarz, B. "Hermeneutik und Sachkontakt." In *Hermeneutik als Weg heutiger Wissenschaft,* ed. V. Warnach. 31–36.

Scott, C. E. "Gadamer's *Truth and Method.*" *Anglican Theological Review* 59 (1977):63–78.

Schriven, M. "Verstehen Again." *Theory and Decision* 1 (1970):382–386.

Seebohm, T. M. *Zur Kritik der hermeneutischen Vernunft.* Bonn, 1972.

Smith, P. C. "The Ethical Dimension of Gadamer's Hermeneutical Theory." *Research in Phenomenology* 18 (1988):75–92.

———. "Gadamer on Language and Method in Hegel's Dialectic." *Graduate Faculty Philosophy Journal* 5 (1975):53–72.

———. "Gadamer's Hermeneutics and Ordinary Language Philosophy." *Thomist* 43 (1979):296–321.

———. "H.-G. Gadamer's Heideggerian Interpretation of Plato." *Journal of the British Society for Phenomenology* 12 (1981):211–230.

Stegmüller, W. "Der sogenannte Zirkel des Verstehens." In *Natur und Geschichte: Zehnter deutscher Kongreß für Philosophie* (Kiel, 1972), ed. K. Hüber and A. Menne. Hamburg, 1974.

Stobbe, H. G. *Hermeneutik, Ein ökumenisches Problem: Eine Kritik der katholischen Gadamer-Rezeption.* Zurich, 1981.

Stover, D. "Linguisticality and Theology: Applying the Hermeneutics of Hans-Georg Gadamer." *Studies in Religion/Sciences religieuses* 5 (1975–1976):34–44.

Strauss, L., and H.-G. Gadamer. "Correspondence Concerning *Wahrheit und Methode.*" *Unabhängige Zeitschrift für Philosophie* 2 (1978):5–12.

Takeda, S. "Reflexion, Erfahrung und Praxis bei Gadamer." Ph.D. diss., University of Tübingen, 1981.

Thulstrup, N. "An Observation Concerning Past and Present Hermeneutics." *Orbis Litterarum* 22 (1967):24–44.

Tugendhat, E. "The Fusion of Horizons." *Times Literary Supplement,* May 19, 1978, p. 565.

Turk, H. "Wahrheit oder Methode? H.-G. Gadamers 'Grundzüge einer philosophischen Hermeneutik.'" In *Hermeneutische Positionen,* ed. H. Birus. 120–150.

Vandenbulcke, J. *H.-G. Gadamer: Een filosofie van het interpreteren.* Brugge, 1973.

Vattimo, G. "Estetica ed ermeneutica in H. G. Gadamer." *Rivista di estetica* (1963):117–130. (Rpt. in his *Poesia e ontologia.* Milan, 1967. 169–184.)

Velkley, R. "Gadamer and Kant: The Critique of Modern Aesthetic Consciousness." *Interpretation* 9 (1981):353–364.

Verra, V. *Introduzione in H.-G. Gadamer, Hegel e l'ermeneutica.* Naples, 1980. 7–34.

———. "Ontologia ed ermeneutica in Germania." *Rivista di sociologia* (1973):111–140.

———. "Il problema della storia: H. G. Gadamer." In *La filosofia dal 45 a oggi.* Rome, 1976. 59–69.

Vitiis, P. de. "Linguaggio e filosofia della identitá in H. G. Gadamer." *Teoria* (1982):39–53.

Wachterhauser, B. R. "Must We Be What We Say? Gadamer on Truth in the Human Sciences." In his *Hermeneutics and Modern Philosophy.* 219–242.

Wallulis, J. "Philosophical Hermeneutics and the Conflict of Ontologies." *International Philosophical Quarterly* 24 (1984):283–302.

Warnke, G. *Gadamer: Hermeneutics, Tradition and Reason.* Stanford, 1987.

Weinsheimer, J. C. *Gadamer's Hermeneutics.* New Haven, 1985.

Westphal, M. "Hegel and Gadamer." In *Hermeneutics and Modern Philosophy,* ed. B. R. Wachterhauser. 65–86.

Wiehl, R., ed. *Die antike Philosophie in ihrer Bedeutung für die Gegenwart: Kolloquium zu Ehren des 80. Geburtstag von Hans-Georg Gadamer.* Heidelberg, 1981.

Wright, K. "Gadamer: The Speculative Structure of Language." In *Hermeneutics and Modern Philosophy,* ed. B. R. Wachterhauser. 193–218.

C) BETTI AND THE OBJECTIVIST ANSWER TO GADAMER

Betti, E. *L'ermeneutica come metodica generale delle scienze dello spirito.* Ed. G. Mura. Rome, 1987.

———. "L'ermeneutica storica e la storicità dell'intendere." *Annali della Facoltá di Giurisprudenza dell'Universitá di Bari* (1961):3–28.

———. *Die Hermeneutik als allgemeine Methodik der Geisteswissenschaften.* Tübingen, 1962.

———. "I principi di scienza nuova di G. B. Vico e la teoria della interpretazione storica." *Nuova rivista di diritto commerciale* 10 (1957):48–59.

———. *Teoria generale della interpretazione.* 2 vols. Milan, 1955.

———. "Zur Grundlegung einer allgemeinen Auslegungslehre." In *Festschrift für E. Rabel.* Tübingen, 1954. 2:79–168.

Secondary Literature

Bianco, F. *Oggettività dell'interpretazione e dimensioni del comprendere: Un'analisi critica dell'ermeneutica di Emilio Betti.* Milan, 1962.

Caiani, L. "Emilio Betti e il problema dell'interpretazione." In his *La filosofia dei giuristi italiani.* Padua, 1955. 163–199.

Crifò, G. "In memoriam: Emilio Betti." *Bulletino dell'istituto di diritto romano* 70 (1967):293–320.

Crifò, G., et al., eds. *Quaderni fiorentini per la storia del pensiero giuridico moderno.* Milan, 1978. (Texts by G. Crifò, A. Schiavone, P. Costa, R. Malter, F. Bianco, A. De Gennaro, H.-G. Gadamer, N. Irti, M. Bretone, and L. Mengoni.)

Di Caro, A. "Metodo e significato nell'ermeneutica di E. Betti." *Hermeneutica* 1 (1982):217–230.

Funke, G. "Problem und Theorie der Hermeneutik: Auslegen, Denken, Verstehen in Emilio Bettis Teoria generale della Interpretazione." *Zeitschrift für philosophische Forschung* 14 (1960):161–181.

Griffero, T. "Ermeneutica e canonicità dei testi," *Rivista di estetica,* n.s., 19–20 (1985):93–111.

———. *Interpretare: L'ermeneutica di Emilio Betti.* Turin, 1988.

Grondin, J. "L'herméneutique comme science rigoureuse selon Emilio Betti (1890–1968)." *Archives de philosophie* 53 (1990):177–198.

Guarino, A. "Una teoria generale dell'interpretazione." *Labeo* 1 (1955):301–313.

Mura, G. "La 'teoria ermeneutica' di Emilio Betti." In E. Betti, *L'ermeneutica come metodica generale delle scienze dello spirito.* Rome, 1987. 5–53.

Rittner, H. "Verstehen und Auslegen als Probleme der Rechtswissenschaft." In *Verstehen und Auslegen,* ed. W. Marx. Freiburg, 1968. 43–65.

Studi in onore di Emilio Betti. Milan, 1962.

Vandenbulcke, J. "Betti-Gadamer: Eine hermeneutische Kontroverse." *Tijdschrift voor Filosofie* 31 (1971):105–113.

D)HERMENEUTICS AND CRITIQUE OF IDEOLOGY

Apel, K.-O. *Der Denkweg des Charles S. Peirce: Eine Einführung in den amerikanischen Pragmatismus.* Frankfurt, 1975.

———. *Diskurs und Verantwortung: Das Problem des Übergangs zur postkonventionellen Moral.* Frankfurt, 1988.

———. *Die Erklären-Verstehen-Kontroverse in transzendental-pragmatischer Sicht.* Frankfurt, 1979.

———. "H.-G. Gadamers *Wahrheit und Methode.*" *Hegel-Studien* 2 (1963):314–322.

———. "Die Herausforderung der totalen Vernunftkritik und das Programm einer philosophischen Theorie der Rationalitätstypen." In *Philosophie und Poesie,* ed. A. Gethmann-Siefert. 1:17–44.

———. Introduction to C. S. Peirce, *Schriften zur Entstehung des Pragmatismus.* Frankfurt, 1967.

———. *Neue Versuche über Erkären und Verstehen.* Frankfurt, 1978.

———. "Szientismus oder transzendentale Hermeneutik?" In *Hermeneutik und Dialektik,* ed. R. Bubner, K. Cramer, and R. Wiehl. 1:105–144.

———. *Transformation der Philosophie.* 2 vols. Frankfurt, 1973.

Apel, K.-O., et al. *Hermeneutik und Ideologiekritik.* Frankfurt, 1971.

Bar-Hillel, Y. "On Habermas' Hermeneutic Philosophy of Language." *Synthese* 26 (1973):1–12.

Bauman, Z. *Hermeneutics and Social Science.* New York, 1978.

Beetham, D. *Max Weber and the Theory of Modern Politics.* London, 1974.

Blanchette, O. "Language, the Primordial Labor of History: A Critique of Critical Theory in Habermas." *Cultural Hermeneutics* 1 (1973–1974):325–382.

Bleicher, J. *Contemporary Hermeneutics: Hermeneutics as Method, Philosophy and Critique.* London, 1980.

Böhler, D. "Philosophische Hermeneutik und hermeneutische Methode." In *Fruchtblätter: Freundesgabe für A. Kelletat,* ed. H. Hartung et al. Berlin, 1977. 15–43.

Böhler, D., and W. Kuhlmann, eds. *Kommunikation und Reflexion: Zur Diskussion der Transzendentalpragmatik. Antworten auf Karl-Otto Apel.* Frankfurt, 1982.

Bormann, C. von. *Der praktische Ursprung der Kritik.* Stuttgart, 1974.

———. "Die Zweideutigkeit der hermeneutischen Erfahrung." In Apel et al., *Hermeneutik und Ideologiekritik.* 83–119.

Broniak, C. "What Is Emancipation for Habermas?" *Philosophy Today* 32 (1988):195–206.

Bubner, R. "Philosophie ist ihre Zeit, in Gedanken erfaßt." In *Hermeneutik und Dialektik,* ed. R. Bubner, K. Cramer, and R. Wiehl. 1:317–342.

———. "Über die wissenschaftstheoretische Rolle der Hermeneutik." In his *Dialektik und Wissenschaft.* Frankfurt, 1973.

———. "Was ist kritische Theorie?" *Philosophische Rundschau* 17 (1969):213–248.

Bubner, R., et al. "Discussion on 'Theory and Practice.'" *Cultural Hermeneutics* 2 (1974–1975):363–366.

Cooper, B. "Hermeneutics and Social Science." *Philosophy of the Social Sciences* 11 (1981):79–90.

Dahrendorf, R. "Zeitgenosse Habermas." *Merkur* 43 (1989):478–487.

Dallmayr, F. R. "Hermeneutics and Historicism: Reflections on Winch, Apel, and Vico." *Review of Politics* 39 (1977):60–81.

———. *Materialien zu Habermas' Erkenntnis und Interesse.* Frankfurt, 1974.

———. "Reason and Emancipation: Notes on Habermas." *Man and World* 5 (1972):79–109.

Dallmayr, F. R., and T. McCarthy. *Understanding and Social Inquiry.* Notre Dame, Ind., 1977.

Gay, W. C., and P. Eckstein. "Bibliographic Guide to Hermeneutics and Critical Theory." *Cultural Hermeneutics* 2 (1974–1975):379–390.

Giurlanda, P. "Habermas' Critique of Gadamer: Does It Stand Up?" *International Philosophical Quarterly* 27 (1987):33–42.

Grondin, J. "Habermas und das Problem der Individualität." *Philosophische Rundschau* 36 (1989):187–205.

Gruner, R. "Understanding in the Social Sciences and Its History." *Inquiry* 10 (1967):151–163.

Habermas, J. *Erkenntnis und Interesse.* Frankfurt, 1968, 1973.

———. *Moralbewußtsein und kommunikatives Handeln.* Frankfurt, 1983.

———. *Nachmetaphysisches Denken: Philosophische Aufsätze.* Frankfurt, 1988.

———. *Der Philosophische Diskurs der Moderne.* Frankfurt, 1985.

———. *Philosophisch-politische Profile.* 2d ed. Frankfurt, 1981.

———. *Theorie des kommunikativen Handelns.* 2 vols. Frankfurt, 1981.

———. "Der Universalitätsanspruch der Hermeneutik." In *Hermeneutik und Dialektik,* vol. 1, ed. R. Bubner, K. Cramer, and R. Wiehl. (Rpt. in K.-O. Apel et al., *Hermeneutik und Ideologiekritik.* 120–159.)

———. "Urbanisierung der Heideggerschen Provinz." In *Das Erbe Hegels,* ed. J. Habermas and H.-G. Gadamer. Frankfurt, 1979.

———. "Wahrheitstheorien." In *Wirklichkeit und Reflexion: Festschrift für W. Schulz.* Pfullingen, 1973. 211–265. (Rpt. in his *Vorstudien und Ergänzungen zur Theorie des kommunikativen Handelns.* Frankfurt, 1984. 127–183.)

————. *Zur Logik der Sozialwissenschaften.* Tübingen, 1967; Frankfurt, 1970.

Honneth, A., and H. Joas, eds. *Kommunikatives Handeln: Beiträge zu Jürgen Habermas' "Theorie des kommunikativen Handelns."* Frankfurt, 1986.

How, A. R. "Dialogue as Productive Limitation in Social Theory: The Habermas-Gadamer Debate." *Journal of the British Society for Phenomenology* 11 (1980):131–143.

Ingram, D. "The Historical Genesis of the Gadamer-Habermas Controversy." *Auslegung* 10 (1983):86–151.

Jay, M. "Should Intellectual History Take a Linguistic Turn? Reflections on the Habermas-Gadamer Debate." In *Modern European Intellectual History,* ed. Dominick LaCapra and Steven Kaplan. Ithaca, 1982.

Kelley, M. "The Gadamer-Habermas Debate Revisited: The Question of Ethics." *Philosophy and Social Criticism* 14 (1988):369–390.

Kisiel, T. "Ideology, Critique and Phenomenology: The Current Debate in German Philosophy." *Philosophy Today* 14 (1970):151–160.

Kockelmans, J. J. "Hermeneutik und Ethik." In *Kommunikation und Reflexion,* ed. D. Böhler and W. Kuhlmann. 649–684.

————. "Toward an Interpretive or Hermeneutic Social Science." *Graduate Faculty Philosophy Journal* 5 (1975):73–96.

Kuhlmann, W. *Reflexive Letztbegründung: Untersuchungen zur Transzendentalpragmatik.* Freiburg, 1985.

Kuhn, H. "Ideologie als hermeneutischer Begriff." In *Hermeneutik und Dialektik,* ed. R. Bubner, K. Cramer, and R. Wiehl. 1:343–356.

Lawrence, F. "Response to 'Hermeneutics and Social Science.'" *Cultural Hermeneutics* 2 (1974–1975):321–325.

Löser, W. "Hermeneutik oder Kritik? Die Kontroverse zwischen H.-G. Gadamer und J. Habermas." *Stimmen der Zeit* 88 (1971):50–59.

Manninen, J., and R. Tuomela, eds. *Essays of Explanation and Understanding: Studies in the Foundations of the Humanities and Social Sciences.* Dordrecht, 1976.

McCarthy, T. *The Critical Theory of Jürgen Habermas.* Cambridge, 1978.

————. "On Misunderstanding 'Understanding.'" *Theory and Decision* 3 (1973): 351–369.

Mendelson, J. "The Habermas-Gadamer Debate." *New German Critique* 18 (1979):44–73.

————. "The Problem of Rationality in Social Anthropology." *Stony Brook Studies in Philosophy* 1 (1974):1–21.

Misgeld, D. "Discourse and Conversation: The Theory of Communicative Competence and Hermeneutics in the Light of the Debate between Habermas and Gadamer." *Cultural Hermeneutics* 4 (1976–1977):321–344.

————. "On Gadamer's Hermeneutics." *Philosophy of the Social Sciences* 9 (1979):221–239.

Okrent, M. "Hermeneutics, Transcendental Philosophy and Social Science." *Inquiry* 27 (1984):23–49.

O'Neill, J., ed. *On Critical Theory.* New York, 1976.

Palmer, R. E. "Response to 'Hermeneutics and Social Science.'" *Cultural Hermeneutics* 2 (1974–1975):317–319.

Parsons, A. "Interpretive Sociology: The Theoretical Significance of Verstehen in the Constitution of Social Reality." *Human Studies* 1 (1978):111–137.

Rabinow, P., and W. M. Sullivan, eds. *Interpretive Social Sciences: A. Reader.* Berkeley, 1979.

Sandkühler, H. J. "Hermeneutik und Ideologiewissenschaft." In *Hermeneutik als Kriterium für Wissenschaftlichkeit?,* ed. U. Gerber. 158–169.

Simon-Schäfer, R., and W. C. Zimmerli, eds. *Theorie zwischen Kritik und Praxis: Jürgen Habermas und die Frankfurter Schule.* Stuttgart, 1975.

Sutherland, D. E. "The Factor of Hermeneutics in Habermas' Critical Theory." In *Research in Sociology of Knowledge, Sciences, and Art.* Westport, Conn., 1979.

"Symposium: Hermeneutics and Critical Theory." *Cultural Hermeneutics* 2 (1974–1975):307–390.

Thompson, J. B. *Critical Hermeneutics: A Study in the Thought of Paul Ricoeur and Jürgen Habermas.* Cambridge, 1981.

Thompson, J. B., and D. Held, eds. *Habermas: Critical Debates.* London, 1982.

Wiggershaus, R. *Die Frankfurter Schule.* Munich, 1986.

Wolff, J. "Hermeneutics and the Critique of Ideology." *Sociological Review* 23 (1975):811–828.

Zaner, R. M. "A Certain Rush of Wind: Misunderstanding Understanding in the Social Sciences." *Cultural Hermeneutics* 1 (1973–1974):383–402.

Zimmerli, W. C. "Ist die kommunikationstheoretische Wende ein Ausweg aus dem 'Hermeneutikstreit'?" In *Theorie zwischen Kritik und Praxis,* ed. R. Simon-Schäfer and W. C. Zimmerli. 95–122.

E) RICOEUR

Ricoeur, P. *Le conflit des interprétations: Essais d'herméneutique.* Paris, 1969.

——. *De l'interprétation: Essai sur Freud.* Paris, 1965.

——. *Du texte à l'action: Essais d'herméneutique.* 2 vols. Paris, 1986.

——. *Freud and Philosophy.* Trans. Denis Savage. New Haven, 1970.

——. "Funktion der Metapher in der biblischen Sprache." *Metapher: Zur Hermeneutik religiöser Sprache,* ed. E. Jüngel and P. Ricoeur. Munich, 1974.

——. "La métaphore et le problème central de l'herméneutique." *Revue philosophique de Louvain* 70 (1972):93–112.

——. *La métaphore vive.* Paris, 1975.

——. "Phénoménologie et herméneutique." In *Phänomenologische Forschungen,* vol. 1: *Phänomenologie Heute: Grundlagen und Methodenprobleme.* Freiburg, 1975. 31–71. (Rpt. in his *Du texte à l'action.* 39–73.)

————. *Philosophie de la volonté,* pt. 1: *Le volontaire et l'involontaire.* Paris, 1950; pt. 2: *Finitude et culpabilité.* Paris, 1950; vol. 1: *L'homme faillible.* Paris, 1960; vol. 2: *La symbolique du mal.* Paris, 1960.

————. *Soi-même comme un autre.* Paris, 1990.

————. *Temps et récit,* vol. 1. Paris, 1983; vol. 2: *La configuration du temps dans le récit de fiction.* Paris, 1984; vol. 3: *Le temps raconté.* Paris, 1985.

Secondary Literature

Bollnow, O. F. "Paul Ricoeur und die Probleme der Hermeneutik." In his *Studien zur Hermeneutik.* 1:224–294.

Bouchindhomme, C., and R. Rochlitz, eds. *"Temps et récit" de Paul Ricoeur en débat.* Paris, 1990. (Essays by J.-P. Bobillot, C. Bouchindhomme, R. Bubner, C. Bremond, J. Grondin, J. Leenhardt, R. Rochlitz, and P. Ricoeur.)

Bourgeois, P. "Paul Ricoeur's Hermeneutical Phenomenology." *Philosophy Today* 16 (1972):20–27.

Bres, Y. P. "Ricoeur: Le règne des herméneutiques ou 'un long détour.'" *Revue philosophique de la France et de l'Etranger* 94 (1969):425–429.

Clayton, P. "Ricoeur's Appropriation of Heidegger: Happy Marriage or Holzweg?" *Journal of the British Society for Phenomenology* 20 (1989):33–47.

Crossan, J. D. "Paradox Gives Rise to Metaphor: Paul Ricoeur's Hermeneutics and the Parables of Jesus." *Biblical Research* 24–25 (1979–1980):20–37.

Gerhart, M. "Paul Ricoeur's Hermeneutical Theory as Resource for Theological Reflection." *Thomist* 39 (1975):496–527.

Hengel, J. W. van den. *The Home of Meaning: The Hermeneutics of Paul Ricoeur.* Washington, D.C., 1982.

Kemp, P. "Phänomenologie und Hermeneutik in der Philosophie Paul Ricoeurs." *Zeitschrift für Theologie und Kirche* 67 (1970):335–347.

Klemm, D. E. *The Hermeneutical Theory of Paul Ricoeur.* Lewisburg, Pa., 1983.

Lapointe, F. H. "A Bibliography on Paul Ricoeur." *Philosophy Today* 16 (1972):28–33; 17 (1973):176–182.

————. "Paul Ricoeur und seine Kritiker: Eine Bibliographie." *Philosophisches Jahrbuch* 86 (1979):340–356.

Lawlor, L. "Dialectic and Iterability: The Confrontation between Paul Ricoeur and Jacques Derrida." *Philosophy Today* 32 (1988):181–194.

Mudge, L. S. "Paul Ricoeur on Biblical Interpretation." *Biblical Research* 24–25 (1979–1980):38–69.

Mukengebantu, P. "Expliquer et Comprendre: Spécificité de l'herméneutique de Paul Ricoeur." Ph.D. diss., University of Laval (Quebec), 1988.

Vansina, F. D. *Paul Ricoeur: Bibliographie systématique de ses écrits et des publications consacrées à sa pensée (1935–84).* Leewen, 1985.

Vansina, F. D., and L. Garcia, eds. *Paul Ricoeur: Une bibliographie systématique.* Louvain, 1983.

Waldenfels, B. "Paul Ricoeur: Umwege der Deutung." In his *Phänomenologie in Frankreich*. Frankfurt, 1983. 226–335.

F) POSTMODERN HERMENEUTICS

Baynes, K., J. Bohman, and T. McCarthy, eds. *After Philosophy: End or Transformation?* Cambridge, 1987. (Contributions by R. Rorty, J.-F. Lyotard, M. Foucault, J. Derrida, D. Davidson, M. Dummett, H. Putnam. K.-O. Apel, J. Habermas, H.-G. Gadamer, P. Ricoeur, A. MacIntyre, H. Blumenberg, and C. Taylor.)

Bernasconi, R., and D. Wodd, eds. *Derrida and Différance*. Evanston, Ill., 1985.

Caputo, J. D. "From the Deconstruction of Hermeneutics to the Hermeneutics of Deconstruction." In *The Horizons of Continental Philosophy: Essays on Husserl, Heidegger, and Merleau-Ponty*, ed. H. J. Silverman, A. Mickunas, T. Kisiel, and A. Lingis. Dordrecht, 1988. 190–204.

———. "Hermeneutics as the Recovery of Man." In *Hermeneutics and Modern Philosophy*, ed. B. R. Wachterhauser. 416–445.

———. *Radical Hermeneutics: Repetition, Deconstruction, and the Hermeneutic Project*. Bloomington, Ind., 1987.

Culler, J. *On Deconstruction*. Ithaca, 1982.

Derrida, J. *De la grammatologie*. Paris, 1978.

———. *Eperons: Les styles de Nietzsche*. Paris, 1967.

———. *Marges de la philosophie*. Paris, 1972.

———. *La voix et le phénomène*. Paris, 1967.

Ferraris, M. "Derrida 1975–1985: Sviluppi teoretici e fortuna filosofica." *Nuova corrente* 93–94 (1984):351–377.

Foucault, M. *L'archéologie du savoir*. Paris, 1969.

———. *Les mots et les choses: Une archéologie des sciences humaines*. Paris, 1966.

———. *L'ordre du discours*. Paris, 1971.

Frank, M. *Die Grenzen der Verständigung: Eine Geistergespräch zwischen Lyotard und Habermas*. Frankfurt, 1988.

———. *Das Sagbare und das Unsagbare: Studien zur neuesten französischen Hermeneutik und Texttheorie*. Frankfurt, 1980.

———. *Was ist Neostrukturalismus?* Frankfurt, 1984.

Frank, M., G. Raulet, and W. van Reijen, eds. *Die Frage nach dem Subjekt*. Frankfurt, 1988.

Gasché, R. "Deconstruction as Criticism." *Glyph* 6 (1979):177–216.

———. "Joining the Text: From Heidegger to Derrida." In *The Yale Critics,* ed. J. Arac, W. Godzich, and W. Martin. 156–175.

———. *The Tain of the Mirror: Derrida and the Philosophy of Reflection*. Cambridge, Mass., 1986.

Hörisch, J. *Die Wut des Verstehens: Zur Kritik der Hermeneutik*. Frankfurt, 1988.

Hoy, D. C. "Forgetting the Text: Derrida's Critique of Heidegger." *Boundary 2* 8 (1979):223–235.

——. "Must We Say What We Mean? The Grammatological Critique of Hermeneutics." *Review of the University of Ottawa* 50 (1980):411–426. (Rpt. in *Hermeneutics and Modern Philosophy*, ed. B. R. Wachterhauser. 397–419.)

——. "Taking History Seriously: Foucault, Gadamer, Habermas." *Union Seminary Quarterly Review* 34 (1979):85–95.

——, ed. *Foucault: A Critical Reader.* New York, 1986. (Essays by I. Hacking, R. Rorty, M. Walzer, C. Taylor, J. Habermas, H. L. Dreyfus, P. Rabinow, D. C. Hoy, E. W. Said, B. Smart, M. Jay, M. Poster, and A. I. Davidson.)

Lyotard, J.-F. *La condition postmoderne: Rapport sur le savoir.* Paris, 1979.

——. *Le différend.* Paris, 1983.

——. "Grundlagenkrise." *Neue Hefte für Philosophie* 26 (1986):1–33.

Madison, G. B. *The Hermeneutics of Postmodernity: Figures and Themes.* Bloomington, Ind. 1988.

——. *Understanding: A Phenomenological Pragmatic Analysis.* Westport, Conn., 1982.

Marquard, O. "Frage nach der Frage, auf die die Hermeneutik die Antwort ist." *Philosophisches Jahrbuch* 88 (1981):1–19. (Rpt. in his *Abschied vom Prinzipiellen.* Stuttgart, 1981. 117–146.)

——. *Schwierigkeiten mit der Geschichtsphilosophie.* Frankfurt, 1973, 1976.

Michelfelder, P., and R. E. Palmer, eds. *Dialogue and Deconstruction: The Gadamer-Derrida Encounter.* Albany, 1989. (Essays by H.-G. Gadamer, J. Derrida, F. Dallmayr, P. Forget, M. Frank, J. Simon, J. Risser, D. Shepherdson, G. B. Madison, H. Rapaport, D. G. Marshall, R. Shusterman, D. F. Krell, R. Bernasconi, J. Sallis, J. D. Caputo, N. Oxenhandler, and G. Eisenstein.)

Natoli, S. *Ermeneutica e genealogia: Filosofia e metodo in Nietzsche, Heidegger, Foucault.* Milan, 1981.

Orr, L. *De-Structuring the Novel: Essays in Postmodern Hermeneutics.* Troy, 1982.

——. "The Hermeneutical Interplay." *Journal of Thought* 16 (1981):85–98.

Palmer, R. E. "Postmodernity and Hermeneutics." *Boundary 2* 5 (1977):363–393.

——. "Toward a Postmodern Interpretive Self-Awareness." *Journal of Religion* 55 (1975):313–326.

Rorty, R. *Consequences of Pragmatism.* Minneapolis, 1982.

——. *Philosophy and the Mirror of Nature.* Princeton, 1979.

——. "Der Vorrang der Demokratie vor der Philosophie." *Zeitschrift für philosophische Forschung* 42 (1988):3–17.

Rosen, S. *Hermeneutics as Politics.* Oxford, 1987.

Sallis, J., and J. D. Caputo. "Radical Hermeneutics: Repetition, Deconstruction, and the Hermeneutic Project." *Man and World* 22 (1989):251–256.

Shapiro, G. *Postmodernism.* New York, 1989.

Silverman, H. J. "Phenomenology: From Hermeneutics to Deconstruction." *Research in Phenomenology* 14 (1984):19–34.

Silverman, H. J., and D. Ihde, eds. *Hermeneutics and Deconstruction.* New York, 1985. (Essays by B. Magnus, T. M. Seebohm, C. O. Schrag, G. Nicholson, P. A. Heelan, V. Descombes, W. Marx, F. Rodi, M. Murray, D. Carr, M. E. Blanchard, J. Margolis, A. Lingis, R. Gasché, J. D. Caputo, T. Sheehan, N. J. Holland, S. H. Watson, G. L. Ormiston, and D. Oskowski.)

Silverman, H. J., and G. E. Aylesworth, eds. *The Textual Sublime: Deconstruction and Its Differences.* New York, 1989.

Vattimo, G. *Le avventure della differenza.* Milan, 1980.

———. "Ergebnisse der Hermeneutik." In his *Jenseits vom Subjekt: Nietzsche, Heidegger und die Hermeneutik.* Graz, 1986. 119–147.

———. *La fine della modernità: Nichilismo ed ermeneutica nella cultura postmoderna.* Milan, 1985.

———, ed. *La sécularisation de la pensée.* Paris, 1988. (Essays by A. A. Gargani, R. Rorty, P. A. Rovatti, G. Vattimo, F. Crespi, S. Givone, J. Rolland, A. Dal Lago, M. Ferraris, G. Carchia, and H.-G. Gadamer.)

Vattimo, G., and P. A. Rovatti, eds. *Il pensiero debole.* Milan, 1987.

Wellmer, A. *Zur Dialektik von Moderne und Postmoderne: Vernunftkritik nach Adorno.* Frankfurt, 1985.

Welsch, W. *Unsere postmoderne Moderne.* Weinheim, 1987.

———. "Vielheit ohne Einheit? Zum gegenwärtigen Spektrum der philosophischen Diskussion um die 'Postmoderne.'" *Philosophisches Jahrbuch* 94 (1987):111–141.

4. Areas of Applied Hermeneutics

A) THEOLOGICAL HERMENEUTICS

Biser, E. *Theologische Sprachtheorie und Hermeneutik.* Munich, 1970.

Bornkamm, G. "Die Theologie Rudolf Bultmanns in der neueren Diskussion: Zum Problem der Entmythologisierung und Hermeneutik." *Theologische Rundschau,* n.s. 28 (1963):33–141.

Bultmann, R. *Geschichte und Eschatologie.* 2d ed. Tübingen, 1964.

———. *Glauben und Verstehen: Gesammelte Aufsätze.* 4 vols. Tübingen, 1952.

———. "Das Problem der Hermeneutik." *Zeitschrift für Theologie und Kirche* 47 (1950):47–49.

Bultmann, R., and K. Jaspers. *Die Frage der Entmythologisierung.* Munich, 1954.

Casper, B. "Die Bedeutung der philosophischen Hermeneutik für die Theologie." *Theologische Quartalschrift* 148 (1968):283–302.

Coreth, E. "Hermeneutik und Metaphysik." *Zeitschrift für katholische Theologie* 90 (1968):422–450.

Dinkler, E., ed. *Zeit und Geschichte: Dankesgabe an Rudolf Bultmann zum 80. Geburtstag.* Tübingen, 1964.

Ebeling, G. "Art: Hermeneutik." In *Religion in Geschichte und Gegenwart*, 3d ed. Tübingen, 1959. 3:243–262.

———. "Die Bedeutung der historisch-kritischen Methode für die protestantische Theologie und Kirche." *Zeitschrift für Theologie und Kirche* 47 (1950):1–46.

———. *Einführung in die theologische Sprachlehre*. Tübingen, 1971.

———. "Wort Gottes und Hermeneutik." *Zeitschrift für Theologie und Kirche* 56 (1959):224–251.

———. *Wort und Glaube*. 3 vols. Tübingen, 1962–1975.

Feneberg, P. "Der Begriff des Verstehens in der Literaturwissenschaft: Untersuchung einer hermeneutischen Frage im Blick auf die Theologie." *Zeitschrift für Theologie und Kirche* (1969):184–195.

Fruchon, P. *Existence humaine et révélation: Essais d'herméneutique*. Paris, 1976.

Fuchs, E. "Alte und neue Hermeneutik." In *Hören und Handeln: Festschrift für Ernst Wolf zum 60. Geburtstag*, ed. H. Gollwitzer and H. Traub. Munich, 1962. 106–132.

———. "Glauben und Verstehen." *Zeitschrift für Theologie und Kirche* 66 (1960):345–353.

———. *Hermeneutik*. Bad Cannstatt, 1954; Tübingen, 1970.

———. "Das hermeneutische Problem." In *Zeit und Geschichte*, ed. E. Dinkler. 357–366.

———. *Marburger Hermeneutik*. Tübingen, 1968.

———. "Das Neue Testament und das hermeneutische Problem." *Zeitschrift für Theologie und Kirche* 58 (1961):198–266.

———. *Zum hermeneutischen Problem in der Theologie: Die existenziale Interpretation*. 2d ed. Tübingen, 1965.

Funk, R. W. "The Hermeneutical Problem and Historical Criticism." In *The New Hermeneutic*, ed. J. M. Robinson and J. B. Cobb, Jr. 164–197.

———. *Language, Hermeneutics and the Word of God: The Problem of Language in the New Testament and Contemporary Theology*. New York, 1966.

———, ed. *History and Hermeneutic*. Tübingen, 1967.

Gabus, J.-P. *Critique du discours théologique*. Neuchâtel, 1977. 106–116.

Geffré, C. "La crise de l'herméneutique et ses conséquences pour la théologie." *Revue des sciences religieuses* 52 (1978):268–296.

Hasenhüttel, G. "Die Radikalisierung der hermeneutischen Fragestellung durch Rudolf Bultmann." In *Mysterium Salutis*, vol. 1: *Die Grundlagen heilsgeschichtlicher Dogmatik*, ed. J. Feiner and M. Löhrer. Einsiedeln, 1965. 428–440.

Hecker, K. "Philosophische Prolegomena zu einer theologischen Hermeneutik." *Catholica* 23 (1969):62–82.

Hilberath, B. J. *Theologie zwischen Tradition und Kritik: Die philosophische Hermeneutik Hans-Georg Gadamers als Herausforderung des theologischen Selbstverständnisses*. Düsseldorf, 1978.

Jaspert, B., ed. *Rudolf Bultmanns Werk und Wirkung.* Darmstadt, 1984.

Jüngel, E. "Metaphorische Wahrheit: Erwägungen zur theologischen Relevanz der Metapher als Beitrag zur Hermeneutik einer narrativen Theologie." In *Metapher,* ed. E. Jüngel and P. Ricoeur. 71–122.

Kasper, W. "Tradition als Erkenntnisprinzip: Zur theologischen Relevanz der Geschichte." *Theologische Quartalschrift* 155 (1975):198–215.

Kerygma and History: A Symposium on the Theology of R. Bultmann. New York, 1962.

Lorenzmeier, T. *Exegese und Hermeneutik: Eine vergleichende Darstellung der Theologie Rudolf Bultmanns, Herbert Brauns und Gerhard Ebelings.* Hamburg, 1968.

Moltmann, J. "Existenzgeschichte und Weltgeschichte: Auf dem Wege zu einer politischen Hermeneutik des Evangeliums." In *Perspektiven der Theologie: Gesammelte Aufsätze.* Munich, 1968. 128–146.

O'Collins, G. "Hans-Georg Gadamer and Hans Küng: A Reflection." *Gregorianum* 58 (1977):561–566.

Ommen, T. B. *The Hermeneutic of Dogma.* Missoula, Mont., 1975.

Pannenberg, W. "Hermeneutik und Universalgeschichte." *Zeitschrift für Theologie und Kirche* (Rpt. in his *Grundfragen systematischer Theologie: Gesammelte Aufsätze.* 2d ed. Göttingen, 1971. 91–122.)

———. "Über historische und theologische Hermeneutik." In his *Grundfragen systematischer Theologie: Gesammelte Aufsätze.* 2d ed. Göttingen, 1971. 123–158.

———. *Wissenschaftstheorie und Theologie.* Frankfurt, 1973.

Pöggeler, O. "Hermeneutische Philosophie und Theologie." *Man and World* 7 (1974):158–176.

"Il problema della demitizzanione." *Archivio di filosofia* (1961).

Rahner, K. "Theologische Prinzipien der Hermeneutik eschatologischer Aussagen." *Zeitschrift für katholische Theologie* 82 (1960):137–158.

Robinson, J. M. "Hermeneutics since Barth." In *The New Hermeneutic,* ed. J. M. Robinson and J. B. Cobb, Jr. 1–77.

Schäfer, R. "Die hermeneutische Frage in der gegenwärtigen evangelischen Theologie." In *Die hermeneutische Frage in der Theologie,* ed. O. Loretz and W. Strolz. Freiburg, 1968. 426–466.

Schillebeeckx, E. *Glaubensinterpretation: Beiträge zu einer hermeneutischen und kritischen Theologie.* Mainz, 1971.

Schultz, W. "Wesen und Grenzen der theologischen Hermeneutik." *Zeitschrift für Theologie und Kirche* 46 (1938):283–304.

Stachel, G. *Die neue Hermeneutik: Ein Überblick.* 2d ed. Munich, 1968.

Thiselton, A. C. *The Two Horizons: New Testament Hermeneutics and Philosophical Description with Special Reference to Heidegger, Bultmann, Gadamer, and Wittgenstein.* Grand Rapids, Mich., 1980.

Turner, G. "Wolfhart Pannenberg and the Hermeneutical Problem." *Irish Theological Quarterly* 39 (1972):107–129.

Westphal, M. "Hegel, Pannenberg, and Hermeneutics." *Man and World* 4 (1971): 276–293.

Wilson, B. A. "Bultmann's Hermeneutics: A Critical Examination." *Philosophy of Religion* 8 (1977):169–189.

b) Literary Hermeneutics

Arac, J., W. Godzich, and W. Martin, eds. *The Yale Critics: Deconstruction in America.* Minneapolis, 1983.

Arthur, C. E. "Gadamer and Hirsch: The Canonical Work and the Interpreter's Intention." *Cultural Hermeneutics* 4 (1976–1977):183–197.

Barner, W. "Rezeptionsästhetik—Zwischenbilanz (III): Neuphilologische Rezeptionsforschung und die Möglichkeit der klassischen Philologie." *Poetica* 9 (1977):499–521.

Bubner, R. "Über einige Bedingungen gegenwärtiger Ästhetik." *Neue Hefte für Philosophie* 5 (1973):38–73. (Rpt. in his *Ästhetische Erfahrung.* Frankfurt, 1989.)

Buck, G. "Hermeneutics of Texts and Hermeneutics of Action." *New Literary History* 12 (1980):87–96.

Dostal, R. J. "Kantian Aesthetics and the Literary Criticism of E. D. Hirsch." *Journal of Aesthetics and Art Criticism* 38 (1980):299–306.

Forget, P., ed. *Text und Interpretation.* Munich, 1984.

Fuhrmann, M., H. R. Jauß, and W. Pannenberg, eds. *Poetik und Hermeneutik IX: Text und Applikation. Theologie. Jurisprudenz und Literaturwissenschaft im hermeneutischen Gespräch.* Munich, 1981.

Göttner, H. *Die Logik der Interpretation: Analyse einer literaturwissenschaftlichen Methode unter kritischer Betrachtung der Hermeneutik.* Munich, 1973.

Griffero, T. "L'ermeneutica ricognitiva di E. D. Hirsch." *Rivista di estetica,* n.s., 16 (1984):77–91.

———. "Il problema dell'intenzione autorale nella critica anglosassone." *Rivista di estetica,* n.s., 14–15 (1983):181–187.

———. *La problematica ermeneutica in E. D. Hirsch.* Turin, 1982.

Grimm, G., ed. *Literatur und Leser: Theorien und Modelle zur Rezeption literarischer Werke.* Stuttgart, 1975.

———, ed. *Rezeptionsgeschichte: Grundlegung einer Theorie: Mit Analysen und Bibliographie.* Munich, 1977.

Harari, J. V., ed. *Textual Strategies.* Ithaca, 1979.

Hirsch, E. D. *The Aims of Interpretation.* Chicago, 1976.

———. "Three Dimensions of Hermeneutics." *New Literary History* 3 (1972):245–261.

———. "Truth and Method in Interpretation." *Review of Metaphysics* 18 (1965):488–507.

———. *Validity in Interpretation.* New Haven, 1967.

Hohendahl, P. U. "Introduction to Reception Aesthetics." *New German Critique* 10 (1977):29–63.

Holenstein, E. *Linguistik, Semiotik, Hermeneutik: Plädoyers für eine strukturale Phänomenologie.* Frankfurt, 1976.

Hoy, D. C. *The Critical Circle: Literature and History in Contemporary Hermeneutics.* Berkeley, 1978.

Ijsseling, S. "Hermeneutics and Textuality." *Research in Phenemenology* 9 (1979):1–16.

Iser, W. *Der Akt des Lesens: Theorie ästhetischer Wirkung.* 2d ed. Munich, 1984.

———. *Die Apellstruktur der Texte.* Constance, 1974. (Rpt. in *Rezeptionsästhetik,* ed. R. Warning. 228–252.)

Japp, U. *Hermeneutik: Der theoretische Diskurs, die Literatur und die Konstruktion ihres Zusammanhanges in den philologischen Wissenschaften.* Munich, 1977.

Jauß, H. R. *Ästhetische Erfahrung und literarische Hermeneutik.* Frankfurt, 1982.

———. *Entstehung und Strukturwandel der allegorischen Dichtung.* Heidelberg, 1968.

———. *Literaturgeschichte als Provokation.* Frankfurt, 1970.

———. "Negativität und Identifikation: Versuch zur Theorie der ästhetischen Erfahrung." In *Poetik und Hermeneutik IV,* ed. H. Weinrich. 263–339.

———. "Paradigmenwechsel in der Literaturwissenschaft." In *Methoden der deutschen Literaturwissenschaft,* ed. V. Zmegac. Frankfurt, 1972. 274–290.

———. "Theses in the Transition from the Aesthetics of Literary Works to a Theory of Aesthetic Experience." In *Interpretation of Narrative,* ed. M. J. Valdes and O. J. Miller, Toronto, 1978. 137–147.

———. "Zur Abgrenzung und Bestimmung einer literarischen Hermeneutik." In *Poetik und Hermeneutik IX,* ed. M. Fuhrmann, H. R. Jauß, and W. Pannenberg. 459–481.

———, ed. *Poetik und Hermeneutik I: Nachahmung und Illusion.* Munich, 1964.

———, ed. *Poetik und Hermeneutik III: Die nicht mehr schönen Künste: Grenzphänomene des Ästhetischen.* Munich, 1968.

Jauß, H. R., and W. Godzich. *Aesthetic Experience and Literary Hermeneutics.* Minneapolis, 1982.

Juhl, P. D. *Interpretation: An Essay on the Philosophy of Literary Criticism.* Princeton, 1980.

Leibfried, E. *Literarische Hermeneutik: Eine Einführung in ihre Geschichte und Probleme.* Tübingen, 1980.

Madison, G. B. "Eine Kritik an Hirschs Begriff der 'Richtigkeit.'" In *Seminar: Die Hermeneutik und die Wissenschaften,* ed. H.-G. Gadamer and G. Boehm. 393–425.

Man, P. de. *Allegories of Reading.* New Haven, 1979.

———. *Blindness and Insight.* 2d ed. Minneapolis, 1983.

————. *The Resistance to Theory.* Minneapolis, 1985.

————. *The Rhetoric of Romanticism.* New York, 1986.

Mandelkow, K.-R. "Problem der Wirkungsgeschichte." *Jahrbuch für Internationale Germanistik* 2 (1970):71–84.

McKnight, E. V. *Meaning in Texts: The Historical Shaping of a Narrative Hermeneutics.* Philadelphia, 1978.

Mecklenburg, N. *Kritisches Interpretieren: Untersuchungen zur Theorie der Literaturkritik.* Munich, 1972.

Medina, A. *Reflection, Time and the Novel: Toward a Communicative Theory of Literature.* Boston, 1979.

Meiland, J. "Interpretation as Cognitive Discipline." *Philosophy and Literature* 2 (1978):23–45.

Metscher, T. "Literature and Art as Ideological Form." *New Literary History* 11 (1979):21–39.

Miller, J. H. "The Critic as Host." *Critical Inquiry* 3 (1977):439–447.

————. "Deconstructing the Deconstructeurs." *Diacritics* 2 (1975):24–31.

————. *Fiction and Repetition: Seven English Novels.* Oxford, 1982.

Muto, S. "Reading the Symbolic Text: Some Reflections on Interpretation." *Humanitas* 8 (1972):169–191.

Nassen, U., ed. *Texthermeneutik: Äktualität, Geschichte, Kritik.* Paderborn, 1979.

Palmer, R. E. "Allegorical, Philological and Philosophical Hermeneutics." *Review of the University of Ottawa* 50 (1980):338–360.

————. "Phenomenology as Foundation for a Post-Modern Philosophy of Literary Interpretation." *Cultural Hermeneutics* 1 (1973–1974):207–223.

Pasternack, G. *Theoriebildung in der Literaturwissenschaft: Einführung in Grundlagen des Interpretationspluralismus.* Munich, 1975.

Piché, C. "Expérience esthétique et herméneutique philosophique." *Texte* 3 (1984):179–191.

Pitte, M. van de. "Hermeneutics and the 'Crisis' of Literature." *British Journal of Aesthetics* 24:2 (1983):99–112.

Seeburger, F. "The Distinction between 'Meaning' and 'Significance': A Critique of the Hermeneutics of E. D. Hirsch." *Southern Journal of Philosophy* 17 (1978):249–262.

Staiger, E. *Die Kunst der Interpretation.* Zurich, 1955.

Stierle, K. "Text als Handlung und Text als Werk." In *Poetik und Hermeneutik IX,* ed. M. Fuhrmann, H. R. Jauß, and W. Pannenberg. 537–545.

"Symposium: Hermeneutics, Post-Structuralism, and Objective Interpretation." *Papers on Language and Literature* 7 (1981):48–87.

Szondi, P. *Einführung in die literarische Hermeneutik.* Frankfurt, 1975. *(Introduction to Literary Hermeneutics,* trans. M. Woodmansee, with a foreword by J. Weinsheimer. London, 1994.)

Wachterhauser, B. "Interpreting Texts: Objectivity or Participation?" *Man and World* 19 (1986):439–457.

Warneken, B. J. "Zu H. R. Jauss' Programm einer Rezeptionsästhetik." In *Sozialgeschichte und Wirkungsästhetik,* ed. P. U. Hohendahl. Frankfurt, 1974. 290–296.

Warning, R., ed. *Rezeptionsästhetik: Theorie und Praxis.* Munich, 1975.

Weimar, K. *Historische Einleitung zur literaturwissenschaftlichen Hermeneutik.* Tübingen, 1975.

Weinrich, H., ed. *Poetik und Hermeneutik IV: Positionen der Negativität.* Munich, 1975.

Weinsheimer, J. *Philosophical Hermeneutics and Literary Theory.* New Haven, 1991.

Wellek, R. "Zur methodischen Aporie einer Rezeptionsgeschichte." In *Geschichte— Ereignis und Erzählung,* ed. R. Koselleck and W. D. Stempel. Munich, 1973. 515–517.

Zimmerman, B. *Literaturrezeption im historischen Prozess: Zur Theorie einer Rezeptionsgeschichte der Literatur.* Munich, 1977.

C) HERMENEUTICS AND PRACTICAL PHILOSOPHY

Bernstein, R. J. *Beyond Objectivism and Relativism: Science, Hermeneutics and Praxis.* Philadelphia, 1983.

Bianco, F. "Validità e limiti del modello ermeneutico nelle scienze sociali." *Paradigmi* 6:16 (1988):69–87.

Bruns, G. L. "On the Tragedy of Hermeneutical Experience." *Research in Phenomenology* 18 (1988):191–204.

Bubner, R. "Eine Renaissance der praktischen Philosophie." *Philosophische Rundschau* 22 (1975):1–34.

———. *Geschichtsprozesse und Handlungsnormen: Untersuchungen zur praktischen Philosophie.* Frankfurt, 1984.

———. *Handlung, Sprache und Vernunft: Grundbegriffe praktischer Philosophie.* Frankfurt, 1982.

———. *Zur Sache der Dialektik.* Stuttgart, 1980.

Buck, G. "Hermeneutics of Texts and Hermeneutics of Action." *New Literary History* 12 (1980):87–96.

———. *Hermeneutik und Bildung: Elemente einer verstehenden Bildungstheorie.* Munich, 1981.

———. "The Structure of Hermeneutic Experience and the Problem of Tradition." *New Literary History* 10 (1978):31–47.

Da Re, A. *L'etica tra felicità e virtù.* Bologna, 1986.

Höffe, O. *Praktische Philosophie: Das Modell des Aristoteles.* Munich, 1971.

Hollinger, R. "Practical Reason and Hermeneutics." *Philosophy and Rhetoric* 18:2 (1985):113–122.

Hookway, C., and P. Petit, eds. *Action and Interpretation*. Cambridge, 1978.

Hoy, T. *Praxis, Truth and Liberation: Essays on Gadamer, Taylor, Polanyi, Habermas, Gutierrez, and Ricoeur*. Baltimore, 1988.

Jung, H. J. "A Hermeneutical Accent on the Conduct of Political Inquiry." *Human Studies* 1 (1978):48–82.

Kamper, D. "Hermeneutik—Theorie einer Praxis?" *Zeitschrift für allgemeine Wissenschaftstheorie* 5 (1974):39–53.

Kemp, P. "Le conflit entre l'herméneutique et l'éthique." *Revue de métaphysique et de morale* 91 (1986):115–131.

Klemm, D. E., ed. *Hermeneutical Inquiry*, vol. 3: *The Interpretation of Existence*. Atlanta, 1986.

Lawrence, F. "Dialectic and Hermeneutic: Foundational Perspectives on the Relationship between Human Studies and the Project of Human Self-Constitution." In *Philosophy and Social Theory: A Symposium, Stony Brook Studies in Philosophy* 1 (1974):37–59.

Luckmann, R. "Zum hermeneutischen Problem der Handlungswissenschaften." In *Poetik und Hermeneutik IX*, ed. M. Fuhrmann, H. R. Jauß, and W. Pannenberg. 513–523.

Madison, G. B. *The Logic of Liberty*. New York, 1986.

Marquard, O. *Apologie des Zufälligen: Philosophische Studien*. Stuttgart, 1986.

Marsch, J. L. "Objectivity, Alienation, and Reflection." *International Philosophical Quarterly* 22 (1982):130–139.

Nassen, U. *Studien zur Entwicklung einer materialen Hermeneutik*. Munich, 1979.

Nörr, D. "Das Verhältnis von Fall und Norm als Problem der reflektierenden Urteilskraft." In *Poetik und Hermeneutik IX*, ed. M. Fuhrmann, H. R. Jauß, and W. Pannenberg. 395–407.

Otto, E. "Die Applikation als Problem der politischen Hermeneutik." *Zeitschrift für Theologie und Kirche* 71 (1974):145–180.

Packer, M. J., and R. B. Addison, eds. *Entering the Circle: Hermeneutic Investigation in Psychology*. New York, 1989.

Page, C. "Axiomatics, Hermeneutics, and Practical Rationality." *International Philosophical Quarterly* 27 (1987):81–100.

Pavlovic, K. R. "Science and Autonomy: The Prospects for Hermeneutic Science." *Man and World* 14 (1981):127–140.

Pfafferott, G. *Ethik und Hermeneutik: Mensch und Moral im Gefüge der Lebensform*. Königstein, 1981.

Pöggeler, O. "Die ethische-politische Dimension der hermeneutischen Philosophie." In *Probleme der Ethik*, ed. G.-G. Grau. Munich, 1972.

Rabinow, P., and W. M. Sullivan, eds. *Interpretive Social Sciences: A Reader*. Berkeley, 1979.

Raulet, G. "Hermeneutik im Prinzip der Dialektik." In *Ernst Blochs Wirkung: Ein Arbeitsbuch zum 90. Geburtstag*. Frankfurt, 1975. 284–304.

Rickman, H. P. "Recent Anglo-Saxon Philosophy of the Social Sciences." *Dilthey-Jahrbuch* 2 (1984):322–338.

Riedel, M. *Für eine zweite Philosophie.* Frankfurt, 1988.

———. *Urteilskraft und Vernunft: Kants ursprüngliche Fragestellung.* Frankfurt, 1989.

———, ed. *Rehabilitierung der praktischen Philosophie.* 2 vols. Freiburg, 1972–1974.

Ritter, J. "Die Aufgabe der Geisteswissenschaften in der modernen Gesellschaft." In his *Subjektivität.* Frankfurt, 1974. 105–140.

———. *Metaphysik und Politik: Studien zu Aristoteles und Hegel.* Frankfurt, 1969.

Rosso, F. *Ermeneutica come ontologia della libertà: Studio sulla teoria dell'interpretazione di Luigi Pareyson.* Milan, 1980.

Rurak, J. "The Imaginative Power of Utopias: A Hermeneutic for Its Recovery." *Philosophy and Social Criticism* 8 (1981):184–206.

Rutt, T. "Die hermeneutische Dimension der Erziehungswirklichkeit." In *Hermeneutik als Weg heutiger Wissenschaft,* ed. V. Warnach. 113–120.

Santiago Guervos, L. E. "Filosofía práctica y hermenéutica." *Estudios Filosóficos* 35 (1986):7–26.

Schönherr, H.-M. A. "Ökologie als Hermeneutik: Ein wissenschaftstheoretischer Versuch." *Philosophia Naturalis* 24:3 (1987):311–332.

Shapiro, M. J. *Language and Political Understanding: The Politics of Discursive Practices.* New Haven, 1981.

Siemek, M. "Marxism and the Hermeneutic Tradition." *Dialectics and Humanism* 2 (1975):87–103.

Simon, M. A. *Understanding of Human Action: Social Explanation and the Vision of Social Science.* New York, 1981.

Taylor, C. *Human Agency and Language: Philosophical Papers I.* Cambridge, 1985.

———. "Understanding in Human Science." *Review of Metaphysics* 34 (1980):25–55.

Tellenbach, H. "Hermeneutische Akte in der klinischen Psychiatrie." In *Hermeneutik als Weg heutiger Wissenschaft,* ed. V. Warnach. 139–144.

Truzzi, M., ed. *Subjective Understanding in the Social Sciences.* Reading, Mass. 1974.

Turner, S., and D. Carr, eds. "The Process of Criticism in Interpretive Sociology and History." *Human Studies* 1 (1978):138–152.

Vollrath, E. *Die Rekonstruktion der politischen Urteilskraft.* Stuttgart, 1977.

Volpi, F. "La rinascità della filosofia pratica in Germania." In *Filosofia pratica e scienza politica,* ed. C. Pacchiani. Abbano Terme, 1980. 11–97.

Waldenfels, B. *Der Spielraum des Verhaltens.* Frankfurt, 1980.

Walhout, D. "Hermeneutics and the Teaching of Philosophy." *Teaching Philosophy* 7 (1984):303–312.

Wright, G. H. von. *Explanation and Understanding.* Ithaca, 1971.

———. *Philosophical Papers,* vol. 1: *Practical Reason.* Oxford, 1983.

D) HERMENEUTICS AND THEORY OF SCIENCE

Abel, T. "The Operation called 'Verstehen.'" *American Journal of Society* 54 (1948):211–218. (Rpt. in *Readings in the Philosophy of Science,* ed. H. Feigl and M. Brodbeck. New York, 1953.)

Acham, K. "Hermeneutik und Wissenschaftstheorie aus der Sicht des Kritischen Rationalismus: Zum Verhältnis von Hermeneutik und Sozialwissenschaften." In *Hermeneutik als Kriterium für Wissenschaftlichkeit?,* ed. U. Gerber. 102–128.

Albert, H. *Die Wissenschaft und die Fehlbarkeit der Vernunft.* Tübingen, 1982.

———. "Theorie, Verstehen und Geschichte." *Zeitschrift für allgemeine Wissenschaftstheorie* 1 (1970):2–23.

———. *Traktat über kritische Vernunft.* 4th ed. Tübingen, 1980.

———. *Transzendentale Träumereien: K.-O. Apel und sein hermeneutischer Gott.* Hamburg, 1975.

Antiseri, D. "Epistemologia, ermeneutica e storiografia." *Archivio di filosofia* 44 (1974):264–270.

Baumgart-Thome, Y. *Das Problem der Geisteswissenschaften in der analytischen Philosophie und Wissenschaftstheorie: Unter besonderer Berücksichtigung der Rekonstruktion der Hermeneutik.* Meisenheim, 1978.

Bubner, R. "Transzendentale Hermeneutik?" In *Wissenschaftstheorie der Geisteswissenschaften: Konzeption, Vorschläge, Entwürfe,* ed. R. Simon-Schäfer and W. C. Zimnerli. 56–70.

———. "Über die wissenschaftstheoretische Rolle der Hermeneutik: Ein Diskussionsbeitrag." In his *Dialektik und Wissenschaft.* Frankfurt, 1973. 89–111.

Chisholm, R. M. "Verstehen: The Epistemological Question." *Dialectica* 33 (1979):233–246.

Conolly, J. M., and T. Keutner, eds. *Hermeneutics Versus Science? Three German Views: Essays by H.-G. Gadamer, E. K. Specht, and W. Stegmüller.* Notre Dame, Ind., 1988.

Crowley, C. B. *Universal Mathematics in Aristotelian-Thomistic Philosophy: The Hermeneutics of Aristotelian Texts Relative to Universal Mathematics.* Washington, D.C., 1980.

Ebeling, G. *Kritischer Rationalismus? Zu H. Alberts Traktat über kritische Vernunft.* Tübingen, 1973.

Feyerabend, P. K. *Against Method.* London, 1974.

———. *Erkenntnis für freie Menschen.* Frankfurt, 1980.

Follesdal, D. "Hermeneutics and the Hypothetico-Deductive Method." *Dialectica* 33 (1979):319–336.

———. "The Status of Rationality Assumptions in Interpretation and in the Explanation of Explanation." *Dialectica* 36 (1982):302–316.

Freundlieb, D. *Zur Wissenschaftstheorie der Literaturwissenschaft: Eine Kritik der transzendentalen Hermeneutik.* Munich, 1978.

Gerber, U., ed. *Hermeneutik als Kriterium für Wissenschaftlichkeit? Der Standort der Hermeneutik im Gegenwärtigen Wissenschaftskanon* (Loccumer Kolloquium 2). Loccum, 1972.

Gründer, K. "Hermeneutik und Wissenschaftstheorie." *Philosophisches Jahrbuch* 75 (1967–1968):152–165.

Gutting, G. "Paradigms and Hermeneutics: A Dialogue on Kuhn, Rorty, and the Social Sciences." *American Philosophical Quarterly* 21 (1984):1–16.

Heelan, P. A. "Perception as a Hermeneutical Art." *Review of Metaphysics* 37 (1983):61–76.

———. "Towards a Hermeneutics of Science." *Main Currents* 28 (1971):85–93.

Heintel, E. "Verstehen und Erklären." In *Hermeneutik als Weg heutiger Wissenschaft*, ed. V. Warnach. 67–76.

Helmholtz, H. von. "Über das Verhältnis der Naturwissenschaft zur Gesammtheit der Wissenschaft." In his *Vorträge und Reden*. 3d ed. Braunschweig, 1884.

Hempel, C. G. "Erklärung in Naturwissenschaft und Geschichte." In *Erkenntnisprobleme der Naturwissenschaft*, ed. L. Krüger. Cologne, 1970. 215–238.

———. "Wissenschaftliche und historische Erklärung." In *Theorie und Realität*, ed. H. Albert. 2d ed. Tübingen, 1972. 237–261.

Janssen, P. "Die hermeneutische Bestimmung des Verhältnisses von Natur und Geisteswissenschaft und ihre Problematik." In *Natur und Geschichte: X. Deutscher Kongreß für Philosophie*. Hamburg, 1973. 363–370.

Joseph, G. "Interpretation in the Physical Sciences." *Southern California Law Review* 58 (1985):9–14.

Kamper, D. *Philosophie der Geisteswissenschaften als Kritik ihrer Methoden*. The Hague, 1978.

Kimmerle, H. "Die Funktion der Hermeneutik in den positiven Wissenschaften." *Zeitschrift für allgemeine Wissenschaftstheorie* 5 (1974):54–73.

Kisiel, T. "Hermeneutic Models for Natural Science." In *Die Phänomenologie und die Wissenschaften*. Freiburg, 1976. 180–190.

———. "Scientific Discovery: Logical, Psychological, or Hermeneutical?" In *Explorations in Phenomenology*, ed. D. Carr and E. S. Casey. The Hague, 1973. 263–284.

Kolb, J. "Hermeneutik in der Physik." In *Hermeneutik als Weg heutiger Wissenschaft*, ed. V. Warnach. 85–99.

König, E. "Wissenschaftstheoretische Überlegungen zur Interpretation historischer Texte." In *Natur und Geschichte: X. Deutscher Kongreß für Philososphie*. Hamburg, 1973. 379–386.

Krüger, L. "Über das Verhältnis der hermeneutischen Philosophie zu den Wissenschaften." In *Hermeneutik und Dialektik*, ed. R. Bubner, K. Cramer, and R. Wiehl. 1:3–30.

Kuhn, T. S. *The Structure of Scientific Revolutions*. 2d ed. Chicago, 1970.

Lakatos, I. "Falsification and the Methodology of Scientific Research Programs." In *Criticism and the Growth of Knowledge,* ed. I. Lakatos and A. Musgrave. Cambridge, 1970.

Lawrence, F. "Dialectic and Hermeneutic: Foundational Perspectives on the Relationship between Human Studies and the Project of Human Self-Constitution." *Stony Brook Studies in Philosophy* 1 (1974):37–59.

Lorenzen, P. "Szientismus versus Dialektik." In *Hermeneutik und Dialektik,* ed. R. Bubner, K. Cramer, and R. Wiehl. 1:57–72.

MacIntyre, A. "Contexts of Interpretation: Reflections on Hans-Georg Gadamer's *Truth and Method." Boston University Journal* 24:1 (1976):41–46.

———. "Epistemological Crises, Dramatic Narrative and the Philosophy of Science." *Monist* 60 (1977):453–472.

Patzig, E. "Erklären und Verstehen: Bemerkungen zum Verhältnis von Natur- und Geisteswissenschaften." *Neue Rundschau* 84 (1973):392–413.

Popper, K. R. *Conjectures and Refutations.* London, 1965.

———. *Logik der Forschung.* 6th ed. Tübingen, 1976.

———. *The Poverty of Historicism.* 2d ed. London, 1960.

Poster, M. "Interpreting Texts: Some New Directions." *Southern California Law Review* 58 (1985):15–18.

Rickert, H. *Die Grenzen der naturwissenschaftlichen Begriffsbildung: Eine logische Einleitung in die historischen Wissenschaften.* 5th ed. Tübingen, 1929.

———. *Kulturwissenschaft und Naturwissenschaft.* 6th ed. Tübingen, 1926.

Rohs, P. *Die Vernunft der Erfahrung: Eine Alternative zum Anarchismus der Wissenschaftstheorie.* Meisenheim, 1979.

Seiffert, H. "Hermeneutik und Wissenschaftstheorie: Hermeneutik und wissenschaftstheoretische Positionen." In *Hermeneutik als Kriterium für Wissenschaftlichkeit?,* ed. U. Gerber. 40–47.

Simon-Schäfer, R., and W. C. Zimmerli, eds. *Wissenschaftstheorie der Geisteswissenschaften.* Hamburg, 1975.

Stegmuller, W. "Die sogenannte Methode des Verstehens." In his *Probleme und Resultate der Wissenschaftstheorie und analytischen Philosophie.* Berlin, 1969. 1:360–375.

———. "Der sogenannte Zirkel des Verstehens." In *Natur und Geschichte: Zehnter deutscher Kongreß für Philosophie* [Kiel, 1972], ed. K. Hüber and A. Menne. Hamburg, 1973.

Taylor, C. "Interpretation and the Sciences of Man." *Review of Metaphysics* 25 (1971):3–51.

Thurnher, R. "Erklärung in genetischen und systematischen Zusammenhängen." *Dialectica* 33 (1979):189–200.

Warnach, V., ed. *Hermeneutik als Weg heutiger Wissenschaft: Ein Forschungsgespräch.* Salzburg, 1971.

Wieland, W. "Möglichkeiten der Wissenschaftstheorie." In *Hermeneutik und Dialektik,* ed. R. Bubner, K. Cramer, and R. Wiehl. 1:31–56.

Wright, G. H. von. *Explanation and Understanding.* Ithaca, 1971.

E) HERMENEUTICS AND LANGUAGE

Apel, K.-O. *Der Denkweg den Charles S. Peirce: Eine Einführung in den amerikanischen Pragmatismus.* Frankfurt, 1975.

————, ed. *Sprachpragmatik und Philosophie.* Frankfurt, 1981.

Batey, R., and J. H. Gill, "Fact, Language, and Hermeneutic: An Interdisciplinary Exploration." *Scottish Journal of Theology* 23 (1970):13–26.

Blumenberg, H. *Arbeit am Mythos.* Frankfurt, 1981.

Bubner, R. "Wohin tendiert die analytische Philosophie?" *Philosophische Rundschau* 34 (1987):257–281.

Coseriu, E. *Synchronie, Diachronie und Geschichte: Das Problem des Sprachwandels.* Munich, 1974.

Danto, A. C. *Analytical Philosophy of History.* Cambridge, Mass., 1965.

Davidson, D. *Inquiries into Truth and Interpretation.* Oxford, 1984.

Deetz, S. "Hermeneutics and Research in Interpersonal Communication." In *Interpersonal Communication* ed. J. Pilotta. 1–14.

Fahrenbach, H. "Die logischhermeneutische Problemstellung in Wittgensteins *Tractatus.*" In *Hermeneutik und Dialektik,* ed. R. Bubner, K. Cramer, and R. Wiehl. 2:25–54.

Fischer-Lichte, E. *Bedeutung: Probleme einer semiotischen Hermeneutik und Ästhetik.* Munich, 1979.

Grondin, J. "Hermeneutical Truth and Its Historical Presuppositions: A Possible Bridge between Analysis and Hermeneutics." In *Anti-Foundationalism and Practical Reasoning,* ed. E. Simpson. Edmonton, 1987. 45–58.

Hülsmann, H. "Hermeneutik und Sprache." In *Hermeneutik als Weg heutiger Wissenschaft,* ed. V. Warnach. 101–111.

Hyde, M. J. "Philosophical Hermeneutics and the Communicative Experience: The Paradigm of Oral History." *Man and World* 13 (1980):81–98.

Joy, M. "Rhetoric and Hermeneutics." *Philosophy Today* 32 (1988):273–285.

Kimmerle, H. "Metahermeneutik. Applikation: Hermeneutische Sprachbildung." *Zeitschrift für Theologie und Kirche* 64 (1967):221–235.

Klemm, D. E., ed. *Hermeneutical Inquiry,* vol. 1: *The Interpretation of Texts.* Atlanta, 1986.

Lohmann, J. *Philosophie und Sprachwissenschaft.* Berlin, 1965.

Malbon, E. S. "Structuralism, Hermeneutics, and Contextual Meaning." *Journal of the American Academy of Religion* 51 (1983):207–230.

Meztger, M. "Sprachgestalt und Sachverhalt als Frage an die Auslegung." *Zeitschrift für Theologie und Kirche* 64 (1967):372–391.

Outlaw, L. "Language and Consciousness: Toward a Hermeneutic of Black Culture." *Cultural Hermeneutics* 1 (1973–1974):403–413.

Palermo, J. "Pedagogy as a Critical Hermeneutic." *Cultural Hermeneutics* 3 (1975–1976):137–146.

Parret, H., M. Sbisà, and J. Verschueren, eds. *Possibilities and Limitations of Pragmatics.* Amsterdam, 1982.

Perelman, C. *Le champ de l'argumentation.* Brussels, 1970.

———. *Rhétorique et philosophie.* Paris, 1952.

Perelman, C., and L. Olbrechts-Tyteca. *La nouvelle rhétorique: Traité de l'argumentation.* 2d ed. Paris, 1970.

Pilotta, J., ed. *Interpersonal Communication: Essays in Phenomenology and Hermeneutics.* Washington, D.C., 1982. (Essays by S. Deetz, M. J. Hyde, J. J. Pilotta, A. Mickunas, D. Ihde, D. H. Cegala, E. A. Behnke, H. J. Silverman, T. L. Widman, T. M. Seebohm, and A. Lingis.)

Plessner, H. "Zur Hermeneutik nichtsprachlichen Ausdrucks." In *Das Problem der Sprache: Achter deutscher Kongreß für Philosophie,* ed. H.-G. Gadamer. Munich, 1967. 555–566.

Rajachman, J., and C. West, eds. *Post-analytic Philosophy.* New York, 1985.

Risenhuber, K. "Hermeneutik und Sprachanalyse: Ansätze zu einem Gespräch." *Zeitschrift für katholische Theologie* 101 (1979):374–385.

Schmidt, K. "Der hermeneutische Zirkel: Untersuchungen zum Thema: Übersetzen und Philosophie." *Die pädagogische Privinz* 21 (1967):472–488.

Schökel, L. A. "Hermeneutics in the Light of Language and Literature." *Catholic Biblical Quarterly* 25 (1963):371–386.

Seebohm, T. M. "The Significance of the Phenomenology of Written Discourse for Hermeneutics." In *Interpersonal Communication,* ed. J. Pilotta. 141–160.

Seung, T. K. *Semiotics and Thematics in Hermeneutics.* New York, 1982.

———. *Structuralism and Hermeneutics.* New York, 1982.

Simon, J. *Philosophie des Zeichens.* Berlin, 1989.

———. *Sprachphilosophie.* Freiburg, 1981.

———. *Wahrheit als Freiheit: Zur Entwicklung der Wahrheitsfrage in der neueren Philosophie.* Berlin, 1978.

Todorov, T. *Symbolisme et interprétation.* Paris, 1978.

Tugendhat, E. *Selbstbewußtsein und Selbstbestimmung: Sprachanalytische Interpretationen.* Frankfurt, 1979.

———. *Vorlesungen zur Einführung in die sprachanalytische Philosophie.* Frankfurt, 1976.

Weinberger, C., and O. Weinberger. *Logik, Semantik, Hermeneutik.* Munich, 1979.

Zimmerman, J. *Wittgensteins sprachphilosophische Hermeneutik.* Frankfurt, 1975.

Zuck, J. E. "The New Hermeneutic of Language: A Critical Appraisal." *Journal of Religion* 52 (1972):397–416.

F) HERMENEUTICS AND LAW

Bobbio, N. *Il positivismo giuridico.* Turin, 1961.

Esser, J. "Die Interpretation im Recht." *Studium Generale* 7 (1954):372–379.

Garet, R. R. "Comparative Normative Hermeneutics: Scripture, Literature, Constitution." *Southern California Law Review* 58 (1985):35–134.

Haba, E. P. "Sur une 'méthodologie' de l'interprétation juridique." *Archives de philosophie du droit* 18 (1973):371–383.

Hart, H. L. A. *The Concept of Law.* Oxford, 1961.

Hoy, D. "Interpreting the Law: Hermeneutical and Poststructuralist Perspectives." *Southern California Law Review* 58 (1985):135–176.

Kriele, M. "Besonderheiten juristischer Hermeneutik." In *Poetik und Hermeneutik IX,* ed. M. Fuhrmann, H. R. Jauß, and W. Pannenberg. 409–412.

Levinson, Sanford, and Steven Mailloux. *Interpreting Law and Literature: A Hermeneutic Reader.* Evanston, Ill., 1988.

Marini, G. *Savigny e il metodo della scienza giuridica.* Milan, 1967.

Mayer-Maly, T. "Hermeneutik und Evidenz im Recht." In *Hermeneutik als Weg heutiger Wissenschaft,* ed. V. Warnach. 127–130.

Mootz, F. J. "The Ontological Basis of Legal Hermeneutics: A Proposed Model of Inquiry Based on the Work of Gadamer, Habermas, and Ricoeur." *Boston University Law Review* 68:3 (1988):523–560.

Nörr, D. "Triviales und Aporetisches zur juristischen Hermeneutik." In *Poetik und Hermeneutik IX,* ed. M. Fuhrmann, H. R. Jauß, and W. Pannenberg. 235–246.

Otte, G. "Hermeneutik und Wissenschaftstheorie aus der Sicht des Rechtswissenschaftlers." In *Hermeneutik als Kriterium für Wissenschaftlichkeit?,* ed. U. Gerber. 155–156.

Perry, M. J. "The Authority of Text, Tradition, and Reason: A Theory of Constitutional 'Interpretation.'" *Southern California Law Review* 58 (1985):551–602.

Savigny, F. K. *Geschichte des römischen Rechts im Mittelalter,* vol. 6. Heidelberg, 1815–1831; vol 7. Heidelberg, 1834–1851.

———. *System des heutigen römischen Rechts,* vol. 8. Berlin, 1840–1849.

———. *Vermischte Schriften.* 5 vols. Leipzig, 1850.

Schroth, U. "Hermeneutik und Gesellschaftstheorie aus der Sicht der Rechtswissenschaftlichkeit." In *Hermeneutik als Kriterium für Wissenschaftlichkeit?,* ed. U. Gerber. 170–171.

Simon, L. "The Authority of the Constitution and Its Meaning: A Preface to a Theory of Constitutional Interpretation." *Southern California Law Review* 58 (1985):603–646.

Solari, G. *Storicismo e diritto privato.* Turin, 1940.

Thibaut, A. F. J. *System des Pandektenrechts.* 2 vols. 2d ed. Jena, 1803.

———. *Theorie der logischen Auslegung des römischen Rechts.* Altona, 1806. (Rpt. Düsseldorf, 1966, with an intro. by L. Geldsetzer.)

———. *Ueber die Nothwendigkeit eines allgemeinen bürgerlichen Rechts für Deutschland.* Heidelberg, 1814.

———. *Versuche über einzelne Teile der Theorie des Rechts.* 2d ed. Jena, 1817.

Viehweg, T. *Topik und Jurisprudenz: Ein Beitrag zur Rechtswissenschaftlichen Grundlagenforschung.* 3d ed. Munich, 1953.

Wiacker, F. "Friedrich Karl von Savigny." *Zeitschrift der Savigny-Stiftung für Rechtsgeschichte* (1955):1–38.

G) HERMENEUTICS AND HISTORY

Baumgartner, H. M. *Kontinuität und Geschichte: Zur Kritik und Metakritik der historischen Vernunft.* Frankfurt, 1972.

Baumgartner, H. M., and J. Rüsen, eds. *Seminar Geschichte und Theorie: Umrisse einer Historik.* Frankfurt, 1976.

Daly, G. "History, Truth, and Method." *Irish Theological Quarterly* 47 (1980):43–55.

Dray, W. "Explaining What Is History." In *Theories of History,* ed. P. Gardiner. Glencoe, Ill., 1959.

———. *Laws and Explanation in History.* Oxford, 1957.

———. *Perspectives on History.* London, 1980.

———, ed. *Philosophical Analysis & History.* New York, 1966.

Faber, K. G. *Theorie der Geschichtswissenschaft.* Munich, 1971.

Gründer, K. "Verständiges Leben in der Geschichte: Grundaspekte der Hermeneutik der Gegenwart." In *Spiegel und Gleichnis: Festschrift für Jacob Taubes,* ed. N. W. Bolz and W. Hübener. Würzburg, 1983. 239–251.

Koselleck, R. *Vergangene Zukunft: Zur Semantik geschichtlicher Zeiten.* Frankfurt, 1979.

Lotze, J. "Geschichtlichkeit und Tradition." In *Ermeneutica e tradizione* (Archivio di filosofia). Padua, 1963. 289–300.

Lübbe, H. *Geschichtsbegriff und Geschichtsinteresse.* Basel, 1977.

Mandelbaum, M. *The Problem of Historical Knowledge: An Answer to Relativism.* New York, 1967.

Marrou, H.-I. *De la connaissance historique.* Paris, 1959.

Minogue, K. R. "Method in Intellectual History: Quentin Skinner's Foundations." *Philosophy* 56 (1981):533–552.

Mommsen, W. J., ed. *Theorie der Geschichtswissenschaft.* Cologne, 1972.

Rüsen, J. *Für eine erneuerte Historik: Studien zur Theorie der Geschichtswissenschaft.* Stuttgart, 1976.

———, ed. *Historische Objektivität: Aufsätze zur Geschichtstheorie.* Göttingen, 1975.

Savile, A. "Historicity and the Hermeneutic Circle." *New Literary History* 10 (1978):49–70.

Schnädelbach, H. *Geschichtsphilosophie nach Hegel: Die Probleme des Historismus.* Freiburg, 1974.

———. *Vernunft und Geschichte: Vorträge und Abhandlungen.* Frankfurt, 1987.

Simmel, G. *Vom Wesen des historischen Verstehens.* Berlin, 1918.

Skinner, Q. "Hermeneutics and the Role of History." *New Literary History* 7 (1975):209–232.

———. "Meaning and Understanding in the History of Ideas." *History and Theory* 8 (1969):1–53.

Theunis, F. "Hermeneutik, Verstehen und Tradition." In *Ermeneutica e tradizione* (Archivio di filosofia). Padua, 1963. 263–288.

Tully, James, ed. *Meaning and Context: Quentin Skinner and His Critics.* Princeton, 1988.

Veyne, P. *Comment on écrit l'histoire: Essai d'épistémologie.* Paris, 1971.

White, H. "Interpretation in History." *New Literary History* 4 (1973):281–314.

Index